PSYCHIATRY AND THE HUMANITIES, VOLUME 7

Assistant Editor
Gloria H. Parloff

Editorial Assistants
Carolyn Wheaton
Katherine S. Henry

Published under the auspices of the
Forum on Psychiatry and the Humanities
The Washington School of Psychiatry

Taking Chances:
Derrida,
Psychoanalysis,
and Literature

Edited by
Joseph H. Smith, M.D.
and
William Kerrigan, Ph.D.

The Johns Hopkins University Press

BALTIMORE AND LONDON

©1984 Forum on Psychiatry and the Humanities
of the Washington School of Psychiatry
All rights reserved
Printed in the United States of America

Originally published, 1984
Second printing, 1985
Johns Hopkins Paperbacks edition, 1988

The Johns Hopkins University Press
701 West 40th Street
Baltimore, Maryland 21211
The Johns Hopkins Press Ltd., London

LIBRARY OF CONGRESS CATALOGING IN PUBLICATION DATA

Main entry under title:

Taking chances.

(Psychiatry and the humanities; v. 7)
Includes essay by Jacques Derrida.
Includes index.
1. Psychoanalysis and literature—Addresses, essays,
lectures.   2. Derrida, Jacques—Addresses, essays,
lectures.   I. Smith, Joseph H., 1927–.
II. Kerrigan, William, 1943–.   III. Derrida,
Jacques.   IV. Series.
RC321.P943   vol. 7   616.89s   [801´.92]   83-49198
[PN56.P92]
ISBN 0-8018-3232-2
ISBN 0-8018-3749-9 (pbk.)

Contents

v

Introduction

WILLIAM KERRIGAN

AND

JOSEPH H. SMITH

> Why bastard? Wherefore base,
> When my dimensions are as well compact,
> My mind as generous, and my shape as true,
> As honest madam's issue? Why brand they us
> With base? With baseness? Bastardy base? Base?
>
> —*King Lear*

In October 1982 Jacques Derrida delivered from a written text the Weigert Lecture commissioned by the Forum on Psychiatry and the Humanities. A subsequent state of this text opens the volume at hand, in which form the editors have become its deliverers or mailmen. Here, then, is your postmodernism.

Since readers of this book may often feel deprived of regulative certainties, we might as well begin with what, chances are, everybody knows. Poets both anticipate and defy psychoanalysis. Superstition, like a naïve metaphysics, projects psychic contents onto the world at large. Psychoanalysis is a science.

Frequently repeated and elaborated by Freud, such statements are often read as earned summation. The founder, standing on the achievements of his movement and allowing himself some time alone with a vista no one has ever seen before, takes a sweeping glance at a few broad prospects on the civilized terrain. Literature confirms us, and yet, by keeping the secret of sublimation, remains truer than we know. As science has already taught us, superstition must not prevail, and now there is something to put in its place, a new interpretation of dreams, omens, uncanniness, and demonic possession to drive out the old, which it is also an interpretation of. Impatient and universalizing philosophy has received its due rebuke. The future of psychoanalysis converges with that of science. Sharing the values of the natural sciences, eschewing all other *Weltanschauungen,* psychoanalysis takes its place among them.

Psychoanalysts familiar with the work of Hans Loewald, Roy Schafer, and others know how much this concept of psychoanalysis is currently being revised. We are arriving at a post-Strachean, post-Rapaportian vision of Freud and of experience, not altogether different from Derrida's interpretation.

Freud's desire for systematic explanation culminated in David Rapaport's (1967) Freud. Rapaport drew from Freud a concept of hierarchical development arising out of the interplay of drive and defense in interaction with others resulting, at its highest point, in the capacity for logical, scientific understanding. Where Freud was found to be less than systematic his conclusions were dismissed in favor of what would be logically consistent with a tighter, though often more complex, system. It is a kind of reading necessary for understanding Freud and an essential preliminary for any deconstructive move. One cannot, that is, attempt to deconstruct psychoanalysis without first having a grasp of what its system, if logically consistent, would be.

But the whole idea that logical consistency and the scientific method can lead us to the truths or truth governing human existence is the Platonic bias of Western thought that Derrida questions. He reads Freud as Freud read himself and others—with an eye toward the contingent, the haphazard, the chance event or lapse. He is the strong poet of that which Freud, not altogether wrongly, named "overdetermination"—a concept that itself originally masked or sought to set limits on the universality of overdetermination. Everything is overdetermined. Every meaning supplements—that is, extends or replaces others. The paradoxical or oxymoronish aspect is that if every event is shaped by multiple determinants, then overdetermination itself is the vehicle of chance entering the scene, or rather the vehicle by which chance was always already on and in the scene. If "there is never anything *but* overdetermination" (Derrida, 1981, p. 346), and if, as Freud wrote (*S.E.* 11:137, cited by Derrida herein), "we are all too ready to forget that in fact everything to do with our life is chance . . . chance which nevertheless has a share in the law and necessity of nature, and which merely lacks any connection with our wishes and illusions," overdetermination and chance are always co-implicated. Here is the place where Freud and

Derrida meet. This is the point of Derrida's deepest, though ambivalent, indebtedness to Freud. Without this play of/on/in the mind guaranteed by overdetermination or supplementarity—without the interplay, that is, of language, desire, drive, and defense—no definite meaning could be and because of it no meaning can be absolutely definite—and no discipline as well.

Regarding disciplines, as everybody knows, there is trouble at every boundary. Take psychoanalysis and literature. If works of psychoanalysis prove that works of literature *mean* psychoanalysis, or inevitably pass through it on the way to whatever else they may mean, what is the difference? Is psychoanalysis willing to say that it is literature? If it does, will scientists be willing to say that literature/psychoanalysis is a science? On the other side of the border, psychoanalysis outrages or disappoints certain literary critics able to believe themselves in charge of distinctly literary values. It may appear to reduce the reference of the work; or it may seem, if psychoanalysis itself is what the literary work is supposed to mean, as in Lacan's famous seminar on "The Purloined Letter" (1972; see Felman, 1980, p. 138), possessive: why should literature always arrive at psychoanalysis when there are, after all, so many intellectual destinations clamoring to receive this especially popular sort of letter? Little seems to be at stake in these disputes beyond prestige, which is not to say that prestige is a little thing in human affairs. But when the relationship of psychoanalysis to neighboring discourses is seen as summary and afterthought, the truth, character, and future of psychoanalysis do not really depend on the settlement of these disputes. Freud may have assessed the terrain wrongly. That would not affect the ground he stands on.

In the way Derrida reads Freud, these questions of boundary extend as far down as one can see into the origins of Freud's peculiar science. Perhaps we need to be reminded that the founder was a master of the questionable boundary, placing concepts between the somatic and the psychic, inside and outside, meaning and nonsense. What everybody knows about psychoanalysis because Freud told them, and told them at emphatic moments, is neither summary nor survey. Those familiar propositions manifest a tense intellectual birth, the differentiation of a new term—"psychoanalysis"—taking place among other terms and battling for autonomy. Most kinds of autonomy, however, are fraught with illusion. To Derrida, psychoanalysis is from the beginning and in its essence a discipline trying to take place by trying to take a place, inevitably in the fray, taking chances. It will always be forced to reconceive itself (not just of itself) as through time the boundaries keep shifting.

Consider the texts. Are the means by which Freud distinguished psychoanalysis from literature themselves psychoanalytic (scientific, transparent) or literary (metaphorical, theatrical, rhetorical)? Behind

major strategic distinctions lie problems that the distinctions seem
designed, in part, to obfuscate. In previous work (1975, 1980) Derrida
has tracked the progress of this denying isolation as it joins with a self-
denial—the creation of an unbiased observer in texts that know, in some
ways more fully than any previous texts, that this observer cannot be
other than a fiction. Rather like Freud, who was often amused and
chagrined at having built such an edifice from the detritus of human
behavior, Derrida sees himself "ambushing and pouncing upon some of
Freud's shorter texts prudently left in corners, animal machines lying in
wait in the shadows and menacing the security of a space and a logic"
(1975, p. 39). The cat is out of the mailbag. He pounces, and he does
not let go until he is finished (to be continued).

As theme, method, and source of wonder, reflexivity dominated the
great philosophies of consciousness. This doubling back fixed mind in
the presence of itself, and for reasons that Derrida has explored, this
security of autoaffection was rendered in great chains of preferential
metaphors extending from and toward the speaking voice. Derrida is a
philosopher of writing, but he intends "to demonstrate that the traits
that can be recognized in the classical, narrowly defined concept of
writing . . . . [iterability beyond the presence of the writer, the force
writing carries to break with its context, and the spacing that constitutes
the written sign] . . . . are generalizable. They are valid not only for all
orders of 'signs' and for all languages in general but, moreover, beyond
semiolinguistic communication, for the entire field of what philosophy
would call experience" (Derrida, 1977, p. 181).

In *La carte postale,* where he directs us in the sole substantive
footnote to "Mes Chances," Derrida endeavors to make of the circulation of letters by mail a structural metaphor as acute and serviceable to
deconstruction as speaking was to philosophies of consciousness. Writing
about his reading of writing, he makes legible a negative reflexivity of
error—texts that move forward by doubling back through derivatives on
an original exclusion. In order to maintain their bounds, say what they
want to say, the texts Derrida deconstructs hide from their own creature,
the unthinkable. Otherwise how could we think? What above all distinguishes the postmodernist analysis is the methodological necessity of
including itself in the issue and the problem, accepting responsibility for
its own reflexivity of error. Postmodernist discourse wants to field its
rebound—to abandon a tradition of self-certainty, to stand aside from
the conditions of sense defined in this tradition, without lapsing into
mere unintelligibility. The outsider's accusation of massive contradiction
("What you say refutes what you say") is an ancient *topos* of philosophical argument, used particularly against the skeptics. Thus Thomas
Browne: "The Skeptics that affirmed they know nothing, even in that

opinion confute themselves, and thought they knew more than all the world beside" (1977, p. 128). Do you not intend your argument against intentional meaning? Are you not doing what you oppose? This is reason's version of the argument against throwing the stone: it could with equal justice be thrown back. But in postmodernism the rebound of statement upon itself is not suffered passively or received in embarrassment, as somehow silencing, but actively embraced. Discourse has been reconstituted about precisely this instability.

Hence a deep kinship between Freud and the deconstructionist: both are in the fray, on the margins, never quite to coincide with a traditional "good sense" and therefore prompting doubts about their capacity for self-regulation. They take a chance. Though often ignored or forgotten or made light of, the possibility of rebound can never be lifted from psychoanalytic writing, where any interpretation may snap back upon itself and proliferate in the mazy folds of its context. The threat is engulfment in infinite regress (an interpretation that requires an interpretation that in turn . . .), and in the work of Freud this threat was inseparable from a monstrous entrapment in autobiography, a writing about "Freud" rather than "psychoanalysis." Its fixed reference lost in the vertigo of self-reference, such a discourse would be analogous to a proper name—not a science, but a certain discipline of self-scrutiny disseminated by transferential identifications. So Freud controlled the doses of self-examination, and in such a way, perhaps, that he created a new sort of text, neither science as he thought of it nor literature as he thought of it.

Derrida has grown to appreciate Freud's abilities, as a writer, to release undecidability while retaining self-regulation. In this book Samuel Weber speaks of two kinds of deconstruction: the "classical" one, which hopes to preserve for itself an exteriority to the intentions of the text being read, and a more recent or recently prominent one that forfeits this exteriority by allowing itself to become, in Derrida's words, "an example of that of which it speaks or writes." An evolving fascination with the second style of reading can be discerned in the difference between the early "Freud and the Scene of Writing" (1978), with its enthusiastic program for purifying psychoanalysis of its naïve reiteration of philosophy, and the present "Mes Chances." To be sure, there is still an accusation of dogmatism. But Freud's manipulation of context seems in most respects a lucky performance. It is as if Derrida has consented to be one station of Freud's "beyond."

In "good sense" concepts and instances are brought together definitively (in reply to initiating questions such as "What concept is this an instance of?" and "What instances is this a concept of?"). It implies finished instances and stable concepts. In his effort to be responsibly beyond this sort of sense, Derrida strives not to be illustrative while also not producing a discourse of the proper name. Like the barber with the sign in his window I SHAVE ALL YOU VILLAGERS AND ONLY YOU VILLAGERS WHO DO NOT SHAVE YOURSELVES (the only game in town), he has set up shop to disrupt the logic of exemplification. There is a close shave with chance, and Derrida's razor does not work like the one Occam borrowed from Aristotle to sharpen the structure of exemplification: often enough the vanity lies in reducing assumptions to an impregnable few.

The tradition Derrida wants to dismantle found chance abhorrent. Why is Edmund base? Because he is a sport, a mongrel, a stray cat, an outlaw. Because, as an ill-chance, a bastard outside the system, he has less right to be. Because, looking as human as anyone else, he demands that we examine the differences that make him base. It is not a question we have been eager to address. Interpretation (literary, scientific, super- stitious, psychoanalytic) opposes chance: "It is not by accident that . . . ." Classically, beyond the physics of the atomists, chance was accorded some dignity and moral force only in the public careers of politics and warfare: the die is cast, you bet your life, and if you win, you could just as well not have. Usually *fortuna* has about it a sense of the willed, the meant, the exemplary; its victims are being made an example of. Philosopher after influential philosopher has expressed belief in some power of unwavering principle behind the throne of *fortuna*. God does not play dice with the universe.

But in our languages, Derrida observes, elaborate semantic con- tinua link chance with fate. Although a spoken word resonates in its etymology, fate is also something written (on the wall, in the stars, in a book or a ledger: your sentence). But, as that very resonance would suggest, the text involved in this major metaphor for fate is a non- Derridean writing, which is to say, a stable, permanent, eternal writing safe from the vicissitudes of chance. Fate pulls unfolding time back into the past and precedent. It drives out chance from a reign of law. It interprets everything. It encourages philosophies of adjustment: the stoic must live his life as though his life were through. Chance may sometimes be conceived as the opposite of fate—an affinity with the future, with gratuitous gift rather than fatal payment. But another intuition has placed chance beyond opposition or difference, outside system but not nothing: Chaos. (Epicurus, in one of the stories handed down by Diogenes Laertius, "took up philosophy when disgruntled because the schoolmasters could not explain the meaning of 'chaos' in Hesiod to him" [1969, p. 209].) Here interpretation is utterly repelled. Removing the structure of entities and thus the structure of illustrable concepts, Chaos is the mythic counterpart to the proper name with its *"marked insignificance."* Chance has always threatened this, evoking a state without cuts and differences, where Edmunds really are indistinguishable from Edgars.

Fate was woven deep in the texture of psychoanalysis. If we must place him among the philosophers, Freud has at least as much in common with the stoics as with the German romantics. Adjustment to *Ananke* is his repeated advice, even as his theory gives full acknowledgment to the extremity of will's insistence (energy, cash, fulfillment)—a conflict between two kinds of "necessity" symmetrical with the two sides of the stoic tradition, philosophical treatises advising discipline in the face of inexorable circumstances and tragic dramas representing inexorable, unconfinable passions.[1] Psychoanalysis is attuned to the fixations, returns, and repetitions of the indestructible past. How does chance operate in its economy of psychic determinism?

It is a break in the rebounding. The coachman at the end of *The Psychopathology of Everyday Life* drove Freud to the wrong address. Because his malpractice could not have been influenced by Freud's intentions at whatever level, Freud will not file a brief. This could not be, in the interpretative system called psychoanalysis, a meaningful event. Only a superstitious man interprets such an event. There are times when a coincidence is just a coincidence, and the constant pressure of becoming the unfinishable example of a self-consuming theory, the victim of one's own compulsion to interpret, subsides. Then, in this time of relaxation, an ideal differentiation occurs. Severed from superstition or autobiography and aligned with science, regulated, autonomous, psychoanalysis takes its place. Chance, the close associate of proper names, has here made room for a proper conceptual one: psychoanalysis, *genus* science. A diminutive descendant of the beasts of primordial Chaos has been good enough to slip inside and mark a difference. Pounce.

Where Freud fell silent in the presence of chance, Derrida urges interpretation, extending the web of coincidence from the faulty coachman to Freud himself and the aged patient to Freud's mother. Definitely the wrong address? Definitely by chance? No dice. Even here or especially here, there is rebound, and Freud's suspension of interpretation becomes itself interpretable.

Derrida invites us to reckon his score. Has he established that the ominous coach ride is indeed interpretable? Well, maybe, and maybe there are at least two questions here, one about establishing and one about the ride. Freud decided on coincidence. Coincidence: the bastard that looks legitimate; the interpreter's temptation; a case where the world steps aside from the declarative mode into a subjunctive "as if" that is not contrary to fact, since this "as if" *is* the fact. As we reckon the score, Derrida has collapsed the *appearance* of meaning in Freud's coincidence back into a *possibility,* abandoning chance at the level of event in order to reintroduce chance at the level of interpreting or establishing. We are left suspended between coincidence and meaning, chance and fate. So Derrida must also field the rebound: his shot has missed. Is it by accident that, at just the section of "Mes Chances" where he considers the neatly bounded differentiation of psychoanalysis proper at the conclusion of the *Psychopathology,* Derrida should for the first time advance his own proper name, "deconstruction," and map it onto the differentiation of psychoanalysis by remarking that a certain sympathy for superstition is a happy trait in deconstructing? The French mouser is some kind of copycat.

Derrida's interpretations often radicalize rather than diminish chance. Neither his examples nor his example illustrate in the conventional way. They question, make questionable, and often because they are questionable. His reader is beset by uncertain tone (is this wit or proposition?), by multiplicate meanings activated in enmeshed words, aware always, therefore, of difference within the text itself, and the possibility of error and mistake both in its statement and our construction of its statement. Derrida exhibits and occasions chance. This is not necessarily a bad thing. There is *mes chances* as *méchance*: lapse and mistake, as Derrida has asserted in so many of his texts, belong to the essence of iteration. But so too, he reminds us here, does the sport of sublimation, the happy chance, *Chance Elysée.* "The Purloined Letter," Derrida has written, "makes of chance as writing what we shall be careful not to call 'the real subject' of the tale" (1975, p. 102). What *shall* we call it? The chance of the tale. Derrida has stolen writing from the old metaphor for fate and rethought it as a major new metaphor for chance. And the proper/generic name for the taking of this chance is "deconstruction."

With a fragment of the *Phaedrus,* the rolling stones of an ellipsis, and the assertion that we will or should follow the links when he is gone, Derrida takes leave of us. A short visit, but the other contributors to this volume give a likely impression of the effects this man might have, might even intend to have, on psychoanalysis. There might be, as Alan Bass suggests, an end to the dogmatic warfare for ownership of the "true" psychoanalysis sometimes conducted in the language of metapsychology. There might even be an end to metapsychology: if for Lacan there was too little philosophy in Freud, for Derrida there is too much. There might be prolonged investigations of the rebound in Freud's texts, such as that performed by Avital Ronell, wherein the traditional questions of intellectual history (how did Goethe influence Freud?) become inseparable from the ideas and implications, the "textual problematics," of psychoanalysis itself. There might be, as Samuel Weber implies there ought to be in his meditation on a moment when Derrida, noting

that Freud forgets Nietzsche, proceeds to forget Heidegger, some attention given to the moves and gestures peculiar to readings of Freud. Some
of the works of expulsion performed by founding distinctions may serve
political interests, and as David Carroll proposes, one benefit
of Derrida's iconoclasm toward psychoanalytic dogma might be a wider
appreciation of the ideological self-deceit arising from these institutional
contests.

J. Hillis Miller's essay about the chances of happening on a particular text and choosing to receive it may occasion us to reflect on the style
in which the life of learning has customarily been conducted. The scholar
poses as master—thorough, exact, custodian of a field of texts and
policeman of things said about them. Professional training encourages
the stance. Reading is a responsibility or the discharge of a debt, and if a
chance, primarily a chance to get ahead. The production of writing
becomes patently involved in competition, prestige, and territorial
impulse, which in turn lends urgency to the "right reading" and the
exposure of the "wrong reading." This idealization ignores the throws of
chance that lead us from text to text, as somehow our eyes pause at one
book on the library shelves, and the sense of good fortune at having
received in a proper way some few of these letters (Freud, say, or Derrida)
that should underwrite our responsibility for them, and has perhaps
brought some of us to this book right here.

NOTES

1. These remarks are indebted to Gordon Braden's forthcoming study, *Anger's
Privilege: Renaissance Tragedy and the Senecan Tradition*. Perhaps too little attention has been given in the many recent discussions of Poe's "The Purloined Letter"
to the fact that the letter Dupin delivers derives ultimately from Seneca, whose very
name means suicide (*se necans*).

REFERENCES

Browne, T. *The Major Works.* Edited by C. A. Patrides. New York: Penguin, 1977.
Derrida, J. "The Purveyor of Truth." *Yale French Studies* 52 (1975): 30–113.
———. "Signature, Event, Context." Translated by S. Weber and J. Mehlman. In
    Glyph 1. Johns Hopkins Textual Studies. Baltimore: Johns Hopkins University
    Press, 1977.
———. "Freud and the Scene of Writing." In *Writing and Difference.* Translated by
    A. Bass. Chicago: University of Chicago Press, 1978.
———. *La carte postale.* Paris: Flammarion, 1980.
———. *Dissemination.* Translated with an Introduction and additional notes by
    B. Johnson, Chicago: University of Chicago Press, 1981.

Felman, S. "On Reading Poetry: Reflections on the Limits and Possibilities of Psychoanalytic Approaches." In J. H. Smith, ed., *The Literary Freud: Mechanisms of Defense and the Poetic Will,* vol. 4 of *Psychiatry and the Humanities.* New Haven: Yale University Press, 1980.

Freud, S. *Standard Edition of the Complete Psychological Works.* London: Hogarth, 1953–74: *Leonardo da Vinci and a Memory of His Childhood* (1910), vol. 11.

Lacan, J. "The Seminar on 'The Purloined Letter.' " Translated by J. Mehlman. *Yale French Studies* 48 (1972): 39–72.

Laertius, D. *Lives of the Philosophers.* Translated by A. Caponigri. Chicago: Gateway, 1969.

Rapaport, D. *The Collected Papers of David Rapaport.* Edited by M. Gill. New York: Basic Books, 1967.

Taking Chances:
Derrida, Psychoanalysis, and Literature

1　My Chances/*Mes Chances:*
A Rendezvous with Some
Epicurean Stereophonies

JACQUES DERRIDA

How should one go about calculating the age of psychoanalysis? Not everything under which psychoanalysis falls can be simply relegated to the manifestation of its name; but under this name it remains a rather young venture. One can contemplate its chances—those of yesterday and tomorrow.

You are perhaps wondering why I chose the theme of *la chance* when, according to the specific terms of our program or contract, I should speak to you about the relation of the one to the other, psychoanalysis to literature—that other thing of an incalculable age at once immemorial and altogether recent. Did I choose this theme haphazardly or by chance? Or, what is more likely, perhaps it was imposed upon me in that chance offered itself for the choosing as if I had fallen upon it, thus leaving me with the illusion of a free will. All this involves a very old story, which, however, I shall not endeavor to recount.

For the moment let us treat "Psychoanalysis" and "Literature" as presumably proper names. They name events or a series of events about which we can rightfully suppose the *singularity* of an irreversible process and a historical existence. On the basis of this singularity alone, their transaction with chance already gives us something to reflect upon.

If I may now make use of the apostrophe, let me tell you this much at once: I do not know to whom I am speaking. Whom is this discourse or lecture addressing here and now? I am delivering it to you, of course, but that doesn't change the situation much. You will understand why I say this. And once you find this intelligible, it becomes at least possible to demonstrate that, beginning with the first sentence, my lecture has not simply and purely missed its destination.

You understand very well why I am asking myself such questions as: to whom, in the final analysis, will this lecture have been destined? and, Can one speak here of destination or aim? What are my chances of reaching my addressees if, on the one hand, I calculate and prepare a place of *encounter* or if, on the other, I hope, as we say in French, to *fall* upon them by accident?

Regarding those to whom I now speak, I do not know them, so to speak. Nor do I know you who hear me. I do not even know if, according to your declared interests or professional affiliations, the majority among you belong to the "world" of psychiatry, as the title borne by this school tends to suggest, to the "worlds" of psychoanalysis, to one and the other, to one or the other, or to the "worlds" of science, literature, the arts, or the humanities. It is not certain that such "worlds" exist. Their frontiers are those of "contexts" and justificatory procedures currently undergoing rapid transformation. Even if I had at my disposition some information that might clarify this subject, it would still remain overly vague and general; I would have to make rough calculations and hold a lecture of loosely woven netting, counting on my chances in a way somewhat analogous to fishing or hunting. How indeed could I aim my argument at some singular destination, at one or another among you whose proper name I might for example know? And then, is knowing a proper name tantamount to knowing someone?

There. I have just *enumerated* the themes of my lecture. They are all presented in what was just said, including the theme of numbers, which has been added just now to the enumeration. This amounts to what I would like to discuss with you, but I shall have to do so in the dim light of a certain indetermination. I impart my words a bit haphazardly, trying my luck in front of you and others, yet what I say at this chance moment has more chance of reaching you than if I had delivered it to chance without speaking of this. Why? Well, at least because these effects of chance appear to be at once produced, multiplied, *and* limited by language.

Language, however, is only one among those systems of *marks* that claim this curious tendency as their property: they *simultaneously* incline toward increasing the reserves of random indetermination *as well as* the capacity for coding and overcoding or, in other words, for control and self-regulation. Such competition between randomness and code disrupts the very systematicity of the system while it also, however, regulates the restless, unstable interplay of the system. Whatever its singularity in this respect, the linguistic system of these traces or marks would merely be, it seems to me, just a particular example of the law of destabilization.

Even here, among us, the effects of chance are at once multiplied and limited (that is, relatively tempered or neutralized) by the multiplicity of languages and codes that, while they are engaged in intense translational activity, overlap at each instant. Such activity transforms not only words, a lexicon, or a syntax (for example, from French into English) but also nonlinguistic marks, mobilizing thus the near totality of the present context and even that which might already exceed it. The text that I am now reading should be publishable; I was aware of this when writing this summer. It is destined in advance to addressees (*destinaires*) who are not easily determinable or who, as far as any possible calculation is concerned, in any case command a great reserve of indetermination. And this in turn involves, as I shall try to show, the most general structure of the mark. Running my chances over your heads, I therefore address myself to addressees unknown to you or me. But while waiting and in passing, this falls, as the French saying goes, upon you.

What do I or could I conceivably mean by declaring these addressees "unknown" to you and me? What criteria would one use in order to arrive at a decision regarding them? Not necessarily the criteria of self-conscious knowledge. For I could be addressing myself to an unconscious and absolutely determined addressee, one rigorously localized in "my" unconscious, or in yours, or in the machinery programming the partition of this event. Moreover, everything that comes to mind under the words "consciousness" or "unconscious" already presupposes the possibility of these marks in addition to all the possible disruptions connected with the destining of dispatches (*envois à destiner*). In any case, the fact that the proper name or the idiom of the other is a matter of ignorance to us does not mean that we know nothing about her or him. Despite the fact that I do not know you or can barely see you while addressing myself to you, and that you hardly know me, what I have been saying is, as of a moment ago, reaching you—regardless of the trajectories and translations of signs that we address to each other in this twilight. What I have been saying comes at you, to encounter and make contact with you. Up to a certain point it becomes intelligible to you. The "things" that I throw, eject, project, or cast (*lance*) in your direction to come across to you fall, often and well enough, upon you, at least upon certain of those among you. The things with which I am bombarding you are linguistic or nonlinguistic signs: words, sentences, sonorous and visual images, gestures, intonations, and hand signals. Within the range of our calculations we can count on certain probabilities. On the basis of numerous indices, we form, you and I, a certain schematic idea of one another and of the place where contact could be made. We certainly count on the calculating capacity of language, with its code and game, with what regulates its *play* and plays with its regulations. We count on that which is destined to random chance (*ce qui destine au hasard*), while at the same time reducing chance. Since the expression *"destiner au hasard"* can have two syntaxes and therefore can carry two meanings in French, it is at once of sufficient determination *and* indetermination to leave room for the chances to which it speaks in its course (*trajet*) and even in its "throw" (*"jet"*). This depends, as they say, on the context; but a context is never determined enough to prohibit all possible random deviation. To speak in the manner of Epicurus or Lucretius, there is always a chance open to some *parenklisis* or *clinamen*. *"Destiner au hasard"* could mean resolutely "to doom," "abandon," "yield," or "deliver" to chance itself. But it can also mean to destine something unwittingly, in a haphazard manner or at random. In the first of these cases, one destines to chance without involving chance, whereas in the second, one does not destine to chance but chance intervenes and diverts the destination. The same can be said for the expression "to believe in chance": to believe in chance can just as well indicate that one believes in the existence of chance as that one does *not*, above all, believe in chance, since one looks for and finds a hidden meaning at all costs.

For a while now, I have been speaking to you about chance (*du hasard*), but I do not speak haphazardly (*au hasard*). Calculating my chances of reaching you through my speech (*parole*), I have above all spoken to you of speech. I thought that speaking to you about chance and language would give me the greatest chances of being pertinent, that is, of touching on my subject by touching you. This presupposes that, between us, there reigns a good number of contracts or conventions or what Lucretius would call explicit or implicit "federations." The organizers of this encounter have prescribed, for instance, that the dominant language here be English. And everything that I say should relate to something like the chances between psychoanalysis and literature, taking into account earlier works—among others, my own.

I shall cast out *two questions,* then. Once these questions are cast, imagine that suddenly (*d'un seul coup*) they become two dice. Afterward (*après coup*), when they have fallen, we shall try to see, if something still remains to be seen, at what sum they arrive between them: in other words, what their constellation means. And whether one can read my fortune (*mes chances*) or yours.

To Usher in the Fall

The first and preliminary question, as if thrown on the threshold, raises the issue of the downward movement. When chance or luck are under consideration, why do the words and concepts in the first place impose the particular signification, sense, and direction (*sens*) of a downward movement regardless of whether we are dealing with a throw or a fall? Why does this sense enjoy a privileged relation to the non-sense or insignificance which we find frequently associated with chance? What would such a movement of descent have to do with luck or chance (*la chance ou le hasard*)? From what viewpoint can these be related (and we shall see how precisely, in this place, vision comes to be missing)? Is our attention engaged by the ground or the abyss? As you know, the words "chance" and "case" descend, as it were, according to the same Latin filiation, from *cadere,* which—to indicate the sense of the fall—still resounds in "cadence," "fall" (*choir*), "to fall due" (*échoir*), "expiry date" (*échéance*), as well as in "accident" and "incident." But, apart from this linguistic family, the same case can be made for *Zufall* or *Zufälligkeit,* which in German means "chance," for *zufallen* (to fall due), *zufällig,* the accidental, fortuitous, contingent, occasional—and the word "occasion" belongs to the same Latin descent. A *Fall* is a case; *Einfall,* an idea that suddenly comes to mind in an apparently unforeseeable manner. Now, I would say that the unforeseeable is precisely the case, involving as it does that which falls and is not seen in advance. Is not what befalls us or descends upon us, as it comes from above, like destiny or thunder, taking our faces and hands by surprise—is this not exactly what thwarts our expectation and disappoints our *anticipation*? Grasping everything in advance, anticipation (*antipare, ante-capere*) does not let itself be taken by surprise; there is no chance for it. Anticipation sees the *objectum* coming ahead, faces the object or *Gegenstand* that, in philosophical German, was preceded by the *Gegenwurf* in which the movement of the throw (*jet, werfen*) can once again be perceived. The *ob-jectum* (*ob-jet*) is kept under view or hand, within sight or *intuitus,* while it puts a handle on the hand or *conceptus,* the *Begreifen* or *Begriff.* And when something does not befall us "by accident" ("*par hasard*"), as the saying or belief goes, then one can also fall oneself. One can fall well or badly, have a lucky or unlucky break—but always by dint of not having foreseen—of not having seen in advance and ahead of oneself. In such a case, when man or the subject falls, the fall affects his upright stance and vertical position by engraving in him the detour of a *clinamen,* whose effects are sometimes inescapable.[1]

For the time being, let us be content to take note of this law or coincidence, which in an odd way associates chance and luck with a descending movement, a finite throw (which is supposed therefore to fall vertically again), the fall, the incident, the accident, and, most certainly, coincidence. The attempt to submit chance to thought implies in the first place an interest in the *experience* (I emphasize this word) of that which happens unexpectedly (*ce qui arrive imprévisiblement*). Indeed, there are those of us who are inclined to think that unexpectability conditions the very structure of an event. Would an event that can be anticipated and therefore apprehended or comprehended, or one without an element of absolute encounter, actually be an event in the full sense of the word? There are those who lean toward the assumption that an event worthy of this name cannot be foretold. We are not supposed to see it coming. If what comes and then stands out horizontally on a horizon can be anticipated then there is no pure event. No horizon, then, for the event or encounter, but only verticality and the unforeseeable. The alterity of the other—that which does not reduce itself to the economy of our horizon—always comes to us from above, indeed, from the above.

This singular *experience* brings us into contact with what *falls* "well" or "badly," as we would say in French (roughly meaning what falls opportunely or not), which, as such, constitutes fortune or luck (*une chance*). Depending on the context and cases, of which there are quite a few, such luck is a stroke of luck. This amounts to a pleonastic expression: to have luck is to have good luck. In other cases—the unfortunate ones—luck is *bad luck* (*une malchance*). What are the chances of my losing at a game or for the neutron bomb to be dropped? Bad luck (*malchance*) is when one is out of luck; having *no luck* (*pas de chance*); however, it is at the same time in a very significant way a phenomenon of luck or chance—an "infelicity" as the Austinian theory of speech acts would have it—designating accidental or parasitical deviations in the production of performatives, promises, orders, or oaths—and, precisely, contracts.

Bad luck (*malchance*) is *méchance*. We could say that a spiteful person (*le méchant*) plays on bad luck (*malchance*) and on "*méschéance*," which is an Old French word that associates being down on one's luck with spite and meanness (*méchanceté*). The mean, spiteful person falls short (*le méchant méchoit*), which is another way of saying that he is demeaned and loses his standing (*il déchoit*), first in the sense of mischance and then, if we shift the sense a bit, allowing it to deviate in turn, in the sense of that which brings him to do evil.

If I stress the multiplicity of languages, and if I play on it, you should not take this for a mere exercise or a gratuitous and fortuitous display. As I make my way from digression to deviation I wish to demonstrate a certain interfacing of necessity and chance, of significant and insignificant chance: the marriage, as the Greek would have it, of *Anankè*, of *Tukhè* and *Automatia*.

In any case, we can note the incidence in a system of *co*incidences of that which itself is prone to fall (well or badly) *with* something else, that is, at the same time or in the same place as something else. This is also the sense that the Greek gives to *symptôma*, a word meaning a sinking in or depression, a collapse but also a coincidence, a fortuitous event, an encounter or unfortunate event. Finally, we have the symptom as sign—a clinical one, for example. The clinic, let it be said in passing, names the integral space of the retiring or bedridden position, which is the position of illness par excellence, and thus, one invariably "falls" ill.

The same semantic register supposes the idea of whatever falls (*ce qui est échu*) to someone's lot—that lottery said to be attributed, distributed, dispensed, and sent (*geschickt*) by the gods or destiny (*moira, nemein, nomos, Schicksal*), the fatal or fabulating word, the chance circumstances of heredity, the game of chromosomes—as if this gift and these givens obeyed, for better or for worse, the order of a throw coming down from above. We are in fact dealing with a logic and *topos* of the dispatch (*envoi*). Destiny and destination are dispatches whose descending trajectories or projections can meet with perturbation, which, in this case, means interruption or deviation. Within the same register we find (but can we speak in this case of a lucky find or a chance encounter?) the unforeseeable and inexplicable fall from grace into original sin or, in terms of the mythology of Plato's *Phaedrus,* we find the disseminating fall of the soul in a body, just as well as *lapsus* or "slip" (which, as you know, means fall). The *lapsus,* when revealing its unconscious destination and manifesting thus its truth, becomes, for psychoanalytical interpretations, a symptom.

At this point we necessarily fall upon Democritus, Epicurus, and Lucretius again. In the course of their fall in the void, atoms are driven by a supplementary deviation, by the *parenklisis* or *clinamen* that, impelling an initial divergency, produce the "concentration of material (*systrophè*) thus giving birth to the worlds and things they contain" (J. and M. Bollack, H. Wissmann, *La Lettre d'Epicure,* p. 182.3). The *clinamen* diverges from simple verticality, doing so, according to Lucretius, "at an indeterminate moment" and "in indeterminate places" (*incerto tempore . . . incertis locis; De natura rerum,* 2.218.9). Without this declension, "nature would have never created anything" (224).

This deviation alone can change the course of an imperturbable destination and an inflexible order. Such erring (elsewhere I call it "destinerring") can contravene in the laws of destiny, in conventions or contracts, in agreements of *fatum* (*fati foedera,* 2.254). I emphasize the word "contract" for reasons that will soon become clear. But here I must ask you to allow me a brief digression toward a classical philological problem concerning the indeterminate reading of the word *voluptas* or *voluntas* (2.257). The mere difference of a letter introduces a *clinamen* precisely when Lucretius is at the point of explaining the extent to which the *clinamen* is the condition of the freedom and will or voluptuous pleasure that has been wrested from destiny (*fatis avolsa*). But in all cases the context leaves no doubt as to the link between *clinamen,* freedom, and pleasure. The *clinamen* of the elementary principle—notably, the atom, the law of the atom—would be the pleasure principle. The *clinamen* introduces the play of necessity and chance into what could be called, by anachronism, the determinism of the universe. Nonetheless, it does not imply a conscious freedom or will, even if for some of us the principle of indeterminism is what makes the conscious freedom of man fathomable.

When I have the names of Epicurus and Lucretius appear here, a kind of *systrophè* takes place in my discourse. For Epicurus, condensation or density—the systrophic relief—is in the first place a twisted entanglement and concentrated turn of atoms (mass, swarm, turbulence, downpour, troop) that produces the seed (*semence*) of things, the *spermata,* the seminal multiplicity (inseminal or disseminal). A number of elements are gathered up in the turbulent whirl of the *systrophè* that I bring to you. They ingather in their turn and follow several turns. Which ones? For what diverse and overlapping reasons might I have provoked this Epicurean downpour? They number at least three.

1. The atomic elements, the bodies that fall in the void, are often defined, particularly by Lucretius, as letters (*littera*). And inside their *systrophè* they are seeds (*spermata, semina*). The indivisible element, the *atomos* of the literal dissemination produced by the supplement of deviation, is the *stoikheion,* a word at once designating the graphic element as well as the mark, the letter, the trait, or the point. This theory of literal dissemination is also in turn a discourse on incidents and accidents *as* symptoms and even, among others, as "symptoms of the soul." And in order to account for the possibility of speaking of these psychic symptoms (*peri ten psuchen ta sumptômata*) Epicurus rejects the theories of the "incorporeal" soul (*Letter to Herodotus*, 67.8–12).

2. In consideration of the principal movement in the literal scattering of seeds (*semences*), should one interpret verticality as a fall, as the displacements proceeding from up to down in view of man or a finite being—and, precisely, proceeding from his view, within his horizon? Epicurus seems to reject this perspective: "In the infinite," he proposes, "one should not speak of up and down: we know that if what is above our heads were transferred to the infinite, it would never appear to us in the same way. . . ." "Now, the universe is infinite from two points of view; first, through the number of bodies it contains and then through the immensity of the void that it encompasses" (according to Diogenes Laertes). Let us retain at least this much: the sense of the fall in general (as symptom, lapsus, incident, accidentality, cadence, coincidence, expiration date [*échéance*], luck, good luck, and *méchance*) is conceivable solely in the situation and places or space of finitude, within the multi-

ple relations to the multiplicity of elements, letters, or seeds (*semences*).

An admittedly violent condensation could precipitate the Epicurean interpretation of the disseminating dispersion into the Heideggerian analytic of *Dasein*. Apparently a fortuitous connection, this systrophic precipitation would, however, be that much more necessary given that *Dasein* as such does not reduce itself to the current and metaphysical characters of *human existence or experience* (that of man as subject, soul or body, ego, conscious or unconscious). In the case of *Dasein*, Heidegger analyzes the finitude of thrownness (*Geworfenheit, l'être-jeté*, thrownness into existence, into the "there," into a world, into uncanniness, into the possibility of death, into the "nothing," the thrown Being-with-one-another). This *Geworfenheit* or thrownness is not an empirical character among others, and it has an essential rapport to dispersion and dissemination (*Zerstreuung*) as the structure of *Dasein*. Originarily thrown (*jeté*), *Dasein* is not only a finite being (Kant's *intuitus derivativus*) that, as *subject* (*sujet*), would be passively subjected to the objects that it does not create and that are as if *thrown* ahead to encounter it. Neither *subjectum* nor *objectum*—and even before this opposition—*Dasein* is *itself thrown*, originarily abandoned to fall and decline or, we could say, to chance (*Verfallen*). *Dasein*'s chances are, in the first place and also, its falls. And they are always mine, *mes chances*, each time related to its relation to itself, to a *Jemeinigkeit*, a mineness (an "in each case mine") that does not come down to a relation to an ego or an I (*Ich, moi*). Heidegger is certainly precise on this point (*Sein und Zeit*, sec. 38): the fall (*Verfallenheit, déchéance*) of *Dasein* should not be interpreted as the "fall" ("*Fall*," "*chute*") from an original, purer, and more elevated state. We are surely not dealing with a question of the "corruption of human nature." Yet one is all the more struck by certain analogies with such a discourse. All the more so, given Heidegger's rather pronounced silence regarding Democritus, to whom he alludes only briefly when considering the relationship between Galileo and Democritus in *Die Frage nach dem Ding* (1935–62, pp. 61–62), and again—in a context that is, however, of greater interest to us—in "Democritus and Plato" (p. 162) and to *rythmos* in "*Vom Wesen und Begriff der Physis*" (*Wegmarken*, p. 338). To my knowledge he cites Epicurus but once, when interpreting his *Lathè biôsas*, "life in hiding," in *Aletheia* (1943). We shall limit ourselves to this reference here. Even if the affinities were purely lexical and apparently fortuitous, should they be considered as insignificant, as accidental, or, in the same vein, as symptoms? Is it insignificant that Heidegger isolates three structures or types of movements in connection with the fall into inauthenticity (*Uneigentlichkeit*)? These comprise the suspension in the void (*den Modus eines bodenlosen Schwebens*), the fall as a catastrophic downward plunge (*Absturz: "Wir nennen diese 'Bewegtheit' des Daseins in seinem eigenen Sein den Absturz"*), and turbulence (*"die Bewegtheit des Verfallens als Wirbel,"* sec. 38, "Falling and Thrownness").

That would be the first and far too schematically exposed reason for situating Heidegger's analytic here. The other concerns the place that has to be ceded to Heidegger in Lacanian theory. This is also a point that I tried to urge in my interpretation of Lacan's Seminar on Poe's "Purloined Letter." All this belongs to the context and contract of our encounter; the deviation of another systrophe will no doubt lead us here again.

3. Despite the difference or the shift in context, the indivisibility of letters plays a decisive role in the debate where, it seems to me, the most serious strategic stakes are being called. They are made in terms of a psychoanalytic problematic that addresses determinism, necessity or chance, writing, the signifier and the letter, the simulacrum, fiction or literature. Here I must refer you to "The Purveyor of Truth," where I introduced the term *"atomystique* of the letter" in order to place it in question: it sustains Lacan's entire interpretation of "The Purloined Letter," and particularly of its circular, ineluctable, and predetermined return to the point of departure despite all the apparently random incidents. The letter, Lacan claims, shows little tolerance for partition. I have tried to demonstrate that this axiom was dogmatic and inseparable from a whole philosophy of psychoanalysis. Indeed, it made the entire analytical interpretation possible while it also assured that interpretation of its hermeneutic power over the kind of writing we call literary. However, this power also argues a powerlessness and a lack of comprehension. Without returning to a published debate, I shall quickly indicate the point toward which my present aim is inclined. The phenomenon of chance as well as that of literary fiction, not to mention what I call writing or the trace in general, do not so much lead up to the indivisibility but to a certain divisibility or internal difference of the so-called ultimate element (*stoikheion,* trait, letter, seminal mark). I prefer to call this element—which, precisely, is no longer elementary and indivisible—a *mark* for reasons that I have explained elsewhere and to which I shall return again.

A diversion of atomism is at issue, then, if not one of an antiatomism. Why would the Epicurean doctrine be shielded from the *clinamen?*—from this *clinamen* whose doctrine—a properly Epicurean one—was supposed to have rerouted, according to Marx, the tradition of Democritus? Why do we refrain from applying the *clinamen* to Epicurus's name, and in his name itself?

If I gave this lecture the title of *Mes chances,* it was in order to address the issue of my chances and luck. My chances are well known;

they sum up the experience of "my" work, as well as that of "my" teaching and "my" texts. To be in luck (*avoir de la chance*) is, according to the French idiom, often to fall upon or to fall as you are supposed to, to "fall well," at the opportune moment, to find something by chance, to chance upon the right encounter in step with the irresponsibility of making a good find. "The Purveyor of Truth," for instance, begins by repeating the expression "*si ça se trouve*" (if it is found) at least three times. In common French that means, "if by chance. . .," "if by accident. . . ." Now, the moment has come to present to you, with my chances, what I have just found or lucked upon.

First stroke of luck: Première chance. "The Murders in the Rue Morgue" can also be read as a preface to "The Purloined Letter." After Dupin is presented by the narrator, the reference to the name of Epicurus and his theories is not long in coming. Is this pure chance? Is it insignificant? Dupin reminds the narrator how he had been *thrown* upon a pile of street stones ("a fruiterer . . . thrust you"), and how he had "stepped upon one of the loose fragments, slipped, slightly strained [his] ankles." He adds: "You kept your eyes upon the ground—glancing, with a petulant expression, at the holes and ruts in the pavement (so that I saw you were still thinking of the stones), until we reached the little alley . . . which has been paved, by way of experiment, with the overlapping and riveted blocks. Here your countenance brightened up, and, perceiving your lips move, I could not doubt that you murmured the word 'stereotomy' [science of the cut or division], a term very affectedly applied to this species of pavement. I know that you could not say to yourself 'stereotomy' without being brought to think of atomies, and thus of the theories of Epicurus; and since, when we discussed this subject not very long ago, I mentioned to you how singularly yet with how little notice, the vague guesses of that noble Greek had met with confirmation. . . ." I cut here in order to suggest that besides "the late nebular cosmogony," to quote Dupin, and besides the physical sciences, the above confirmation to which the old science gives rise could well be genetics, psychoanalysis, the "theory" (*la pensée*) of writing or literature. Without wishing to engage a reading of Poe's text at this time, I shall stress an element of structure that seems important to me. The reference to atomism and to the name of Epicurus is itself only a minuscule atom, a detail of the text, an incident, a literal trait in the series of which it nevertheless seems to give a reading.

But the incident's inscription within the series is accompanied in a most significant manner. The narrator himself explains how Dupin, the creator and analyst, "a Bi-Part Soul," "a double Dupin—the creative and the resolvent," *divines* the narrator's mind. And he recounts that when the narrator believes the other to fathom his soul, he is in truth only analyzing symptoms and saying *"peri ten psukhen ta sumptō-mata,"* to recall Epicurus's letter to Herodotus once again. Instead of divining—by intuition, luck, or chance—he enters calculations built upon the accidents in a story of a fall, and he symptomalizes contingency. You will remember that Dupin and the narrator err without a goal; they hang about aimlessly (*au hasard*). Then, all of a sudden, Dupin links his argument to the narrator's inner and silent reverie, as if transmission of thought or telepathy had come to pass. In the manner of an analyst, Dupin explains, however, that instead of divining he had actually calculated. Indeed, he had made calculations, but in a way that reckons with apparently random (*hasardeux*) incidents that are very small, minuscule, quasi-atomic particles and that, curiously, have an essential relationship to the throwing, ejecting, and trajecting movement of the fall. Dupin interprets these *cases* as symptoms. The narrator asks: " 'How was it possible you should know I was thinking of—?' Here I paused, to ascertain beyond a doubt whether he really knew of whom I thought." Baudelaire translates "to know" each time, rightly and wrongly, as "to divine." A little later, the narrator asks: "Tell me, for Heaven's sake, . . . the method—if method there is—by which you have been able to fathom my soul in this matter" (which Baudelaire translates as *dans le cas actuel,"* in this actual case). If we had the time to reconstitute the most minuscule grains of the systrophic and analytic calculation approved in Dupin's response, we would once again find evidence of the "little," the "throw," the "fall."

These issues arise with the "diminutive figure" of a boy who made him "unfitted for tragedy," and with a man who has thrown himself at the narrator ("the man who ran up against you") and who in turn throws him on that pile of street stones that bring stereotomy to mind. "The larger links of the chain run thus—Chantilly, Orion, Dr. Nichols, Epicurus, Stereotomy, the street stones, the fruiterer." While the name of Epicurus forms just one link in the chain, his theory seems nonetheless secretly to command the entire deployment of symptomal analysis. I say "analysis" deliberately, to evoke the solution and resolution that, taking a regressive path toward the elementary particles, disconnects the severed details or incidents. Dupin is presented not only as a "resolvent" analyst but as that type of analyst for whom, according to Baudelaire's slightly deviant yet faithful translation, "all is symptom and diagnostics." This is Baudelaire's translation for "indications" in "all afford, to his apparently intuitive perception, indications of the true state of affairs." Dupin exercises his "analytical power" and "calculating power" par excellence in gamelike situations, for "it is in matters beyond the limits of mere rule that the skill of the analyst is evinced." In such cases, his lucidity is not simply of a mathematical order, but shows itself capable of unmasking the thoughts of the other. The narrator notes as much when his focus shifts to a visibly transferential situation (unless it is countertransferential): Dupin "examines the countenance of his partner . . . counting trump by trump, and honor by honor, through the glances bestowed by their holders upon each. He notes every variation of face as the play progresses, gathering a fund of thought from the differences in the expression. . . . He recognizes what is played through feint, by the manner with which it is *thrown* upon the table" (emphasis added). We are dealing, then, with an expert at that very game that consists in throwing or falling: "A casual or inadvertent word; the accidental dropping or turning of a card, with the accompanying anxiety or carelessness in regard to its concealment, the counting of the tricks, with the order of their arrangement . . . all afford, to his apparently intuitive perception, indications of the true state of affairs." "All for him is symptom and diagnostics," Baudelaire translates. Nor does this prevent the narrator from saying of our Dupin-the-atomist: "There was not a particle of *charlatanism* about Dupin," which Baudelaire translates as "there was not an atom of charlatanism in my friend Dupin." A moment later, this atomist devoid of the smallest atom of charlatanism will say to the narrator as subject: "I knew that you could not say to yourself 'stereotomy' without being brought to think of atomies, and thus to the theories of Epicurus."

Second stroke of luck: Deuxième chance. I shall not have the time to display all my chances. No luck. But if I do not stand much of a chance, it is mostly due to the calculation of a certain *"pas de chance"* (no chance, no luck, and the step of luck) that makes me fall upon the providentially necessary passages of Poe or Baudelaire. *"Méchance"* is not standing a chance, *pas de chance.* All Baudelaire's notes on Poe's life and works open with a meditation on the writing of "not standing a chance":

> There are fatal destinies; there are in the literature of each country men who carry the words *rotten luck* [*guignon*, also "jinxed"] written in mysterious characters on the sinuous folds of their foreheads. Some time ago, an unfortunate man was brought before the tribunals. On his forehead he had a singular tattoo: "doesn't stand a chance" [*pas de chance*]. In this way he carried with him, as does a book its title, the label of his life—and when he took the stand, the cross-examination proved that his existence was in conformity with this sign. Analogous fortunes are to be found in literary history. . . . Is there then a diabolical Providence who prepares misfortune from the cradle? That man, whose somber and desolate talent frightens us, was *thrown* with premeditation into a milieu that was hostile to him [emphasis added].

Four years later, Baudelaire writes another introduction to Poe. Here we find the same tattoo, "Doesn't stand a chance!" (*"Pas de chance!"*) and Providence who "throws" angelic natures downward. And they try in vain to protect themselves, for instance, by blocking all the outlets, by "padding" "the windows against the projectiles of chance"! But "the Devil will enter through the keyhole." Projectiles of chance: this is a matter not only of projection, the throw and the send-off (*le lancer*), but of the missive or dispatch (*l'envoi*) as well, of all the missives in the world. In addition to the dispatch we have the sending back or adverting to (*renvoi*) and, indeed, the boost (*relance*). In poker, *relancer* means to *raise* the stakes, to make a higher bid. One raises or *relances* when one knows how to play with what falls and when, being keen on making it pick up again, one boosts it upward to defer the fall and to cut across the incidence of other bodies in the course of its ups and downs. All of this, of course, comes under the art of coincidence, the simulacra of atoms and the art of the juggler, which, according to Baudelaire, would be Poe's art. Though Poe would go even beyond juggling, Baudelaire uses the term in order "to apply it," he says, "almost as an *éloge* to the noble poet." His "almost" is very subtle, but necessary: In itself juggling would imply too great a mastery in the art of coincidence, which must remain "uncanny." Of this noble poet who bounds and rebounds (*lance et relance*), Baudelaire frequently observes that he "throws himself" (for example, into the grotesque or the horri-ble), that he "hurls challenges at difficulties," or, exceeding this, that "he has been thrown, like a defenseless child, to the hazards of random life."

I have just quoted my chances with regard to Poe's *"pas de chance,"* "not standing a chance," because it comes to light as a preface or postface to "The Purveyor of Truth," the idea (*pensée*) of the missive that it picks up again (*relancée*), and to the haphazardness of missives and the missives of haphazard. You may think that I am juggling. For when chances increase steadily, and too many throws of the dice come to fall well, does this not abolish blind Chance (*le hasard*)? It would be possible to demonstrate that there is nothing random in the concatena-tion of my findings. An implacable program takes shape through the contextual necessity that requires cutting solids into certain sequences (stereotomy), intersecting and adjusting subsets, mingling voices and proper names, and accelerating a rhythm that merely gives the *feeling* of randomness to those who do not know the prescription—which, inciden-tally, is also my case.

From "Literary" Ascendance

If, in addition to Democritus, who engendered Epicurus (via his disciple Nausiphanes), who in turn engendered Lucretius, literature is also at the place of rendezvous, is this by chance? This would be the *second question* that I said a moment ago that I wanted to raise. It leads us again to Freud, supposing that we had ever left him. His texts, when they deal with the question of chance, always revolve around the proper name, the number, and the letter. And, almost fatally, they meet literature, a certain type of literature that uplifts them, each time raising their stakes and marking their limit. Why is this so?

One could initially ask oneself what these elements have in common—these *stoikheia* that include the letter or the trait, the number, and the proper name—such that they are to be found thus associated in the same series and such that their relation to chance would be analogous. That which they have in common, I will claim, is their insignificance in marking (*insignifiance marquante*). This insignificance marks. It belongs to the mark. It is marked but above all re-markable. This re-markable insignificance destines them, makes them enter into the play of the destination, and therein stamps the possible detour of a *clinamen*. That which I here call insignificance is this structure that establishes that a mark in itself is not necessarily linked, even in the form of the reference (*renvoi*), to a meaning or to a thing. Take, for example, the case of the proper name. It has no meaning in itself, at least insofar as it is a proper name. It does not refer (*renvoie*) to anyone; it designates someone only in a given context, for example (and for example only), because of an arbitrary convention. The French name Pierre has no meaning in itself. It is untranslatable, and if in my language it is the homonym of a common noun that not only has a possible referent but also a stable signification (the *pierre* or stone that one can cut to make cobblestone streets) that can lead to confusion, contamination, lapsus, or symptoms, this can bring about a fall while leaving the two "normal" functions of the mark without contact between each other. The proper name Pierre is insignificant because it does not name by means of a concept. It stands for only one person each time, and the multiplicity of Pierres in the world bears no relation to the multiplicity of stones (*pierres*) that form a class and possess enough common traits to establish a conceptual significance or a semantic generality. This will be equally evident in the relation between a numeral and a number and also in that between a number and a thing numbered. Between the meaning of the number 7 and the numerals 7 (Arabic or Roman numerals, the words *sept,* seven, *sieben*) there is no natural, necessary, or intrinsic affiliation. No natural bond, to use Saussurian terminology, between the signified and the signifier. Nor is there a natural bond between the signified (the general meaning of 7, the number 7) and all things (stones, horses, apples, stars or souls, men or women, for instance) that could be found together in groups of 7. One could say the same, *mutatis mutandis*, for all graphic marks, for all traits in general, phonic or not, linguistic or not. The paradox here is the following (I must state it in its broadest generality): to be a mark and to mark its marking effect, a mark must be capable of being *identified,* recognized as the same, being precisely *re-markable* from one context to another. It must be capable of being repeated, re-marked in its essential trait as the same. This accounts for the apparent solidity of its structure, of its type, its *stereotypy.* It is this that leads us here to speak of the atom, since one associates indestructibility with indivisibility. But more precisely, it is not simple since the identity of a mark is also its difference and its differential relation, varying each time according to context, to the network of other marks. The ideal iterability that forms the structure of all marks is that which undoubtedly allows them to be released from any context, to be freed from all determined bonds to its origin, its meaning, or its referent, to emigrate in order to play elsewhere, in whole or in part, another role. I say "in whole or in part" because by means of this essential insignificance the ideality or ideal identity of each mark (which is only a differential function without an ontological basis) can continue to divide itself and to give rise to the proliferation of other ideal identities. This iterability is thus that which allows a mark to be used more than once. It is more than one. It multiplies and divides itself internally. This imprints the capacity for diversion within its very movement. In the destination (*Bestimmung*) there is thus a principle of indetermination, chance, luck, or of destinerring. There is no assured destination precisely because of the mark and the proper name; in other words, because of this insignificance.

If I speak of the mark or the trace rather than the signifier, letter, or word, and if I refer these to the Democritian or Epicurian *stoikheion* in its greatest generality, it is for two reasons. First of all, this generality extends the mark beyond the verbal sign and even beyond human language. Thus I hesitate to speak of the "arbitrariness of the sign" in the manner of Hegel and Saussure. Then, within this very frame of reference, I prefer to diverge in turn from strict atomism and the atomistic interpretation of the *stoikheion.* My *clinamen,* my luck, or my chances (*mes chances*) are what lead me to think of the *clinamen* beginning with the divisibility of the mark.

Let me come back to literature, to the work of art, to the oeuvre in general or at least to that which one names as such in the tradition of our culture. Without the mark there is certainly no oeuvre. Each oeuvre, being absolutely singular in some respect, must have and admit the proper name. This is the condition of its iterability as such. From whence comes, perhaps, the general form of the privilege that it retains for us in our experience inasmuch as it is the locus of luck and of chance. The oeuvre provokes us to think of the event. This in turn challenges our attempts to *understand* luck and chance, to envisage them, to take them in hand, or to inscribe them within an anticipatory horizon. It is at least because of this that they are oeuvres and that they create an event, thereby challenging any program of reception. Oeuvres befall us. They speak about or unveil that which befalls *in* its befalling upon us. They overpower us inasmuch as they explain themselves with that which falls from above. The oeuvre is vertical and slightly leaning.

Freud often said that poets and artists—although he attempted to include their lives and oeuvres within the horizon of psychoanalytic knowledge (to make them lie down horizontally in the clinic)—had always anticipated and indeed overwhelmed the discourse of psychoanalysis. In the sense of filiation as well as authority, literature would be an ascendant akin to a house, a family, or a lineage. But what, more precisely, is at issue in this play of titles?

I will now take my chances with Freud's text. As you may already suspect, I am going to proceed somewhat by chance, without a horizon, as if with my eyes closed.

Third stroke of luck. By chance, I fall initially upon an example. By definition, there are nothing but examples in this domain. Freud tries to *understand* the forgetting of a proper name. He wants, therefore, in understanding, to efface the appearance of chance in the relation between a certain proper name and its having been forgotten. Which proper name? As if by chance, that of a disciple of Epicurus. In the third chapter of *The Psychopathology of Everyday Life,* "The Forgetting of Names and Sets of Words":

> Here is an example of name-forgetting[2] with yet another and very subtle motivation which its subject has explained himself: "When I was examined in philosophy as a subsidiary subject I was questioned by the examiner about the teachings of Epicurus, and after that I was asked if I knew who had taken up his theories in later centuries. I answered with the name of Pierre Gassendi, whom I had heard described as a disciple of Epicurus while I was sitting in a café only a couple of days before. To the surprised question how I knew that, I boldly answered that I had long been interested in Gassendi. The result of this was a certificate *magna cum laude,* but also unfortunately a subsequent obstinate tendency to forget the name Gassendi. My guilty conscience is, I think, to blame for my inability to remember the name in spite of all efforts; for I really ought not to have known it on that occasion either."

Now, Freud continues, to understand that, one must know that this subject attached great value to the title of doctor (Freud does not say, as I do, to the title of professor) "and [for how] many other things it has to serve as a substitute."

The person who has forgotten the proper name of the disciple of Epicurus is someone who is referring himself back to the time when he himself was a disciple, a student appearing before his masters at the moment of an examination. Freud has only to cite, to reproduce the interpretation of this disciple forgetting the name of a disciple, in identifying himself purely and simply, without taking the slightest initiative in interpretation, with this disciple who explains why he does not by chance forget the name of a disciple of Epicurus. To exaggerate slightly, one could say that Freud simultaneously identifies and transfers a symptom that could be called: the disciple of Epicurus and the forgetting of his name. I leave it to you to explore further; but never forget that throughout the history of Occidental culture the Democritian tradition, in which the names of Epicurus and his disciples are recorded, has been submitted since its origin (and initially under the violent authority of Plato) to a powerful repression. One can now follow its symptomatology, which begins with the effacement of the name of Democritus in the writings of Plato, even though Plato was familiar with his doctrine. Plato probably feared that one would draw some conclusion with respect to the proximity, indeed to the filiation, of some of his philosophemes. I leave it to you to investigate further this path as well.

I have just named Democritus after having in fact only spoken of his disciples and of the disciples of his disciples: Epicurus, Lucretius, Gassendi. Now the *fourth stroke of luck*: here is the master in person in Freud's text, the father Democritus, as analyst and the one who deciphers symptoms. This is not the only reason that I will cite this passage at the end of chapter 9 of *Psychopathology* ("Symptomatic and Chance Actions"). In the same passage (is this by chance?) Freud also reminds us of the privilege of literature and the priority of the poet. The latter has already said everything that the psychoanalyst would like to say. The psychoanalyst therefore can only repeat and indebt himself within a filiation; in particular, on the subject of symptomal deciphering of seemingly insignificant accidents. The absolute precursor, the grandfather here is the author of *Tristram Shandy*. I therefore cite Freud citing someone else citing Laurence Sterne (paragraph and citation that Freud added later as if to make amends for something previously forgotten in the earlier edition of 1920):

> In the field of symptomatic acts, too, psycho-analytic observation must concede priority to imaginative writers [*Dichter*]. It can only repeat what they have said long ago. Wilhelm Stross has drawn my attention to the following passage in Laurence Sterne's celebrated humorous novel, *Tristram Shandy:*
> "... And I am not at all surprised that *Gregory of Nazianzum*, upon observing the hasty and untoward gestures of *Julian*, should foretel he

would one day become an apostate;—or that St. *Ambrose* should turn his
Amanuensis out of doors, because of an indecent motion of his head,
which bent backwards and forwards like a flail;—or that *Democritus*
should conceive *Protagoras* to be a scholar, from seeing him bind up a fag-
got, and thrusting, as he did, the small twigs inwards.—There are a thousand unnoticed openings, continued my father, which let a penetrating
eye at once into a man's soul; and I maintain it, added he, that a man of
sense does not lay down his hat in coming into a room,—or take it up in
going out of it, but something escapes, which discovers him."

    In this sequence of citations taking us up to Democritus once again,
the *descendance* will not have escaped you. Freud acknowledges the debt
of the psychoanalyst, and this is also a filiation. This instance is exemplary since it engages Freud with respect to Sterne cited by Stross who in
turn cites, from *Tristram Shandy,* the speech of a father. It is a father who
speaks and whom he makes speak via the mouth of his son from a
thousand unnoticed openings ("a thousand unnoticed openings, continued *my* father, which let a penetrating eye [*ein sharfes Auge*] at once
into a man's soul"). By the mouth of his son, and by that of the poet,
this father will have cited in turn the ancestor of ancestors in this matter—notably, Democritus—the prototype of the analyst who knew how
to diagnose science itself, that is, "scholarship," and the *Gelehrtheit* of
Protagoras, beginning with nothing, with mere twigs. Democritus did
not identify just any symptom. In interpreting—an operation that consisted of *binding up* insignificant things, elementary bundles, in a certain way, of binding them evenly, and not in a haphazard fashion, by
turning them inward—Democritus deciphered a symptom that is quite
simply the symptom of knowledge, of the desire for knowledge, the
libido sciendi, scholarship, the *skholè*: which is simultaneously that
which tends toward laborious study and that which suspends ordinary
activity, the everyday relation to praxis, for this end. Protagoras, a man of
bonds and of disconnections, of the re-solution (*analuein*), is a type of
analyst. That would be the diagnosis that the analyst "Dupin" Democritus pronounces with regard to the symptom. Indeed, there are nothing
but analysts. That is, those who are analyzed in this textual abyss
wherein each is ever more engendered, generated, indebted, affiliated,
subjected, than the one before, all having descended or fallen from a
series of proto-analysts in an eminently divisible chain of proper names
and individuals: Freud, Stross, Sterne, the son and the father in *Tristram
Shandy*, Protagoras, Democritus, etc. Each of them has simultaneously
interpreted and reduced a random series. Each has passed it on to be read
by the other before the other. This chain is heterogeneous; only the
proper names, texts, and situations are different each time, yet all sub-
jects are inscribed and implicated in the scene that they claim to inter-

pret. This overall *"mise en scène"* certainly gives the impression of being predominantly literary. According to what Freud himself said, this would be *Tristram Shandy*. The great rendezvous could be the performative of the oeuvre. It would seem necessary to explore elsewhere the theme of the "rendezvous" (*Zusammentreffen, Zusammenkunft*) in the *Psychopathology*, notably in the last chapter.

The question I have just raised could be referred to as that of science and luck, or determinism and chance, and indeed this is the title of the last chapter of *Psychopathology*—"Determinism, Belief in Chance and Superstition." What happens to an interpretive science when its object is psychic and when it thus implicates in some respect the subject itself of that science? In this form, the question is rather classical. What happens when the "savant" acknowledges his debt or his dependence with regard to apparently nonscientific statements such as, for example, poetic or literary ones? And when an analytic attitude itself becomes a symptom? When there is a tendency to interpret the incidents or accidents that befall us—opportunely or not—by means of the reintroduction of determinism, necessity, or signification, does this signify in turn an abnormal or pathological relation to the real? For example, what is the difference between superstition or paranoia on the one hand, and science on the other, if they all mark a compulsive tendency to interpret random signs in order to reconstitute a meaning, a necessity, or a destination?

Freud asks himself this in the same chapter, and he must do so in a quasi-autobiographical manner. Implicating himself in the situation, he tells us in sum (and here we could parody a Nietzschean title, a type of Freudian *Ecce Homo*): *Why I am a good analyst* or *Why I am above all not superstitious and even less paranoid*; why I am moderate in my desire to interpret, why this desire is simply normal. In other words, why I have a very good relation to chance and am lucky in my transactions with it. And so you see, Freud tells us, what my chances are.

What are his chances?

Let us allow him to tell us a story whose truth or falsity would be of little consequence. Remember that in 1897 he confided to Fliess his conviction that no "index of reality" of any sort exists in the unconscious and that it is impossible to distinguish between truth and a fiction "invested with affect." But, as we shall examine shortly, Freud could only propose his work as scientific—in the classical sense—by reintroducing this limit between *Wahrheit* and *Dichtung,* so to speak.

Here is the exemplary story. It is not a story about vacations, as is the one of the *fort-da* with the mother, and yet it is the same. In this case, upon returning from vacation, we are between two types of *skholè*: leisure and study. When he returns from vacation Freud thinks of the patients that he will see again and initially of an elderly, ninety-year-old

woman about whom he has already spoken and indeed whom he has
already given several years of medical treatment. Each year he wonders
how much time remains for the old woman. One particular day, Freud,
being in a hurry, hires a coachman who, like everyone else in the neighborhood, knew the address of this patient. He knew the destination: all
the problems that we are speaking about fall under the general category
of the address, of forwarding, of the destination, and hence of the thrust
(*jet*) or the project of the dispatch (*projet d'un envoi*). The fall, the
accident, the case always arises to post the dispatch (*envoi*) from some
interruption or detour that creates the symptom. (This is why I allow
myself to record these modest reflections following more patiently elaborated work which is concerned with the relation between psychoanalysis,
literature, and philosophy on the one hand, and the question of the
dispatch [*envoi*] and of the destination on the other.) The coachman—
who knows the address, the correct one—stops, however, in front of
another house, which has the same number (always a question of number) but on a parallel street. Freud reproves the man, who then apologizes. Is this error concerning the address simply an accident or does it
actually mean something? Freud's answer is clear and firm, at least in
appearance: "Certainly not to me, but if I were superstitious
[*abergläubisch*], I should see an omen [*Vorzeichen*] in the incident, the
finger of fate [*Fingerzeig des Schicksals*] announcing that this year would
be the old lady's last."

Along the way, two values of destination superimpose themselves
upon each other: that of the address or place of destination and that of
destiny (*Schicksal*), the dimensions and direction of that which is dispatched, sent, *geschickt*. (One of the meanings of the *adresse* in French,
that is to say, skillfulness [*habilité*], translates the word *Geschick*.) One
wonders, then, if the false address (and the apparent *maladresse* or
blunder of the coachman) do not in advance point toward the true and
correct destination—that is, the coming death of the old woman. Is it
the case that the coachman did not actually go to the correct address, the
one that is appropriate (*où ça tombe bien*), to speak of the accident that
will not fail to occur? Bad luck (*malchance*) or wickedness (*méchance*)
would invert its sign. This will be the chance for the truth to reveal itself.
A lapsus is revealing in the sense that it gives another truth its chance.
The limit between the conscious and unconscious, that is, between the
unconscious "I" and the other of consciousness, is perhaps this possibility for my fortune (*mes chances*) to be misfortune (*malchance*) and for
my misfortune to be in truth fortunate (*une chance*).

Freud claims that he does not stop, in this case, at the revelation of
Schicksal by the *"Adresse"* since he knows that he is not superstitious.
He considers the incident (*Vorfall*) to be an accident or a contingency

without further signification (*eine Zufälligkeit ohne weiteren Sinn*). It would have been otherwise, he continues, if he *himself* had been the origin of the error and if, by distraction and on foot, he had stopped at the wrong address. In that case, there would have been *Vergehen*—mistaken conduct calling for interpretation (*Deutung*). All of this without chance (*Zufall*) in the least. But this was not the case. It was the coachman who was mistaken and Freud is not superstitious. He stresses the point. If he were, he would have stopped at this interpretation. But he does not stop there. Well, not for a long time, since he found it necessary to raise such a question, which shows this hypothesis also to have crossed his mind. He only distinguishes himself from the superstitious person at the moment of concluding at the instant of judgment and not at all during the unfolding of the interpretation. But Freud does not recognize this at any point in the following paragraph since he explains to us everything that distinguishes him from a superstitious man. He will only go as far as admitting that the only thing he has in common with the superstitious man is the tendency, the "compulsion" (*Zwang*) to interpret: "not to let chance count as chance but to interpret it." The hermeneutic compulsion—that is what superstition and "normal" psychoanalysis have in common. Freud says it explicitly. He does not believe in chance any more than the superstitious do. What this means is that they both believe in chance if to believe in chance means that one believes that all chance means something and therefore that there is no chance. Thus we have the identity of non-chance and chance and of misfortune (*mé-chance*) and fortune (*la chance*).

Before examining the criteria proposed by Freud to distinguish between these two hermeneutic compulsions, we shall take a brief detour from this side of these fortunes, although I am less and less sure as to whether they are misfortunes, my fortunes, or those of Freud (*méchance, mes chances ou celles de Freud*). I reread as if for the first time the story of the address and the coachman. One should notice that he seems to have had neither of the two compulsions and not to have asked himself any such questions. Indeed, Freud seems immediately to exclude all communication between the coachman's unconscious and his own. Following my own compulsion again, I immediately said to myself: and what if the old woman were Freud's mother? Certainly you know very well how much he feared the death of his mother, but he was also afraid of dying before her—a double bind. For all kinds of reasons evident in the reading, this patient could not simply be his mother. She could nevertheless *represent* his mother and take her place. Now here is my stroke of luck, *the fifth*, I believe: Freud had already spoken of this old woman in a passage to which I hasten to return, for according to his phantasm that he exhibits and interprets himself, she indeed is his mother. This entails, he tells us, the single example of a medical mistake in his experience as a doctor. Instead of administering two drops of eye lotion in the woman's eyes and giving her the usual injection of morphine, Freud does the opposite: he puts the morphine in her eyes. It is not a dream of injection, as in the case of Irma, but the reality of an instillation, and that of a liquid that he should have injected. Freud is frightened even though there is no real danger. A few drops of morphine at 2 percent in the conjunctival sac would cause no great harm, but in analyzing this disproportionate fear, which is a symptom, he falls upon the common expression *"sich an der Alten vergreifen,"* "to do violence to the old woman," *vergreifen* meaning both "to make a blunder" and "to commit an assault" (cf. Strachey). This puts him on the track of Oedipus and Jocasta. Freud develops this in greater detail in a passage to which I refer you (Chap. 8, *"Das Vergreifen,"* "Bungled Actions"). Most of the symptoms in this chapter are found to be falls (*chutes*).

Let us now return to the inviolable frontiers that Freud wants to sustain at any price between the superstitious and himself. He does not propose a general distinction, however. Speaking in the first person, he uses all of his eloquence to convince us that he is certainly not superstitious: *"Ich unterscheide mich also von einem Abergläubischen in folgendem,* I am therefore different from a superstitious person in the following way. . . ."* All of his declarations are developed explicitly in the mode of "I believe," "I do not believe," I am not superstitious because *"Ich glaube dass"* or *"Ich glaube nicht dass."* What does he not believe? That an event having nothing to do with his psychic life (the coachman's error, for example) could teach him anything about a future reality. But he believes that an apparently nonintentional manifestation of his psychic life unveils something hidden that belongs only to his psychic life. He summarizes this in the following: "I believe in external (real) chance, it is true, but not in internal (psychical) accidental events. With the superstitious person it is the other way round." A rather abrupt way of collecting things and marking limits. Freud forgets to formalize what he has just stated—the relation to the future. I must leave this issue aside. It relates to the laborious distinction that Freud attempts elsewhere between telepathy and thought transmission. I return here once again to the fragment detached from *La carte postale*, entitled: "Telepathy."

"I believe [*Ich glaube*] in external (real) chance, it is true, but not in internal (psychical) chance. With the superstitious person it is the other way round [*Der Abergläubische umgekehrt*]." One must read this vocabulary of belief very carefully. While availing himself of the word "belief" Freud seems in effect to oppose a normal attitude, that of scientific objectivity, to superstitious belief, that of the *Abergläubischer*, which he claims not to have. He opposes one belief to another, a belief to a credulity. He believes in determinism in the internal and psychic domain. This does not mean—and here one must be careful, I believe—that he does not believe in the occurrence of chance in the external world, nor does it mean that he would agree that the world is thrown to chance and to chaos. One could find a thousand declarations by Freud attesting a completely determinist conviction of the positivistic type prevalent in his day. He even hoped one day to see the science of the psyche united, in a certain way, with the biophysical sciences. And in this precise context, which we are analyzing here, he is only interested in the type of *belief*, of attitude or subjective experience appropriate to the founding of scientific objectivity in the circumscribed domain of psychic events. One must not confuse the domains, he tells us, nor their proper causalities. For example, one must not confuse that which in the drive comes from the biophysical and organic with that which is represented in the world of the psyche. These are the limits that the superstitious person does not recognize in his or her disbelief in psychic determinism. Freud, however, does believe in it, and he thus affirms his project of founding psychoanalysis as a positive science. This tradition has been sustained. For example, Lacan follows Freud to the letter on this point, when he says that a letter always arrives at its destination. There is no chance in the unconscious. The apparent randomness must be placed in the service of an unavoidable necessity that in fact is never contradicted.

But we are speaking of chance. In this historical-theoretical conjuncture one might be tempted to calculate the probabilities of the appearance of the event named: psychoanalysis as a project of positive science. This is not my proposal, however.

I do not believe that Freud believes in *actual* chance in external things. For him, the *believing experience* that *finite* beings have of this external world, once the two series, worlds, or contexts are dissociated (inside / outside), is *normally* and *legitimately* the acceptance of chance, of a margin of chance or probability that it would not be normal or serious to want to reduce or exclude. One could then say, as with the classical determinist conception, that the *effects* of chance (empirically verified) appear in the interference of relatively independent series, of "little worlds" that are not closed. The implicit question to which Freud is responding is thus not the larger one of chance (objective or subjective, in things or in us, mathematical or empirical). It is not this question in its modern or classical form. It is only that of the *believing attitude* before the effects of chance, given the two series of causality: psychic / physical, internal / external. Of course these two series or two contextual worlds are only distinguishable from within a culture (or a "world") that therein forms the most general context. It is for us, in the Occident, the culture of common sense that is marked by a powerful scientifico-philo-sophic tradition, metaphysics, technics, the opposition of subject/object (*sujet/objet*), and precisely a certain organization of the throw (*jet*). Through several differentiated relays, this culture goes back at least to Plato, where the repression of Democritus perhaps leaves the trace of a very large symptom. Without being able to take this route today, I will locate only what I have called above a *mark*: in the construction of its concept none of the limits or oppositions that I have just invoked are considered absolutely pertinent or decisive, but rather as presuppositions to be deconstructed.

We also know that in other passages, in other problematic contexts, Freud carefully avoids ontologizing or substantializing the limit between outside and inside, between the biophysical and the psychic. But in the *Psychopathology* and elsewhere he requires this limit not only to protect this fragile, enigmatic, threatened defensive state that one calls "nor-mality" but also to circumscribe a solid context (once again stereotomy), the unity of a field of coherent and determinist interpretation, that which we so calmly call psychoanalysis *itself*. But he already had great difficulties with this in other places where he tackles such formidable issues as that of the drive ("a concept . . . on the frontier between the mental and the physical," *Three Essays, S.E.* 7: 168), of telepathy, or of the transmission of thought. At least to the extent that he circumscribes psychoanalysis, the science of the psyche, so as to separate it from the other sciences, Freud provisionally suspends all epistemological relations to the sciences or to the modern problems concerning chance. He wants, in short, to constitute a science of *experience* (conscious or unconscious) as the rapport of a finite being who is thrown (*jeté*) into the world. And this thrown being projects (*Cet être-jeté projette*).

Precisely at this point it is even more difficult for Freud to sustain this limit that separates him from the superstitious person since they both share the hermeneutic compulsion. If the superstitious person pro-jects (*projette, projiziert*), if he throws (*jette*) toward the outside and ahead of himself the "motivations" that Freud claims to be looking for on the inside, if he interprets chance from the standpoint of an external "event" at the point where Freud reduces it or leads it back to a "thought," it is because essentially the superstitious person does not believe, any more than Freud, in the solidity of the spaces circumscribed by our Occidental stereotymy. He does not believe in the contextualizing and framing but not actual limits between the psychic and the physical, the inside and the outside, not to mention all of the other connected oppositions. More so than Freud, more so than this Freud here, the superstitious person is sensitive to the precariousness of the contextual circumscriptions of the epistemological frames, the *constructs* and the *artifacts* that enable us, for life's convenience and for the mastery of limited networks of knowledge and technics, to separate the psychic from the physical or the inside from the outside. The superstitious person simply has a different experience of this same finitude.

But let us not make the superstitious person into a thinker capable of deconstructing the limits or the oppositions that Freud himself sustained dogmatically here in order to circumscribe the field of a scientific psychoanalysis. Inversely, if I might be permitted to put this forward, some sensitivity to superstition is perhaps not a useless stimulation for the deconstructive desire. But in fact, in the eyes of Freud, the superstitious person, to the same extent as the religious one and the metaphysician, is not the one who places the limits in question in the name of science, of the enlightened, or even in that of deconstruction. It is someone who, respecting these limits, projects on the outside that which is inside and that in which he lives. Through this concept of *projection* (or throwing), the scheme of the *jet* again provides the essential mediation. In the following paragraph Freud describes superstition, modern religion, metaphysics itself as "nothing but psychology projected [*projizierte*] into the external world." (These projections evidently have a fictional structure and, as in the case of the unconscious, one does not distinguish here between reality and "fiction invested with affect.") This paragraph multiplies the analogies, and Freud is overwhelmed by them. Such is always the case whenever he is forced to transgress the limits or the "frames of reference" that are simultaneously convenient and without solidity. Not having the time for a more extensive development, I quote and emphasize the terms which situate the difficulty:

> The obscure recognition (the endopsychic perception, *as it were*) of psychical factors and relations in the unconscious *is mirrored* [*spiegelt sich—es ist schwer, es anders zu sagen*]—*it is difficult to express it in other terms, and here the analogy with paranoia must come to our aid* in the construction of a supernatural reality, which is *destined to be changed back once more by science into the psychology of the unconscious.* One could venture to explain in this way the myths of paradise and *the fall* of man, of God, of good and evil, of immortality and so on, *and to transform metaphysics into metapsychology.* The gap between the paranoiac's displacement and that of the superstitious person is less wide than it appears at first sight. . . . They [primitive human beings] behaved, therefore, just like paranoiacs, who draw conclusions from insignificant signs given them by other people, and just like all normal people, who quite rightly base their estimate of their neighbours' characters on their chance and unintentional actions.

This discourse is built on an impressive series of approximations and declared analogies. It does not only interpret the motif of the fall or decline, of the *méchance* of man as a superstitious projection—or even paranoiac, in any case, of a psychological order. It does not only suggest as in *Totem and Taboo* that there is a certain analogy between paranoid mania and a (deformed) philosophic system. It projects the reconversion into science or into metapsychology of the metaphysical discourse *from which it nonetheless obtains the concepts themselves for this project* and operation—notably, the oppositional limits between the psychic and the physical, the inside and the outside, not to mention all those that depend on them. Playing fiction against fiction, projection against projection, this gesture could appear—depending on the case—naïve or audacious, dogmatic or hypercritical. I will not choose (*trancher*) between them, and indeed I wonder if there really is a choice.

Freud works by playing with the topologies and the conceptual limits of inherited discourses, be they philosophical or scientific. The provisional circumscription of an explanatory context—one might say of a field of knowledge—supposes something like the performative of a convention and a fiction each time, as well as the contract that serves to guarantee new performatives. Freud acknowledges that he does not believe in the substantial value of these limits nor in the definitive character of such circumscriptions. Having taken account of a certain state of the discourse, of discourses, and of many sciences at the same time, having taken account also of the necessity of constituting a theory and a practice, the assignment of such limits is indispensable. But it is indispensable to someone—Freud, for example—at a particular moment in a particular situation. Yet there is nothing relativist or empiricist in this claim. Elsewhere, I have tried to show how the inscription of a proper name, of a certain autobiography, and of a certain fictional projection might be constitutive for psychoanalytic discourse and indeed for the very structure of its occurrence (*événement*). The event of its occurrence thus raises within itself the questions of chance and literature. Not that all fiction and all inscriptions of proper names have had a literary dimension or a relation to the work of art as such; rather, they arise in the place where, between the movement of science—notably when it is concerned with random structures—and that of philosophy, of the arts—literary or not—the limits cannot be actual and static or *solid* but rather only the effects of contextual circumscription. Neither linear nor indivisible, they would arise instead from an analysis that I will call (with some circumspection) *programmatological*, at the intersection of a pragmatics and a grammatology. Open to a different sense of the dispatch (*envoi*) and of dispatches (*envois*), programmatology should always take the situation of the marks into account; in particular that of utterances, the place of senders and addressees, of framing and of the sociohistorical circumscription, and so forth. It should therefore take account of the problematics of randomness in all fields where it evolves: physics, biology, game theory, and the like. In this respect, the advent of psychoanalysis is a complex event not only in terms of its historical probability but in terms of a discourse that remains open and that attempts at each instant to regulate itself—yet affirming its originality—according to the scientific and artistic treatment of randomness, which in the course of this century has undergone continued transformation. This is where one can find overdetermined comings and goings (*allers et retours*), a game of advances and delays upon which I should renounce further speculation but that I wish to illustrate, in conclusion, by a citation. If I conclude with the conclusion of *Leonardo da Vinci and a Memory of His Childhood*, it is for three reasons. These do not exclude the randomness of the moment where, as my exposé is becoming much too long, *la chute* (in French one says *la chute* [the fall] or the *envoi* for the end of a lecture) makes me fall upon this text rather than another. This will be *my last chance*. It is the moment when suddenly (*d'un seul coup*) two dice come to a standstill and we must tally the score. We are thus touching upon the incalculable and the innumerable.

Freud concludes, as you will see, by an allusion to the incalculable and the innumerable. This is the first reason to cite him. But it is precisely a question of the incalculability and the innumerability of the reasons or the causes (*ragioni, causes, Ursachen*) that are in nature and that "never enter experience." Second reason: this allusion to nature as "full of countless causes [*ragioni*] that never enter experience" is a quasi-citation and from an artist. Once again indebtedness and filiation. Freud cites Leonardo da Vinci, whom he had come to recognize as being out of the reach of analytical science by virtue of a certain random enigma. But Freud cites da Vinci approximately citing Shakespeare, or rather Hamlet the son: "*La natura è piena d'infinite ragioni che non furono mai in isperienza*," in place of "There are more things in heaven and earth Horatio / Than are dreamt of in your philosophy." Extending across numerous mediators, the debt is once again acknowledged with respect to the poet or even to a dramatic character that one has so often wished to have lie down on the couch. Literature perhaps need not resist the clinic. To stay with our present argument, let us say that art, in particular the "art of discourse" and literature, only represents a certain power of indeterminacy that sustains the capacity of *performatively* circumscribing its own context for its own event, that of the oeuvre. It is perhaps a kind of freedom, a large margin in the play of this circumscription (*découpe*). This stereotomic margin is very large and perhaps even the largest of all at a certain time in history, but it is not infinite. The appearance of arbitrariness or chance (literature as the place of proper names, if you wish) has to do with this margin. But this is also the place of the greatest symptomatology. Giving the greatest chance to chance, it reappropriates chance itself into necessity or fatality. Literature plays nature for fortune—and art. ("Nature's above art in that respect"— *King Lear.*) Consequently, the third reason for this citation: it appeases the sense of remorse or misfortune ("How malicious is my fortune," says the bastard Edmund in *King Lear*), the regret I feel in not having attempted with you, as I initially projected, an analysis of *King Lear* that would take us beyond Freud's observations in *The Theme of the Three Caskets* (1913). I would have followed the play of Nature and Fortune there, the words "nature" and "fortune," and also the abundantly numerous "letters" (for example, the "thrown letter"), the "wisdom of nature," "prediction" ("there's son against father: the king falls from bias of nature"), "planetary influence" for "a sectary astronomical," of "epicurism," "posts," letters and lips to unseal, "gentle wax" and the "reason in madness" of Lear ("I am even / The natural fool of fortune"). And taking more time, but that will be for another time, I would have attempted to read with you together, between the lines of Shakespeare, Freud and Heidegger's reflections on *Moira* (in *The Theme of the Three Caskets* and in *Moira*). As a solution of compromise between the things I do and do not renounce here, I shall take my chances with the following citation of a citation of a citation. I shall cite Freud citing da Vinci citing Shakespeare. Notice in particular the play of limits and self-limitations that I stress in the passage. These are the strokes (*coups*) and the chances of psychoanalysis. I will be satisfied to propose a title in English for this citation:

SUBLIMING DISSEMINATION

> Instincts and their transformations [*Die Triebe und ihre Umwandlungen*] are at the limit of what is discernible by psycho-analysis. From that point it gives place to biological research. We are obliged to look for the source of the tendency to repression and the capacity for sublimation in the organic foundations of character on which the mental structure is only afterwards erected. Since artistic talent and capacity are intimately connected with sublimation we must admit that the nature of artistic function is also inaccessible to us along psychoanalytic lines. The tendency of biological research to-day is to explain the chief features in a person's organic constitution as being the result of the blending of male and female dispositions, based on [chemical] substances. Leonardo's physical beauty and his lefthandedness might be quoted in support of this view. *We will not, however, leave the ground of purely psychological research.*

Once again deliberate self-limitation gives psychoanalysis its only chance as a science. It circumscribes a context into which external randomness no longer penetrates. Biogenetics is not devoid of randomness and neither is the psyche, but the orders or the random sequences must not communicate or cross over into the same grouping, at least if one wants to distinguish between orders of calculable necessity. There must be no bastardy or hybridization, no accidental grafts between these two generalities, genres, or genealogies. But how is one to eliminate the throws of bastardy's dice?, one could ask the author of *Leonardo*. Is not the concept of sublimation, like that of the drive, precisely the concept of bastardy?

> Our aim remains that of demonstrating the connection along the path of instinctual activity between a person's external experiences and his reactions. Even if psycho-analysis does not throw light on the fact of Leonardo's artistic power, it at least renders its manifestations and its limitations intelligible to us. It seems at any rate as if only a man who had had Leonardo's childhood experiences could have painted the Mona Lisa and the St. Anne, have secured so melancholy a fate for his works and have embarked on such an astonishing career as a natural scientist, as if the key to all his achievements and *misfortunes* [emphasis added] lay hidden in the childhood phantasy of the vulture.
>
> But may one not take objection to the findings of an inquiry which ascribes to accidental circumstances [*Zufälligkeiten*] of his parental constellation so decisive an influence on a person's fate [*Schicksal*]—which, for example, makes Leonardo's fate depend on his illegitimate birth and on the barrenness of his first stepmother Donna Albiera? I think one has no right to do so. If one considers chance [*Zufall*] to be unworthy of determining our fate, it is simply a relapse into the pious view of the Universe which Leonardo himself was on the way of overcoming when he wrote that the sun does not move. We naturally feel hurt that a just God and a kindly providence do not protect us better from such influences during the most defenceless period of our lives. At the same time we are all too ready to forget that in fact every thing to do with our life is chance [*Zufall*], from our origin out of the meeting of spermatozoon and ovum onwards [this is also that which I name, in my language, dissemination—J.D.]—chance which nevertheless has a share in the law and necessity of nature, and which merely lacks any connection with our wishes and illusions. The apportioning of the determining factors of our life between the "necessities" of our constitution and the "chances" [*Zufälligkeiten*] of our childhood may still be uncertain in detail; but in general it is no longer possible to doubt the importance precisely of the first years of our childhood. We all still show too little respect for Nature which (in the obscure words of Leonardo which recall Hamlet's lines) "is full of countless causes [*'ragioni'*] that never enter experience."
>
> Every one of us human beings corresponds to one of the countless experiments in which these "*ragioni*" of nature force their way into experience. [*S.E.* 11:136–37]

Freud loves and looks after Nature.

Among the paths through which Nature erupts in our experience a mistake always remains possible—a *Vergreifen* or bastardy.

In looking after Nature Freud can still mistake the address or *pharmakon*, he can replace the eye drops with morphine, the old woman could be his mother or his mother-in-law, and the "I" of the coachman is perhaps not an other. He is perhaps not good. Maybe a bastard— maybe it is I rereading, under the influence of some drug, the myth of the harnessing and fall of souls in the *Phaedrus*. But Plato too, already, explained that coachmen are always "good" and composed "of good elements" (*ex agatôn*), whereas for other beings there is a mixture. It is true that when Plato makes Socrates speak he cites *Stésichore* (244a) and that prior to the myth he reminds us: *"ouk est' etymos logos ôs an . . . ,"* "there is no true language if. . . ." I leave you to explore further.

NOTES

Translated by Irene Harvey and Avital Ronell.

The Edith Weigert Lecture, sponsored by the Forum on Psychiatry and the Humanities, Washington School of Psychiatry, October 15, 1982.

1. In a certain way this essay proposes an almost silent reading of the word *"tombe"* (tomb) or *"tomber"* (to fall) in *La carte postale*. This is one of the most frequently used words in the *Envois*. Take for example the entry for March 14, 1979: "Somebody else, whom I know well, would unbind himself to run in the other direction. I'll wager that he falls upon you again; I fell in well with you, so I'm staying." On the following day: "If you were insane you would have come to wait for me like a hallucinating woman. I would have run towards you along the platform, near the tracks, and I would have done everything not to fall." If I quote this book, I do so because I find it included in the program of our encounter—it was in a certain sense inscribed in its charter. Don't accuse me, therefore, of being, as you say in English, "self-centered." In truth I always dreamt of writing a *self-centered* text; I never arrived at that point—I always fall upon the others. This will end up by being known.

2. The preceding passage in Freud was concerned with the substitution of the names of Nietzsche and Wilde, among others, for that of Jung, which a woman could not remember, associating Wilde and Nietzsche with the idea of "mental illness." "You Freudians will go on looking for the causes of insanity till you're insane yourselves [*geisteskrank*]." Then: "I can't bear Wilde and Nietzsche. I don't understand them. I hear they were both homosexuals." Nietzsche is also a name that Freud would have very much liked to forget. He occasionally succeeded and he avows this. Concerning chance and chaos there would be a great deal to say at this point in the name of Nietzsche.

REFERENCES

Baudelaire, C. *Edgar Allan Poe: Sa vie et ses ouvrages*. Edited by W. T. Bandy. Toronto: University of Toronto Press, 1973.

Derrida, J. *La carte postale*. Paris: Flammarion, 1980.

Epicurus. *Letters, Principal Doctrines, and Vatican Sayings*. Translated by R. Geer. Indianapolis: Bobbs-Merrill, 1964.

Freud, S. *Standard Edition of the Complete Psychological Works*. London: Hogarth, 1953-74.

The Psychopathology of Everyday Life (1901), vol. 6.

Three Essays on the Theory of Sexuality (1905), vol. 7.

Leonardo da Vinci and a Memory of His Childhood (1910), vol. 11.

"The Theme of the Three Caskets" (1913), vol. 12.

Heidegger, M. *Die Frage nach dem Ding* (1935-62). Tübingen: Niemeyer, 1962.

———. *Wegmarken*. Frankfurt: Klostermann, 1967.

———. *Sein und Zeit*. Frankfurt: Niemeyer, 1977.

———. *Aletheia*, 1943.

Lacan, J. "The Seminar on 'The Purloined Letter.' " Translated by J. Mehlman. *Yale French Studies* 48 (1972): 39-72.

Sterne, L. *Tristram Shandy*. New York: Norton, 1979.

2 The Debts of Deconstruction and Other, Related Assumptions

T o set us on our way, three epigraphs. The first, from the lecture by Jacques Derrida included in this volume, "My Chances/Mes Chances":

> Don't accuse me, therefore, of being, as you say in English, "self-centered." In truth I always dreamt of writing a *self-centered* text; I never arrived at that point—I always fall upon the others. This will end up by being known. [Derrida, note 1]

The second, more to the point perhaps, is from Laurence Sterne's *Tristram Shandy:*

> The Mortgager and Mortgagée differ the one from the other, not more in length of purse, than the Jester and Jestée do, in that of memory. But in this the comparison between them runs, as the scholiasts call it, upon all-four; which, by the bye, is upon one or two legs more than some of the best of Homer's can pretend to;—namely, That the one raises a sum, and the other a laugh at your expense, and thinks no more about it. Interest, however, still runs on in both cases;—the periodical or accidental payments of it, just serving to keep the memory of the affair alive; till, at length, in some evil hour—pop comes the creditor upon each, and by demanding principal upon the spot, together with full interest to the very day, makes them both feel the full extent of their obligations. [Book 1, chap. 12]

33

And finally, the third, which is also the shortest, is taken from the preface to Nietzsche's autobiography, *Ecce Homo:*

> Under these circumstances there is an obligation, against which rebel at bottom my habits, and even more the pride of my instincts, namely, to declare: *Hear me! For I am such and such. Above all, do not mistake me for another!*

I

Readers of Jacques Derrida's *La carte postale* will doubtless recall the following anecdote, recounted in a long footnote early in the *Envois:*

> I feel obliged to note, here and now, that this very morning, August 22, 1979, around 10 A.M., as I was typing this page in view of the present publication, the telephone rings. The United States. The American operator asks me if I will accept a "collect call" . . . from Martin (she says Martine or martini) Heidegger. As is often the case in such situations, which I know only too well, since I must often call collect myself, I can hear vaguely familiar voices at the other end of the intercontinental line: someone is listening to me, awaiting my reaction. What is he going to do with the ghost or the Geist of Martin? I can hardly summarize the entire chemistry of the calculation that led me, very quickly, to refuse ("It's a joke, I do not accept"), after having the name of Martini Heidegger repeated several times, in the hope that the author of the farce would finally be named. Who, in short, pays: the addressee or the sender? Who ought to pay? The question is very difficult, but this morning I thought that I ought not to pay, apart from adding this note of thanks. [*La carte postale,* pp. 25–26]

It is to this "difficult" but decisive question—who pays, the sender or the addressee?—that these remarks will be addressed, in something less than systematic fashion. Let us begin, then, with this anecdote, in which, properly speaking, nothing really happens: unless, that is, the refusal to accept a collect call—one which is obviously a "farce," a "joke"—can be said to constitute an event of sorts. But even as a mere joke, the story is meager, without punch line or *pointe,* it would seem, unless the volatilization of the name "Martin," exchanging its gender or even its species, is to be considered a *pointe.*

And yet, if the fate of a joke depends, above all, upon its timing, this one could not have come at a more propitious moment.

> I know that I will be suspected of having invented the whole thing, because it's too good to be true. But what can I do? It's true, strictly and entirely true, the date, the hour, the contents, etc. The name of Heidegger

had just been written, after "Freud," in the letter I am in the process of transcribing in the machine. [p. 26]

In that letter, as in many others of the *Envois,* the writer—whom, for obvious reasons of convenience, but without seeking to prejudice an issue yet to be discussed, I shall henceforth refer to as "Derrida"—was ruminating upon that "old couple," Socrates and Plato, and in particular, upon their relative positions in the history of philosophy, but also as depicted upon a postcard of an engraving by Matthew Paris. In this letter, Derrida remarks that the drawing calls into question the very "charta" upon which our entire "bildopedic culture" is based, one which prescribes that "Socrates comes *before* Plato," and hence, that "there is between them—and in general—an order of generation, an irreversible sequence of inheritance. Socrates is before, not in front of, but before Plato, hence behind him and the charta binds us to this order." Precisely this "order," however, is silently but all the more effectively *countermanded* by the remarkable postcard, in which "plato" is placed behind a Socrates who, for once, is shown writing.

Of this, Derrida reflects, even Nietzsche suspected nothing:

> He understood nothing of the initial catastrophe. . . . He believed, as did everyone else, that Socrates did not write, that he came before Plato, who wrote more or less under his dictate. . . . From this point of view, N. believed Plato and didn't overturn anything at all. The entire "overturning" has remained within the program of this credulity. [p. 25]

The reference here is, of course, to Heidegger's reading of Nietzsche as the *Umkehrung,* the "overturning" of Platonism. And thus, we arrive at the fateful sentence, resuming all that has preceded, before it itself, perhaps, is resumed in the call that arrives just in time to punctuate its phrase:

> The entire "overturning" has remained within the program of this credulity. And this holds *a fortiori* . . . for Freud and Heidegger. [p. 25]

Small wonder that the ghost or *Geist* of Martine (or martini) Heidegger should have picked this particular moment to intervene, for nothing less than his (her?) credibility and credit had just been called into question. The History of Metaphysics, programming and prescribing its proper overturning, including the very question—and the questioner—of the Meaning of Being: here is an assertion destined to drive the Sage of Todtnauberg straight to the nearest telephone booth in a vain attempt to assert his right of response.

But the call, not surprisingly, was refused, and we can only speculate as to what the response at the other end of the line might have been: amusement, shock, incredulity? "Not accepted; are you certain?" "*Nicht angenommen?*" Nor are we told if the callers ever called back. Or if the call was ever traced.

Indeed, all we do find out is that "my private relationship to Martin does not operate on the same exchange." To this "exchange"—this *standard*—we shall have occasion to return.

II

What *does* pass by the "same standard," it would seem, is Freud's relationship to Nietzsche, at least as it is described in "Speculer—sur 'Freud' " (the second major section of *La carte postale*). It is precisely Freud's refusal to assume his debt toward Nietzsche, and through the latter, toward philosophy in general, that constitutes Derrida's point of departure in posing the question of Freud's speculations. Or rather, it is not simply the refusal of a debt, but the astonishing *ease* with which it is performed, that fascinates Derrida:

> Freud . . . is so much at ease in such an embarrassing situation, he declines the debt with such rapid assurance, with such imperturbable facility that one cannot but wonder whether the debt in question is his at all, or whether it is not the debt of another? [pp. 280–81]

The passage referred to here is from Freud's *Autobiographical Study*, in which he distinguishes the character of his speculation from that of philosophy proper (*S.E.* 20: 59). In this context he mentions the names of Fechner, Schopenhauer, and Nietzsche; if he has deliberately shunned the latter, Freud writes, it is because of the proximity of his insights to the results of psychoanalysis, a proximity that might have threatened Freud's "independence of mind" (*Unbefangenheit*).

What appears remarkable in this acknowledgment, as far as Derrida is concerned, is its matter-of-factness. To decline a debt with such facility is possibly the sign that it is not *one's* debt at all, but rather that of *another*. But, Derrida ruminates, perhaps this is not peculiar to Freud at all:

> What if the debt were always that of another? How one might both feel and not feel, in advance, acquitted and guilty of the debt of another if the latter, lodged in oneself by the effect of a singular topology, returns to itself [*revient à soi*: amounts to the same] in accordance with a filiation that has yet to be thought out . . . ? [p. 281][1]

The brunt of this question, concerning the subject of debt, its "rightful owner" as it were, is concentrated in the untranslatable ambiguity of the French phrase—one that recurs insistently in "Speculer—sur 'Freud' " —*revenir à soi;* for if the subject of debt is another, and if that other is said to "return to the fold," the Self folded into that fold can be either the Other of the Other—that is, "oneself"—or that Other *itself.* Or perhaps both: oneself *as* itself. In which case, however, the Self (*soi*) would begin to lose much of its consoling familiarity, as that instance of synthesis and of identity in which differences are surmounted and alterities contained. Instead, this "self" would begin to acquire an uncanny aspect as a revenant (*à soi*) that never quite succeeds in arriving.

Such a movement of revenants is described in regard to the celebrated *fort-da* game of *Beyond the Pleasure Principle.* The point of view of the narrator, spectator, theoretician, is that of the "PP": the pleasure principle, grandfather of Freudian metapsychology, but no more secure in its place than is the actual "PP" himself, Freud as grandfather of Ernst. Behind the seeming stability and unicity of an apparently proper name, Derrida unravels—or rather, *weaves*—a network of threads (*fils*) within which each place is the overdetermined knot or scene of multiple scenarios: the spectator-speculator is interested in the spectacle he describes not merely as Grandfather (pp), but as father of Sophie, and as double of Ernst, with whom he identifies as the elder brother of a detested, younger rival. One result of such "demultiplication" would be to unleash a power of repetition that no stable structure could ever hope to comprehend, contain, or amortize in the name of truth. In short, the Freudian master-key, the Oedipus complex, would appear as only *one* figure among *others.* This is precisely the claim that emerges from Derrida's reading of the *fort-da:*

> But all the interweavings of fort-da (the scene of writing and of heritage that plays itself out there in ellipse, the abyss of its deferred report, the commutation of places, the leap of generations, the dissymmetry of contracts, in short, everything that *dispatches itself* in a graphics of repetition that dislocates the summary "triangle") can only be called oedipal if one names it, by synecdoche, by means of only one of its effects, one of the most taut, I mean most tightly drawn and determined in its exemplarity. In its notorious and strict sense, the oedipal trait is only a rection for the leading thread of the spool. [p. 362]

But if the "oedipal trait" or triangle "is only a rection"—and the connotations of the word are no less bizarre in French than in English— "only a rection" for the cast of the spool in the game of *fort-da;* if, in other words, it is "only" a reductive, regulative fiction, a part masquerading as the whole, it is nonetheless an ineluctable fiction, without which the trajectory of the spool would lack all determinate direction. The result is to remark the deceptive *necessity* of such reductive structurations:

> If one insists on subsuming the figure of *fort-da*, such as we have seen it functioning, under the name, Oedipus, this amounts to *remarking* a nebulous, vertiginous matrix [*en y remarquant une matrice nébuleuse et plus qu'abyssale*] in terms of only one of its effects, or if you prefer, of its offspring. It is as though one were to pull this nebulous matrix, with its chains of fusions or fissions, its permutations and commutations without end, its disseminations without return, by only one of its threads, only one of its sons [*par un seul de ses fils*]. *It is true that this temptation (to form the trait out of only one of its threads/sons) is not a contingent limitation,* for which one might not have to render an account. For it is as though one wished to have everything devolve upon, return to [*faire revenir à*] one of its sons (threads), in other words, to the mother as matrix, to a mother who would be nothing but that which she is. [p. 362; emphasis added][2]

The problem, which traverses "Speculer—sur 'Freud,' " becomes legible in the passage just cited: how can the noncontingency of the oedipal reduction be *taken into account,* if just some such reduction appears to be the condition of possibility of *accounting* in general? The dilemma is thematized, in "Speculer—sur 'Freud,' " as the problem of psychoanalytic speculation: if Freud, in describing the game of *fort-da,* is not merely representing an instance that can be explained in terms of the more general validity of the Oedipus complex (much less that of the pleasure principle), it is because what he is describing is also, and perhaps above all, his own process of writing, including the organization and articulation of his argument. This, in turn, displaces and reinscribes the significance of the scene that he is attempting to describe but which eludes all comprehension by mirroring, repeating, and dislocating the very theoretical scheme that seeks to comprehend it.

For the details of this dislocation, I must refer you to the text of *La carte postale,* too vertiginously complex to suffer any résumé here. The hermeneutical facet, by contrast, can be summarized, as it is in the following passage, the ramifications of which are by no means limited to the putative "object" of Derrida's text—that is, to "Freud":

> What happens when acts or performances (discourse or writing, analysis or description, etc.) form part of the objects they designate? When they can give themselves as example of that of which they speak or write? There is certainly no gain in self-reflexive transparency, on the contrary. An accounting is no longer possible, an account can no longer be rendered, nor a simple report or *compte rendu* given. And the borders of the whole are neither closed nor open. Their trait is divided. . . . [p. 417]

Derrida describes Freud, in *Beyond the Pleasure Principle*, doing what
he describes, performing the game of *fort-da* with the pleasure principle,
just as Freud describes the boy playing with the spool. But in so doing,
Freud's text does not merely repeat the scene it recounts: the oedipal
triangle ceases to function as frame of reference once it is revealed to be
only one version of a game that vastly transcends it. Hence, the repetition does not produce a "gain in self-reflexive transparency" but rather
something very different. The measure of that difference, however, can
only begin to be gauged when one remarks that the process just
described—by which descriptions participate in what they describe—also
applies, *a fortiori*, to the text that announces this as a general problem.
"Speculer—sur 'Freud' " can in no way be exempted from the "graph-
ics of repetition" it "describes" at work in the descriptions of "Freud."
    We begin to fathom the significance of the quotation marks that set
off the proper name "Freud" in the text that speculates on it. If the
temptation to form a trait out of only one of the threads (sons) of an
irrepressible "matrix"—if this temptation is "not a contingent limitation," and if one cannot, therefore, be dispensed from giving an account
of that noncontingency, then presumably the account will have to deal
with the manner in which an irresistible process of repetition *assumes* the
aspect and the allure of a *proper name*.

III

    "Speculer—sur 'Freud' " can be described as the "interminable
story" (p. 416) of making a name. As such, it also entails the recounting
of an impossible accounting, the story of an ineluctable debt—and guilt
(*Schuld*). No one was more aware of this problem than was Freud, as his
remarks on the indebted, improper character of psychoanalytical discourse, toward the end of *Beyond the Pleasure Principle*, unequivocally
demonstrate: without "the figurative language . . . [of] depth psychology," Freud remarks, "we could not otherwise describe the processes in
question at all, and indeed we could not have become aware of them"
(*S.E.* 18: 60). Commenting on this passage, Derrida exposes the general
law it implies:

> Borrowing is the law. . . . without borrowing, nothing begins, there is no
> proper reserve [*fonds propre*]. Everything begins with the transfer of
> funds, and there is interest in borrowing, it is even the primary interest.
> Borrowing gives you a return, it produces surplus-value, it is the primary
> motor of all investment. One begins thus by speculating, betting on one
> value to produce as though from nothing. And all these metaphors con-
> firm, as metaphors, the necessity of what they say. [p. 410]

If, however, "borrowing is the law" and the beginning of Freud's speculations, this explains why, in contrast to more traditional sciences or
disciplines, psychoanalysis is inseparably bound up with the name of its
founder. If its specificity is indissolubly linked to a fundamental indebtedness, something like a proper name is required in order to hold it
together. But for this very reason, the "property" of that name will be
even more fragile than is ordinarily the case in regard to the sciences.
Freud's speculations, Derrida asserts, seek to take this fragility into
account; they "will have consisted, perhaps, in claiming to pay in
advance, however dearly, the charges of a return-to-the-sender" (p. 353).
But the "claim" is also a pretense (*prétendre*) a "calculation without
basis" (*sans fond*), a manner "to speculate upon the ruin of his
name . . . which keeps what it loses" (p. 353).

Perhaps the most ingenious, most radical stratagem in this project is
that which consists in assuming the debt so totally as to render it inoperative. If "everything" can be said to "begin with the transfer of funds,"
then the very notion of debt itself tends to lose its force. The debt cannot
be paid back,

> perhaps because economy itself has been transgressed; not economy in
> general but an economy in which the principle of equivalence would have
> been forced. All the movements in *trans-* would have violated this princi
> ple, and with it everything that could have assured a payment, a reim
> bursement, an amortization. . . . This effraction—that is, the speculative
> transfer(ence)—would have rendered the debt both infinite or insolvent,
> and hence null and void. It is the economic space of the debt that finds
> itself disorganized [*bouleversé*], immensely enlarged and at the same time
> neutralized. [p. 415]

It is precisely this process that Derrida sees at work in the speculations of
"Freud," endowing the latter with their paradoxical but characteristic
"dual tonality": "Both grave, discouraged, gasping under the burden of
the inexhaustible debt or task; and simultaneously flippant, cavalier,
affirmative" (p. 415). But is a debt thus generalized, necessarily "neutralized"? Does the fact that everything begins with a "transfer"
of funds—with a certain form of borrowing—necessarily "invalidate"
the notion of debt? And what is the relation of such "forcing" of the
principle of equivalence, to that noncontingent limitation at work in the
Oedipus complex, and indeed, in all accounting and accountability?

These questions will compel us to return, in a moment, to the text
in which the problem of *Schuld*—debt and guilt—is exposed in an
unprecedented but decisive manner: to the second book of *The Genealogy of Morals*.

But before embarking upon this inevitable detour, let us first consider the curious position in which we are placed, as readers of "Speculer—sur 'Freud,' " in regard to Nietzsche. This text ("Speculer"), we are informed at its outset in a footnote, is in fact only the third part or "ring" in a chain of readings proceeding, in each of its parts, from a text of Nietzsche's. The first of these "three rings" revolves around the notion of life, the " 'modern' problematics of biology, of genetics, of the epistemology or of the history of the life sciences (readings of Jacob, Canghuilhem, and so forth). The second ring: return to Nietzsche, followed by an explication of the Heideggerian reading of Nietzsche. Finally, here, the third and last ring" (p. 277n).

A certain reading of Nietzsche, then, is absolutely indispensable for the *mise-en-scène* of "Speculer—sur 'Freud.' " This reading, it is suggested, frames the analysis of Freudian speculation. That analysis offers us, here at its beginning, two distinct if interrelated aspects. The first still belongs to what I would describe as the classical "deconstructive" strategy: Freud, it is asserted, always related to Nietzsche in the form of a *denial* (*dénégation*). He mentions him, but only to dismiss him, to dispatch him. This motif is, to be sure, incontrovertible. It is supported not only by the passage from the *Autobiographical Study* cited by Derrida, but by others as well. A perhaps even more striking instance is provided by the minutes of the April 1, 1908, meeting of the Viennese Psychoanalytical Society, devoted to a discussion of the *third* section of *The Genealogy of Morals:*

> Prof. FREUD stresses above all his peculiar relation to philosophy, the abstractions of which were so uncongenial that he finally decided to give up the study of philosophy. Of Nietzsche, too, he is ignorant; an occasional attempt to read him foundered upon an excess of interest. Despite the much noted similarities he could still assure us, he said, that Nietzsche's thoughts had had absolutely no influence upon his own works. . . . Apart from [the motif of] infantilism, the mechanism of displacement is *not* recognized in Nietzsche.[3]

The logic of this response is already sufficiently familiar to readers of *The Interpretation of Dreams:* "No, I haven't read Nietzsche—he is too interesting. No, he hasn't influenced my work and I know nothing of his. Moreover, he has completely failed to recognize the mechanism of displacement." Derrida is thus amply justified in remarking a "denial" here, and then in going on to reveal its effects by pointing up a "return" of Nietzschean motifs in the speculations of Freud. The most striking, most "disruptive" such return relates to the thematics of power. Having analyzed the manner in which Freud pursues the problem of the pleasure principle in *Beyond,* Derrida draws the following conclusion:

It is indeed within the code of power—and not only metaphorically so—
that [Freud's] problematic is situated. The question is always to discover
who is "master" and who "dominates," who has "authority" and the
point to which the PP can exercise power. [p. 431]

Nietzsche, dismissed and avoided by Freud, thus imposes his "code"
upon the latter's speculations, taking his tribute in a debt admitted only
to be denied.

However, this tells only part of the story: there is another "chapter," as it were, which comes not so much at the end but rather at what
appears to be the beginning. And this other aspect, I submit, is no
longer comprehensible within what I have called the classical strategy of
deconstruction. For, as already mentioned, what fascinates Derrida
throughout his reading of "Freud," and above all in the "scene" of the
"denial" of Nietzsche (and of "philosophy"), is the very ease and the
facility with which the putative debt is acknowledged and dispatched by
Freud—*as though it were the debt of another.* Indeed, this aspect of
Freud's *démarche* defines the very project of Derrida's "own" reading,
which he describes as follows:

> I would like to render legible [*donner à lire*] the nonpositional structure
> of *Beyond . . .* , its athetical functioning, in the last instance, which,
> however, amounts to extracting it from the authority of a last instance, or
> indeed from that of any instance at all. [p. 279]

This "nonpositional structure" of Freud's speculation, subtracting it
from "the authority of a last instance, or . . . that of any instance at all,"
would, however, ultimately extract "Freud" from the project of a deconstruction. For the latter necessarily presupposes a governing intention, an
effort to establish meaning, a *will-to-say-something;* what is at work in
Beyond the Pleasure Principle, however, in the "athetical" reading that
Derrida seeks to give it, is almost the opposite: instead of a *vouloir-dire,*
we discover a vouloir-*rien*-dire. As we read in one of the letters of the
Envois (May 18, 1978), what captivates Derrida in *his* reading of *Beyond,*
is precisely the manner in which "it tells us NOTHING [*il ne nous dit
RIEN*], doesn't take a step without then, with the next step, retracting it"
(p. 153).

What *can* be deconstructed here, by contrast, is not an intention to
say nothing, to go nowhere, but rather all those readings of Freud's text
which have tried to make it say something, be intelligent,

> all those readings as partial as [they are] canonical, even academic, [which
> mistake] the essential impossibility of arresting [Freud's text] at a thesis, at
> a conclusion posed in a scientifical or philosophical mode. [p. 279]

This is why even the most powerful "philosophical" theses—such as the Nietzschean theory of the Will-to-Power—cannot have the last word in regard to the speculations of "Freud." "The motif of power" may be "more orginary and more general than the PP," it may be "independent of it and of its Beyond," but it still cannot impose itself fully upon Freud's most daring speculative notions: "The death-drive and the repetition-compulsion, however much they proceed from a drive for power . . . still exceed power" (p. 432).

Nietzsche *almost* has the last word, then, but *not quite*. Not, at least, the Nietzsche of the Will-to-Power. For "there is only power if there is a principle or a principle of principles. The transcendental or meta-conceptual function pertains to the order of power" (p. 432). What, by contrast, Derrida has remarked in the hesitation waltz of Freud's speculations, is a movement that cannot be comprehended by a cognitive scheme of intention: a speculation that is not subordinated to the universal equivalent and supreme value, *truth*.

This, then, is the "Freud" of "Speculer—sur 'Freud' "—the Freud who speculates on the impossible gambit of *writing-himself*; of constructing a network of circulation, of relay stations; and of paying the price in advance:

> [Freud's] speculation will have consisted, *perhaps*, in pretending [*prétendre*] to pay in advance, however dearly, the charges of a return-to-the-sender. [p. 353; emphasis added]

But why, in this most programmatic, most "deconstructive" statement, that little most Nietzschean word, undermining the declarative tone with a barely perceptible hesitation—why the qualifying "perhaps"? Could it not be because of the peculiarly and openly contradictory manner in which Freud "assumes" and radicalizes his "debt," to the point where one can no longer be entirely certain just *whose* debt is at stake? An example of this "dangerous perhaps" (Nietzsche, *Beyond Good and Evil*, p. 10): When the "athetical reading" of "Speculer—sur 'Freud' " declares itself to depend upon an interpretation of *Beyond* that is "selective, slanted [and] discriminating" (*sélective, criblante, discriminante*, p. 279); and when, some pages later, *Freud's* rhetoric is also described as a "slanted strategy" whose "busy selectivity" is "no longer regulated by a reassuring model of science or of philosophy" (p. 298)—then, *who* is repeating *whom*: Freud Derrida or Derrida Freud? And, if one responds that the distinction no longer makes sense, is one prepared to assume the consequences of its disappearance (or indeed, *are* those consequences assumable?)? The response depends, no doubt, on what one means by the word "assume"—a problem to which I shall return. But for the moment, let us note that the "athetical reading" advanced in "Specu-

ler—sur 'Freud,' " by undermining the possibility of establishing a decisive, final instance, "draws the textual performance into a singular
slippage" (*dérive*, p. 279) in which even "deconstruction" loses its foot-
ing. For the impossibility of establishing or identifying a governing
intention also entails the impossibility of assuming that minimal "exteriority"[4] without which deconstruction is unthinkable. By contrast,
"What happens when acts or performances . . . form part of the objects
they designate" is that such exteriority is suspended and the deconstruction also emerges as "an example of that of which it speaks or writes."
Which is doubtless why "deconstruction," in "Speculer—sur 'Freud,' "
is most conspicuously remarked in a scene in which it is a question of
defending its priorities and property rights; I refer you to p. 285 of *La
carte postale,* where the "brand name" of Deconstruction is defended
against the "competition": French Heideggerians and Marxists, who
seek to expropriate the term by rediscovering it in their respective texts of
reference. It is precisely the necessity, and necessary absurdity, of such a
defense that renders Deconstruction incapable of accounting for its
debts, and for the question of debt in general. And it is this, too, which
underscores the novelty of "Speculer—sur 'Freud.' " At the very
moment it is describing Freud's dispatching of Nietzsche, it also, in a
certain sense, dispatches its readers by referring them to analyses that
"Freud" refused to undertake, but that now have been accomplished—
but elsewhere, in a place that remains inaccessible to the reader:

> I will therefore be brief. To proceed in the quickest possible manner, I will
> recall for instance what was said concerning childhood, play and the lack-
> of-debt. What was said in regard to [*à partir de*] Nietzsche. How and with
> what the self-declared child indebts himself in a game that declares itself
> free of debt? Of the lack-of-debt upon which the game speculates in
> secret? And where to situate, according to what topology, the place of such
> a secret? [p. 280]

Where, indeed, situate the secret if not precisely *here,* at this moment in
the text that is beginning to speculate, on "Freud." A game that does
not declare itself to be "without debt," *sans dette,* to be sure, but which
does immediately go on to declare *its other,* "Freud," in hock up to his
ears, and apparently—*perhaps!*—unwilling to pay the bills. Unwilling,
or unable? Yet, what if those bills were not *his* bills at all? Or not simply,
exclusively *his?*

Freud's will and wish not to know of, and not to owe anything to,
Nietzsche thus forms the paradoxical first act of Derrida's speculations, on
"Freud." Paradoxical first, because Freud, Derrida will go on to show, in
fact continues to play the game first "theorized" by Nietzsche—but in

perhaps an even more radical manner, if one of the effects of that debt is to make theory, in a certain sense, impossible. And second, the insistent reference to the "author"—in quotes—of the *theory of debt* (not in quotes) is paradoxical, because it *does* what it purports to *describe:* it refers to a theory of debt (first Nietzsche, then Heidegger), which it then proceeds to withhold. Or rather, to promise: "As far as referring *Sein und Zeit* to *The Genealogy of Morals,* insofar as *Schuldigsein* is concerned, I shall attempt that elsewhere" (p. 282).

Does this place us, as readers, in Derrida's debt—or him in ours? If a text, describing a certain refusal to assume a debt, ostensibly on the part of *Freud,* practices what it preaches, does what it describes, this does not, we now know, lead necessarily to an increase in self-reflexive transparency. But just *where,* then, *does* it lead? Perhaps the "author" of the theory of debt can give us a clue?

IV

It is curious that a promise, or something very much like it, should lead us back to Nietzsche's discussion of debt in *The Genealogy of Morals.* For that discussion, of course, proceeds precisely from Nietzsche's assertion that promising entails nothing less than the "essential problem *of* man" (*Genealogy,* p. 56). The opposition that Nietzsche establishes between "active forgetting," and its disciplining through mnemotechnics—the establishment of memory, of anticipation, and hence, of the ability to promise—recalls in many ways Freud's distinction between primary and secondary processes, with its correlative categories of "perceptual identity" and "identity of thought." In each case, the articulation of the one process with the other, depicted as an apparently genetic development, but with distinctly structural implications, depends upon what both Freud and Nietzsche designate with the word *Hemmung:* literally, "inhibition" or "blockage." Since the very notion of *Hemmung* strongly suggests the interruption or deviation of a continuous movement, it is not entirely surprising for Nietzsche to describe the decisive *Hemmung* as a consequence of the shift of life from water to land; it is this move out of the water and onto terra firma that is both ground and origin of what Nietzsche calls the "internalization of man": the development of a soul, of an interiority arises in direct proportion to the blockage of any discharge into the external world: "The entire inner world . . . expanded and inflated itself . . . in the same measure as outward discharge was *inhibited*" (p. 84; Nietzsche's emphasis).

It is here that Nietzsche situates the origins of the "*schlechtes Gewissen,*" the "guilty conscience," and indeed, of guilt itself. But if Nietzsche introduces this section (sec. 16) by warning his readers that

"my own Hypothesis on the origin of the 'guilty conscience' . . . will not
gain a hearing easily and needs to be pondered, observed and slept over
lengthily" (p. 84), it is not simply because of the phantasmagoric nature
of the explanation, of its obvious lack of refutability. What makes this
"hypothesis" so difficult *to hear,* as it were, is its disruptive implication
for the fundamental opposition that seems to structure the entire three
books of *Genealogy*—that is, ultimately, the opposition between nobility and *ressentiment,* between "active" and "reactive" values and
behavior, between spontaneous self-affirmation and other-directed devi-
ousness. The mythical "hypothesis" does not merely challenge such
oppositions, it subverts the very force of *oppositionality* itself, in accordance with the suspicions uttered at the outset of *Beyond Good and Evil:*

> The fundamental belief of metaphysicians is *the belief* in the oppositions
> of values. It may be questioned whether there are indeed any opposi-
> tions at all . . . rather than simply foreground estimations, preliminary
> perspectives. . . . Indeed, it might even be possible that *what* comprises
> the value of those good and respected things is precisely that they are
> insidiously related, tied to, interlaced with those wicked, seemingly
> opposed things, and perhaps even of the same essence. Perhaps! But who
> is willing to worry about such dangerous perhapses. For that, we will have
> to wait for the arrival of a new kind of philosopher. [*Beyond Good and
> Evil,* p. 10; translation modified, Nietzsche's emphasis]

Nietzsche's hypothesis of the origin of the "guilty conscience" disrupts the governing opposition of his "story" precisely by virtue of its
very *originality*: for what originates with this move from the aquatic to
the land medium is *human being itself,* with *all* of the predicates that
can be attributed to it, including not only the reactive qualities leading
to resentment, but also the active self-affirmation constantly opposed to
it. The move from water to land thus reveals the common origin of both
nobility *and* resentment, active *and* reactive, internalization *and* exter-
nalization. Man only becomes "self-supporting" (*selbsttragend*) by
becoming dependent: "From now on they were supposed to walk on
their feet and 'carry themselves,' whereas hitherto they had been carried
by water: a frightful heaviness lay upon them" (*Genealogy,* p. 84). This
fateful move ashore is described, in German at least, more as the effect
of a witty play-on-words, that is, more as a kind of *repetition* than as a
clear-cut *alternative.* The choice was "entweder *Landtiere* zu werden
[either to become land animals] oder *zugrunde* zu gehen [or to be
destroyed, literally: to be *grounded*]." But this fateful joke is also one
played at the expense of the "theory" that places resentment in opposition to its other: noble, aristocratic self-affirmation. This joke on the

"dramatic" aspect of Nietzsche's story, however, also introduces an element that is perhaps even more *theatrical:* a *spectacle* necessitating the participation of *spectators:*

> Indeed, divine spectators were needed to appreciate the spectacle that thus began and the end of which is not yet in sight. . . . From now on, man is *included* among the most unexpected and most exciting lucky throws in the game played by Heraclitus' 'great child,' be he called Zeus or chance—man evokes interest in himself, a tension . . . as though he were not a goal but only a way, an episode, a bridge, a great promise. [p. 85]

It is only against the backdrop of this spectacle, with its interest, its tension, its promise—but above all, its spectators—that Nietzsche's discussion of *Schuld* can be appreciated.

The development of resentment out of a noble or aristocratic culture is marked by the emergence of the guilty conscience (*schlechtes Gewissen*), in turn characterized by a shift in the notion of *Schuld*. Nietzsche seems to tell us the story of two distinct, and indeed diametrically *opposed* conceptions of *Schuld*. The familiar, moral notion of *Schuld* as *guilt,* he argues, derives from an older, more pragmatic, more "material" notion, *Schuld* as *debt*. The opposition consists in the nature of the obligation thereby designated: whereas *guilt* is construed as a debt that is essentially *unredeemable* (by the debtor, at least), the earlier, more original, more tangible notion of *Schuld* was predicated precisely upon the essential quality of its being *repayable*. Thus, if the essence of debt was originally to be *"abzahlbar,"* if the derived notions of punishment and justice consisted in *Vergeltung*, retribution, it was, Nietzsche contends, because these concepts developed out of "the contractual relationship of creditor and debtor (*Gläubiger und Schuldner*)," which "in turn points back to the fundamental forms of buying and selling, barter, trade, and traffic" (p. 63). In this "prehistoric" period—a prehistory, Nietzsche remarks parenthetically (sec. 9), which "is present in all ages or may always reappear" (p. 71)—the notion of *Schuld* as debt is part of an overriding "logic of compensation" (*Logik des Ausgleichs*), one which prescribes that " 'everything has its price; *all* things can be paid for' " (p. 70). This "logic," which Nietzsche insists is *"fremdartig genug"* (strange enough) (p. 64), seems, at first sight at least, to consist precisely in the overcoming of "strangeness" (*Fremdheit*). For it is marked by what is apparently the unproblematic establishment of equivalences:

> in the oldest and most primitive personal relationship, that between buyer and seller, creditor and debtor . . . one person first confronted another person, one person first *measured itself* against another. Setting prices,

measuring values, devising equivalents, exchanging—this preoccupies the
earliest thinking of man to such an extent that in a certain sense it *is* thinking itself. [p. 70]

I shall return to the "strangeness" of this apparently unproblematic
"logic of compensation." For the moment, however, let us retain the
appearance of its straightforward simplicity, that of the establishment of
a certain identity—"person to person"—by a process of evaluation and
of *measurement* that coincides with "thinking itself." Let us retain this
appearance, because without it, the contrast and opposition between the
two kinds of *Schuld*—debt and guilt—are no longer as clear-cut as
Nietzsche, in the more dramatic, more explicit aspect of his genealogy,
would have us believe. For the shift from the notion of redeemable debt
to that of unredeemable guilt is above all dependent upon the loss of an
unproblematic *standard of measurement,* the loss of binding equivalents. It is striking to note that this loss, the key component of the
genealogy Nietzsche is developing, coincides with the emergence, precisely, of something like a genealogical consciousness. In a celebrated
passage, in which Nietzsche anticipates, in certain respects, Freud's myth
of the development of culture through guilt (*Totem and Taboo*), the
emergence of the "guilty conscience" is portrayed as the result of an
interpretation that is "exceedingly remarkable and perplexing" (the
German word *bedenklich* suggests something both disconcerting *and*
thought-provoking; we shall have occasion to return to this word later, in
another context).

> The civil-law relationship between the debtor and his creditor, discussed
> already at length, has been interpreted in an, historically speaking, exceed-
> ingly remarkable and dubious manner into a relationship in which, to us
> modern men, it is perhaps least intelligible: namely into the relation of
> the present generation to its ancestors. [p. 88]

And, Nietzsche continues, it is through this *Hineininterpretieren* that a
logic emerges that is very different from that earlier analyzed:

> The conviction reigns that it is only through the sacrifices and accomplish-
> ments of the ancestors that the tribe *exists*—and that one has *to pay them
> back* with sacrifices and accomplishments: one thus recognizes a *debt*
> [*Schuld*] that constantly increases, since these forebears never cease, in
> their continued existence as powerful spirits, to accord the tribe new
> advantages and new strength. . . . The *fear* of the forefather and of his
> power, the consciousness of being indebted to him, increases, in accord-
> ance with this logic, in direct proportion to the increase in the power of the
> tribe itself. . . . If one imagines this rude kind of logic carried to its end,

> then the ancestors of the *most powerful* tribes are bound eventually to
> grow to monstrous dimensions through the imagination of growing fear
> and to recede into the darkness of the divinely uncanny and unimagina-
> ble: in the end the ancestor must necessarily be transfigured into a *god*.
> Perhaps this is even the origin of the gods, an origin therefore out of *fear!*
> [pp. 88–89]

Here we would seem to have, quite clearly and unequivocally, the genealogy of resentment: the self-interpretation of the identity of the community situates the origin of that self *elsewhere*, in those forefathers held
to be responsible for everything that the tribe has and is, for its very
existence, its power, and its possibilities. The result coincides with a well-
known jingle of years gone by—"the more you have, the more you
want"—that is, the more you have the more you owe. The "end" of
this "logic" is, then, the establishment of this other as the "uncanny
and unimaginable [*unvorstellbar*: unrepresentable]" God, to whom
"the present generation [die Gegenwartigen]" is tied by an unredeemable debt.

Nietzsche leaves the "origin" of this origin—of the fateful
Hineininterpretieren of exchange relations into, or onto, the axis of
generations—shrouded in darkness, no less uncanny than the effects it is
said to produce. This is, on the one hand, in accordance with his conception of interpretation itself—discussed several sections earlier (sec. 12)—
as a *discontinuous* series of assaults, in which one scheme imposes itself
upon a previous one. And if Nietzsche stresses the discontinuity of these
interpretive impositions, it is precisely because the effectiveness of their
power game depends in part upon creating the illusion of a causal continuity, one which would thereby obscure the violence of the interpretive
intervention as such, by presenting it as the intrinsic essence of the thing
itself.

And yet, even in this general discussion of interpretation, it is clear
that the "sequence of more or less . . . independently operating processes of subjugation" cannot be entirely discontinuous, if only because it
inevitably includes "the resistances encountered, the attempted transfor-
mations of form for the purpose of defense and reaction, and the results
of successful counter-measures" (p. 78).

If it is therefore indisputable that every interpretive imposition is
thus in part determined by the scheme it seeks to dethrone and to
subjugate, by its adversary in the struggle, the complicity of that particular interpretation which "projects" the exchange relationship onto the
genealogical axis, with the notion of *Schuld* it is about to displace, is far
more profound; indeed, it offers us what is perhaps the paradigm of that
interlacing of opposites (*Verhäkelung der Gegensätze*) to which we have
already referred.

The sign of this complicity—between *Schuld* und *Schuld,* guilt and debt—is nothing less than "the origin of the gods," as the uncanny, unrepresentable terminus *ab quo* and *ad quem* of the interminable *Schuld.* For this "origin" of the gods is by no means simply original or unprecedented: in the story Nietzsche is telling, it is itself a somewhat uncanny repetition of *another origin of the gods,* this time in the "pre-historical" world of simple exchange.

For, as we have already mentioned, the "logic" of that exchange, of its *Ausgleichsform,* is in fact less simple than it might first appear. Its *Fremdartigkeit,* its strangeness, lies in the peculiar kind of equivalences that are established. For what is striking, in Nietzsche's account of the "logic of compensation," is that it is ultimately no less "other-directed" than the culture of resentment to which it is opposed. We need only reflect upon the following passage to discover such other-directedness at work in what appears to be the simple assertion of self:

> Let us be clear as to the logic of this form of compensation: it is strange enough. An equivalence is provided by the creditor's receiving, in place of a direct compensation for an injury (that is, in place of compensation in money, land, possessions of any kind) a kind of satisfaction [*Wohlgefühl*] in being granted a kind of pleasure as recompense and compensation—the satisfaction of being permitted to vent, without second thoughts [*unbe-denklich*], his power upon someone who is powerless, the ecstasy "*de faire le mal pour le plaisir de la faire,*" the enjoyment of violating the other. . . . The compensation consists, therefore, in a warrant and right to be cruel. [pp. 64–65]

It is in the exercise of one's power to violate the other, the debtor, that the "universal equivalent" (Marx) is found, which in turn permits one sort of "injury"—a material debt, for instance—to be requited in a manner that, if no less "material," is yet of a quite different order: the production of *suffering* in the *other.*

The "strangeness" of this originary logic, by which the ideas of "debt and suffering" (*Schuld und Leid*) become "uncannily . . . inter-twined" (p. 65), resides precisely in that moment which Freud, as we have seen, thought Nietzsche to have overlooked completely: that of an original, irreducible displacement or substitution. For the "equiva-lence" of debt and suffering is the effect precisely of a substitution, a shift, or a displacement, through which the infliction of suffering becomes the equivalent of a property debt. The body of the debtor *replaces* the possessions he owes. The value of that body is determined by its position within the social hierarchy, in relation to that of the creditor. Society is thus the stage upon which the spectacle of cruelty—suffering as repayment—is acted out upon the body of the other. And society is

implicated because the demonstration of power cannot take place simply
between two persons: it requires witnesses, spectators. It is this, perhaps,
that most distinguishes the other-directed spectacle Nietzsche is describing from the Hegelian master-slave dialectic. For the efficacy of cruelty,
as retribution, does not find its "truth" in the labor of the powerless
other. Rather, the violation of the debtor by the creditor calls for spectators who are not directly involved in this process and yet without whom it
could not operate meaningfully. For, despite the apparently "prehistoric" nature of such processes, what is at stake is the ability of "thinking" to set prices and to establish equivalences, among objects and
phenomena that remain, in a certain sense, incommensurable. "Meaning," therefore, entails precisely the recognition of that incommensurable equivalence that ties suffering to debt. But such recognition can only
come from elsewhere, from others whose alterity has not been drawn into
the power play of retribution. These others are the gods:

> What really arouses indignation against suffering is not suffering as such
> but the senselessness of suffering. . . . So in order to abolish hidden, unde-
> tected, unwitnessed suffering from the world and honestly to deny it, one
> was in the past virtually compelled to invent gods and genii of all heights
> and depths—in short, something that . . . will not easily let an interesting
> painful spectacle pass unnoticed. . . . The entire mankind of antiquity is
> full of tender regard for "the spectator." [chap. 7, p. 68]

"The gods conceived of as the friends of *cruel* spectacles" and the gods
conceived of as the uncanny, unrepresentable ancestors to which the
present descendants—*die Gegenwärtigen*—are irrevocably indebted:
Are these two origins of the gods without a common thread? Or is it not
rather the inextricably ambivalent relation to the Other that is here in
play, in a play that reveals the ostensible opposition of noble and slave,
aristocracy and resentment, to be two versions of a single but highly
ambivalent story. For, if the relation of exchange could be "projectively
interpreted" (*hineininterpretiert*) into the genealogical relation of
present and past, of descendants and ancestors, is it not because those
uncanny "creditors" were already at work in the "contriving of equivalences" itself? The necessity of divine spectators, of the divine *as spectator* and as witness, confirms the irremediable indebtedness of even the
most apparently spontaneous and direct retribution, its dependence
upon an alterity with which it can never dispense, since it is there *in* (*the*)
place of the other that the "standard" of equivalence, the measure of
value, must be established. But since that *place* is never accessible or
determinable other than as that of an (excluded) addressee, the verdict
or testimony that it emits can never be certain. For those spectators never
speak for themselves, but only through others, through riddles or enig-

mas, which in turn must be interpreted. And since interpretation, as Nietzsche well knew, is simply another name for the power play of a certain indebtedness—one, however, that refuses to assume its *Schuld*— the words of those spectators can never do more or other than echo the spectacle they are held to behold.

Their "message," in the story we are rehearsing, is simply: *Schuld*. Debt, guilt: debt as guilt, guilt as debt. And if the two words are one, it is precisely because they seek to be two: *Schuld* as debt seeks to deny the structural dependency of the self upon an other, by confronting that other as creditor to debtor. But despite the cruel self-affirmation of the creditor, his power and self remain indebted to another, whom he cannot control and with whom he can hardly even negotiate. For the creditor needs witnesses and spectators to testify to the (repayment of the) debt. But since that testimony is always mute, always equivocal, always as unreliable as it is indispensable, the repayment of the debt is never assured, never certain—never unequivocally certified or certifiable. And thus, sooner or later, the "friends of *cruel* spectacles" reveal themselves to be the uncanny, unimaginable, *unvorstellbare* gods, whom we must fear and hate as much as love.

V

If the theory of *Schuld* demonstrates, against its explicit assertions, that Schuld *is* Schuld—that is, that debt and guilt are inextricably inter-woven in the irreducible reference to a certain alterity—then this is not without consequences for Derrida's reading of "Freud," or speculating with an unpayable debt. Above all, the generalization of this debt would not necessarily entail its neutralization or nullification (*Carte postale*, p. 415). Nor would its accents be limited to that dual but opposed tonal-ity that Derrida finds in Freud: "serious, discouraged," but also "flip-pant, cavalier, affirmative" (p. 415). Rather, Nietzsche's *Verhäkelung* (interweaving) of debt and guilt should sensibilize us to possibilities of dealing with *Schuld* other than those of affirmation or resignation. Possi-bilities, or tonalities, which, we might expect, often are situated "within" the apparent unity of seemingly single words. I will limit myself here to what might constitute one such instance, in *Beyond the Pleasure Principle*. It occurs at the very beginning of the text, and it allows the reading of "Speculer—sur 'Freud' " to set its scene and get underway.

The way is that strange *"pas au-delà"* that is both a step beyond, and no step at all. In other words, it is the effort of the PP to "write it/ himself"—that is, to send himself a letter without ever moving from the spot, by paying in advance the costs of a return-to-the-sender.

The way, then, taken by "Speculer—sur 'Freud' " is that of rewriting *Beyond the Pleasure Principle* in the discourse or code of that other PP: the Postal Principle. Such a rewriting, a letter in the *Envois* informs us, essentially takes care of itself:

> This whole vocabulary, this entire postal code . . . will go very well with all that imposes itself on me in the reading of *Beyond* . . . , that is with the typology of posting, postures, impostures, and above all, of the position [*Setzung, thesis*], the thesis, the athesis and the hypothesis. And it is the *postal*, the Postal Principle as differential-deferring relay that regularly prevents, delays, dispatches the deposition of the thesis, that prohibits all repose and incessantly deposes, deports and keeps the movement of speculation on the run. [p. 61]

It is perhaps worth remarking here that in the list of words belonging to the postal code that impose themselves in the reading of *Beyond*, one word is conspicuously omitted, although it is inscribed as the key operator of the series—the word "imposition." In what way does the word "imposition," which describes the intervention of the postal code itself, fall under the sway of that code, obey its rules, follow its laws? Or does its unremarked absence, here—and elsewhere—suggest that it is precisely the point at which the postal code ceases to be a code, that is, closed, systematic, self-contained?

The question imposes itself all the more after our brief detour to Nietzsche's *Genealogy*, since it is there that interpretation is described as a process of *imposition*, by which one discourse *prägt sich auf*—impresses itself upon—another. And if the problematic of *Schuld* involves just such an interpretive imposition—ultimately of a certain alterity or exteriority upon that which seeks to exclude it in the name of its self, of its power, and of its property—then we shall not be entirely surprised that just this notion of imposition should impose itself at the very outset of Derrida's reading of "Freud."

That outset, as we have already noted, begins on a double, and equivocal, tone: the one familiar, deconstructive, depicts Freud crassly denying his debt to Nietzsche, to philosophy—that is, to a certain philosophy. The second, or other accent, no longer deconstructive, is the wonderment over the ease with which "Freud" dispatches the debt. But in both cases, the Freud described is shown as a *sender* rather than as a receiver; indeed, he is characterized as one who refuses to receive (the debt or message of Nietzsche), in order more freely to "write himself": write of himself, write to himself, both while apparently only assessing the current state of psychoanalytical theory.

And yet, this is not the whole story either. Freud's ambivalent attitude toward philosophy, his effort to distinguish the nature of the "speculations" of psychoanalysis from those of philosophy, may also, Derrida surmises, comport the effort to redeem, or recognize, a debt that the philosophical notion of speculation has endeavored to exclude. And indeed, although "Speculer—sur 'Freud' " does not make explicit mention of it, a certain aspect of Freud's suspicion of philosophy anticipates its own; for what animates this suspicion is the very *systematic* pretension of philosophy that has provided Derridean deconstruction with its privileged target. Thus, what Freud "rejects" here, at the beginning of *Beyond the Pleasure Principle,* is not simply a debt to philosophy as such—"en coupant court avec tel ascendant 'philosophique' " (in cutting off contact with a particular philosophical predecessor, *Carte postale,* p. 294)—but rather a debt to a philosophy that masks its own constitutive indebtedness with narcissistic claims to construct systematic explanations or arguments.

That this aspect of Freud's relation to "philosophy" would not be explicitly acknowledged in "Speculer—sur 'Freud' " is all the more remarkable in view of the programmatic declaration, by Derrida, just a few pages earlier, that the purpose of his reading of Freud is

> to open [the issue of] what *holds together* [*tient ensemble*] the new position of the question of death in psychoanalysis, the apparently autobiographical point-of-view of Freud, and the history of the analytical movement. What *holds together* does not maintain the form of a system. No concept of system (whether logical, scientific or philosophical) is perhaps capable [*habilité*] of . . . achieving such a bringing-together [*rassemblement*]. Of the latter it itself is only an effect. [p. 290]

Thus, *Freud's* "avoidance" of philosophy, as described in "Speculer—sur 'Freud,' " appears also, and perhaps above all, as a certain avoidance of *"Freud."* The question, "what happens when [descriptions] . . . can give themselves as examples of that about which they . . . write?" folds back upon the text which inscribes it. As does the question posed at the outset of "Speculer—sur 'Freud' ": "Comment spéculer avec cette speculation?" (How to speculate with this speculation?) (p. 296).

The beginnings of a response, or of a strategy, in "Speculer," is, then, as I have indicated, to translate Freud's speculations into the terms of the code that has "imposed itself" upon Derrida's reading of *Beyond,* the postal code. The center of that code, the "postal principle," communicates with what is perhaps the essence of philosophy, the gesture of *setting up,* of *Setzen, thesein, ponere,* while at the same time suggesting that this act, far from being originary and constitutive, is an "effect" of a network of relays, of a circulation that never succeeds in coming full circle. This would be the "athesis" demonstrated by Freud's speculations. But the formulation of this "athesis" seems still inextricably bound up with the deconstructive demasking of a determining intention:

> Perhaps he who bears the name of Freud can neither appropriate the speculative (moment) of this singular speculation, nor identify himself with the speculator of this speculation, without precedent or precursor, nor yet exclude it, detach himself from it, deny [disown: *renier*] the one or the other. [p. 297]

If Freud, then, perhaps never entirely succeeds in sending himself that fateful letter, in prepaying the charges of that return-to-sender, he also, it would seem, can never stop trying, either. And the point of departure of that impossible, if ineluctable, attempt, is "the promissory note [*lettre d'engagement*] that [Freud] *believes* he can send himself circularly, round-robin, specularly" (p. 303; emphasis added).

But does Freud begin his speculations with such a *belief?* Does he begin by writing—by writing off his debt to philosophy, in order to gain the means with which to speculate? If his "speculations" entailed, "within the 'same' word—speculation— . . . a translation . . . from the philosophical concept of speculation in its dominant determination . . . to something else [which], in allowing itself to be excluded [from the philosophical concept] has never ceased to belabor it in the most domestic fashion" (p. 296)—if Freud's speculations entail such an *intraverbal* translation, we may assume that the mechanism of such a translation will, perhaps, also be situated within what appears to be a single word, thereby opening and dividing that word, as well as the code to which it seems to belong.

If the master-word of the postal code that imposes itself in and on "Speculer—sur 'Freud' " is that of *position*, the philosophical act par excellence, it is not surprising that the beginning of Freud's speculations, in *Beyond the Pleasure Principle,* should be described in such terms. Freud introduces that text, you may remember, with a brief survey of the current state of psychoanalytical theory, in particular concerning the pleasure principle: "In the theory of psycho-analysis we have no hesitation in assuming that the course taken by mental events is automatically regulated by the pleasure principle" (*S.E.* 18: 7). Derrida remarks that Freud thus begins on a note of uncertainty that will pervade his entire speculations, imparting to them a character of undecidability that will place them beyond the pale of traditional theory and theorems; what we have, right here at the outset, he writes,

> is neither a confirmation nor a questioning of the well-foundedness [of the pleasure principle]. But that will never become—this is my hypothesis here—either a confirmation or a refutation. Nonetheless, for the moment

let us take note [*prendre acte*] of the following: Freud presents this state of
theory as the possibility of an assumption which can be imprudent: "we
assume *unbedenklich*," without wincing, as if it were self-evident, the
authority of the pleasure principle. [p. 294]

And, Derrida continues, Freud's manner in thus describing the impru-
dence, the *Unbedenklichkeit*, of this *assumption* serves to suspend its
validity, and with it, that of the "law of avoidance" (*loi d'évitement*)—
whether the avoidance of tension, *Unlust*, or Freud's own avoidance of
his philosophical antecedents—or rather, the manner in which it functions and its significance.

It is precisely such a suspension—of the governing assumptions of
psychoanalytical theory—that distinguishes the speculations of psychoanalysis from their philosophical counterparts (or homonyms). Having
begun by describing the nature of the pleasure principle within analytical theory, Freud goes on to assert, as Derrida puts it, that such
" 'speculative hypotheses' " are radically distinct from those of philosophy because they claim no a priori status or validity.

But if their status is determined neither by the dominant, philosophical notions of speculation nor by any other deductive or inductive
scheme, by what is it determined? It is here that the intervention, or
imposition, of the "postal code" demands our attention. For what is at
work in Freud's "speculative hypotheses" is not simply an imposition,
but a *superimposition*, and one which leaves the most suggestive—most
bedenklichen—traces. For the phrase by which Derrida translates Freud
here, thereby drawing him back toward the "philosophy" he ostensibly
seeks to "avoid," as well as into the postal code—marks a slight but
significant shift from the German text. For Freud describes the pleasure
principle not as a "spekulative Hypothese," as the French translation
might lead us to believe, but rather as a "spekulative *Annahme*," a
word that repeats and continues the verb, *anzunehmen*, with which
Freud began his considerations on the state of analytical theory.

Why all this fuss about the translation of *Annahme* by *hypothesis?*
Not merely because Freud, in *Beyond the Pleasure Principle*, repeatedly
resorts to this word, rather than to *Hypothese*, perfectly available in
German, to designate the *assumptions* with which psychoanalysis is destined to operate, but also because the root of the word sets it apart from
that which characterizes "hypothesis," from the "setting up" or "posing" of a *thesis*.[5] For at the core of "assumption," *Annahme*, is not
Setzung, but *Nehmen*, and the difference is *bedenklich* indeed. For "to
take," or "take on," denotes an "activity" that is by no means the same
as "setting: up, out, upon . . . ." Indeed, it is hardly even certain that
this *Nehmen* should be called an "activity" at all, for it also entails

receptivity, a certain passivity or readiness, as much as any spontaneous and clearly delimited "act."

Thus, if Freud begins *Beyond the Pleasure Principle* by both describing and at the same time in a certain sense "suspending" the guiding principles of psychoanalytical theory, by underscoring their character as "assumptions"—and assumptions as such are always to some extent assumed *unbedenklich*, unreflectively—it is not indifferent if he retains the word to designate, in their entirety, the tenuous character of metapsychological concepts. Such *Annahmen*, Freud remarks, apparently to reassure his readers, unlike those of philosophy, have been arrived at "in an attempt to describe and to account for the facts of daily observation in our field of study" (*S.E.* 19: 17). However, one need only recall that such "daily observation" in the "field" of psychoanalysis is, like perception itself, a function of borrowed languages and *Bilderspra-chen*, to realize how tentative the "descriptive" or "observational" status of psychoanalytical assumptions must necessarily be.

It is this precarious, tentative aspect of psychoanalytical thinking that leads Freud, at the conclusion of his brief, introductory résumé, to declare that in such matters, "the least rigid [loosest, most flexible] assumption [*die lockerste Annahme*] will, I believe, be the best one" (my translation; Strachey uses "hypothesis").

If, then, the story of Freud's speculations is not so much one of "hypotheses," or even of "theses," but of *Annahmen*, this modifies the very "postal code" which seeks to impose itself upon it. And it modifies it by revealing a certain process of *imposition* at work. This process installs a peculiar indebtedness at the very core of psychoanalytical thinking. For *to assume assumptions* is not merely to open oneself and one's thought to an exteriority that comes from without: it is to accommodate something that remains, in a certain sense, alien, strange—*fremdartig*, as Nietzsche would say. It is to install a debt at the core of cognition, *owing* at the heart of *knowing*. Such accommodation can only be ambivalent, however, since it inevitably entails a resistance to that which imposes itself, but which can never be simply assimilated or appropriated.

This is why an *Annahme* can never be simply "loose" or *locker*, however desirable that might be. For the force with which it *takes hold* is irresistible: this at least is what emerges at decisive points in the speculations of *Beyond the Pleasure Principle*. This is already explicit in the opening pages of the text, where it becomes clear that, if the pleasure principle has succeeded in installing itself as an *unbedenkliche Annahme*, it is because of its ability to overwhelm any and all resistance: the assumption, Freud writes, has been "forced upon us by psycho-analytic work" (*S.E.* 18: 8).

This is also why, when an *Annahme* is suspended, it is generally only through the force of another, more powerful "assumption." This is the case with the move "beyond the pleasure principle": for what replaces the pleasure principle is not, as Derrida has emphasized, another principle or thesis, or even a hypothesis, but rather the very process of *imposition*, of *assumption* itself. For to assume, *unbedenklich*, in order to "account" for the "facts" of an impossible observation—an "observation" which in fact is nothing but the *reading* of a borrowed, figural language—is to engage in the very process that Freud "thematizes" under the ostensibly descriptive term "repetition-compulsion." The latter does not merely *designate* the irresistible, repetitive movement of the *drives*: it *imposes* itself upon Freud with and as the very same movement it describes: "Here the idea cannot but force itself upon us, that . . . " (my translation; in *S.E.* 18: 36, it appears as "At this point we cannot escape a suspicion . . . ").

If the gesture that marks Freud's speculations is that of an irresistible imposition of *Annahmen*, then this may explain why and how Freud can at the same time deny, acknowledge, and dispatch his indebtedness with that matter-of-factness that so fascinates Derrida. To record the movement of such *assumptions* is to retrace one's dislocation by forces that one can neither determine nor identify; to "assume," in this sense, is both to admit an irreducible dependency, and also to refuse that dependency as a mere "assumption": to recognize the "other" at the very moment one tries to take hold of it.

It is this ambivalent character of the process of assumption, by which its "taking on" is also and inevitably a "taking off," that may account for the curious place *Annahme* occupies within the postal code. For, in German at least, when a letter is returned to its sender, it is often with a stamp affixed to the envelope, that reads: "Annahme verweigert." In this case, however, the question: "Who, in short, pays? The addressee or the sender?" is a lure, for neither pays. Rather, it is the postal system itself that is left holding the bill, which is probably why such systems can never make ends meet.

VI

This almost brings us back full circle to our point of departure, the collect call from Martin(e) or martini Heidegger. The call, you remember, was refused, after the "chemistry" of a calculation impossible to summarize, but for reasons we have in the meanwhile *perhaps* begun to envisage.

And yet, what results when a collect call made in the name of Martin, Martine, or martini Heidegger is refused? "This morning, I thought that I ought not to pay. . . . " But in refusing to accept the charges—*Annahme verweigert*—was the debt reduced?

In the chain of readings in which "Speculer—sur 'Freud' " is situated, Heidegger is doubtless the most important of the missing links. The divisibility of place and the reversibility of time, the superimposition of "fort" upon "da," the destination of the postal network, its "exappropriative" structure—all can be retraced to Heideggerian notions of *Geschick* and *"Da,"* of *Enteignung* and *Ent-fernung,* and of a space in which backward and forward, front and back, near and far, are no longer defined by opposition to each other. The debt to Heidegger is clear, and, in a certain sense, assumed. Why, then, is the collect call, made in his name, refused?

A hint of where the elements of a response might be sought is inscribed in, and around, the same long footnote in which Heidegger and Nietzsche are mentioned in regard to the notion of an unrequitable debt—the note that ends with the promise, or threat, to "refer *Sein und Zeit* to *The Genealogy of Morals,* insofar as *Schuldigsein* (being guilty) is concerned"—but to do it "elsewhere [*ailleurs*]" (*Carte postale,* p. 282). The phrase that occasions this long note reads as follows: "One can be guilty of that of which one considers oneself essentially innocent; indebted to that of which one always feels oneself redeemed in advance" (p. 282). And the ensuing footnote refers the reader to "the existential analytics of Dasein," which "situate the structure of originary *Schuldigsein* (being responsible, being forewarned, or the capacity-of-being responsible, the possibility of having to answer-for before every debt, every fault, and even every determinable law) this side of all subjectivity, of every relation to an object, [prior to] all cognition and above all, prior to all consciousness" (p. 282; compare Heidegger, *Being and Time,* sec. 58, pp. 325–35).

One can be *schuldig*—guilty, responsible, indebted—independently of any act or feeling, intention or awareness, that one may have or do. For instance, the act of refusing to accept a collect call. But when the call is made in the name of a certain Heidegger—however dubious its authenticity may be—that *name* obliges its addressee to at least take note of the discussion of debt, or rather, of being-*Schuldig,* in *Being and Time.*

If, therefore, we follow the hint, promise, or threat, and go to the section of *Being and Time* indicated (sec. 58), what we find is not merely a discussion of debt, or being guilty, but also—and perhaps above all—a scene which is almost the uncanny double of that said to have taken place the morning of August 22, 1979.

For the discussion of *Schuld* in *Being and Time* is also the analysis of a "call" (*Ruf*), or rather, of an "appeal" (*Anruf*). Or perhaps of a telephone call. Indeed, coming to section 58 with that other call in mind, it becomes impossible *not* to read the *Anruf* of conscience (*Gewissen*) as just such a telephone call. In the first place, the call is very definitely long distance: "The call is from afar unto afar" (*Gerufen wird aus der Ferne in die Ferne*) (p. 316). Secondly, the call is in a certain sense uncalled for, it comes as a surprise, interrupting and deranging. Thirdly, if the call deranges, it is because, ultimately, nothing is said: "The call asserts nothing, gives no information about world events, has nothing to tell" (p. 318). It announces nothing, except perhaps a certain nothingness of the called, of the addressee. That is, it recalls the latter to or before its irrevocable *Schuldigsein*—a term whose translation I shall defer, for a moment. But only in order first to proceed to another untranslatable word, which bears even more immediately upon our problem. This word concentrates, as it were, the duplicit, uncanny but also witty, perhaps even *farcical* relation of the two calls, long distance and collect. For the essence of the call of conscience, in *Being and Time,* is that caller and called are, ultimately, the *same*—although by no means simply identical. The call comes from *Dasein* to *Dasein*. In short, "Es [Dasein], hat sich selbst gewählt" (which the English translation presents as, "It has chosen itself" [p. 334]). The untranslatability of this phrase is like that of a good joke. For *wählen* does not simply mean "to choose, elect"; it also, and particularly in combination with "call," means: "to dial." In the long-distance call that says nothing, but calls up a certain debt, *Dasein* therefore *dials* itself. And it is above all the nature of this dialing that suggests why, and in what way, that other collect call had to be refused, by one whose "private relation to Martin does not go by the same line" (*Carte postale*, p. 26).

For it is precisely a question of *standards:* of equivalents, as with Nietzsche, but also of telephone lines, exchanges, and operators (*standardistes*). *Dasein*, we recall, does not simply *dial itself* in *Being and Time*. It dials itself *directly*, without intermediary. Indeed, it is this ability of direct dialing that determines the possibility of the call, as that which interrupts *Dasein*, recalling it to its *Schuldigsein:* "The possibility of its thus getting broken off lies in its being appealed to without mediation [*unvermittelten*: unaided]" (p. 316). The ineluctability of a certain *Vermittlung*, however—and the word also designates the *telephone exchange*—is what *La carte postale* is all about. There is no call, no dispatch, no missive, letter, or communication, without a *Vermittlung;* indeed, the former is an effect, and defect, of the latter. This, too, is recorded and recounted in the annotated story of the collect call that was refused.

All this should not create the impression that there is no telephonic communication which ties me to the ghost of Heidegger, as well as to more than one other. On the contrary, the network of my connections . . .

is rather cluttered and more than one exchange is required to absorb the overload. Simply, my correspondents of this morning should know that . . . my private relation to Martin does not go by the same line. [*Carte postale*, p. 26]

That "private relation" does not go by the "même standard" for the simple reason that it does not go by *le standard du même*, not at least as that *standard* operates in the direct dialing of *Dasein*. For what enables Dasein to call itself directly, without the intermediary of any exchange or any operator, is a certain *sameness*, which notwithstanding the remoteness that separates *Dasein* from itself, nevertheless substantiates the assertion that caller and called are ultimately the *same*.

Indeed, the call is precisely something which *we ourselves* have neither planned nor prepared for nor voluntarily performed, nor have we ever done so. "It" calls, against our expectations and even against our will. On the other hand, the call undoubtedly does not come from someone else who is with me in the world. The call comes *from* me and yet *from beyond* me. [*Being and Time*, p. 320]

To be sure, *Dasein* as the "called" (*als angerufenes*) is differently *da*, there, from the *Dasein* that calls. And indeed, the entire effect of the call operates within the space of this difference. However, what is essential in remarking the distinction between the call of *Dasein*, recalling its *Schuldigsein*, and the collect call refused in *La carte postale*, is that the call of *Dasein* takes place, takes its place, *without the intervention of an operator*. This means that there can never be any doubt as to the nature of the call, of the caller, and what the call recalls: namely, a *Schuldigsein* whose "owner," as it were, is unequivocally determined, as "Dasein itself" (*Dasein Selbst*).

Of course, such clarity is not characteristic of the actual call itself: the Self of *Dasein* that receives the call "remains indefinite and empty in its 'what'. . . . And yet the Self has been reached, unequivocally and unmistakably," even though "That which calls the call, simply holds itself aloof from any way of becoming well-known" (p. 319). But if the Called and the Caller are both indeterminate, the certitude with which the call attains its addressee indicates a level of determination that exceeds that of the call as experienced, that of its *"existentielles Hören."* For the *"existenziale Analyse,"* by contrast, both Caller and Called can be unequivocally determined, and indeed, such absence or elimination of equi-vocation is the condition of the Call itself.

To understand this unequivocal quality of the Call, we must recall the manner in which it operates, without the mediation of operators or exchanges. *Dasein* dials itself, but the Self that it dials is not that which dials. The Self that is called is one that is *lost*—lost in the "one" (*das Man*) of itself, lost in, and as, *one*-self. It is this Self, lost in its *Oneness*, that is interrupted and disrupted by the unexpected, unerring call. The Self is thereby called back and forth, not alternatively, in an oscillating or rocking motion, but at the same time. It is this back-and-forth, back-*as*-forth, that comprises the silent, unuttered message of the call: what Heidegger designates as *Schuldigsein*. Let us, finally, take a closer look at just what this word denotes in *Being and Time*.

The *Schuldigsein* that is called up in the call of conscience addresses *Dasein* in its ability-to-be (*Seinkönnen*); that ability-to-be, however, is characterized by a certain *Nichtigkeit* (nullity, notness). What marks the being of *Dasein* as *schuldig* is that it is inseparable from being-*not*. Not only is *Dasein* "thrown, *not* brought by itself into its There" (as "geworfenes, *nicht* von ihm selbst in sein Da gebracht"), but its very ability-to-be confounds it in a choice (*Wahl*) of possibilities that is ineluctably marked by those it necessarily must reject, the possibilities *not*-chosen:

> In having a potentiality-for-Being, it always stands in one possibility or another: it constantly is *not* other possibilities, and it has waived these in its existentiell projection. Not only is the projection, as one that has been thrown, determined by the nullity of Being-a-basis; *as projection* it is itself essentially *null* [not]. . . . The nullity we have in mind belongs to Dasein's Being-free for its existentiell possibilities. Freedom, however, *is* only in the choice of one possibility—*that is, in tolerating one's not having chosen the others and one's not being able to choose them.* [p. 331; emphasis added in final sentence]

Dasein is thus "as such *schuldig*" because its mode of being is determined by the possibilities it rejects, does *not* choose, as much as by those it does.

The call of conscience, then, recalls *Dasein* to its most basic being, which is to be the basis of a notness or nullity. It is only on this basis, as *Grundsein einer Nichtigkeit*, that *Dasein* can truly care, and take care of its Self. By being thus recalled to this basic "notness," *Dasein* calls upon itself *to accept* the not-possible, that is, "even that thrown entity which it is [*selbst das geworfene Seiende, das es ist, existierend zu übernehmen*]" (p. 333). However "uncanny" this call may be, however indeterminate the caller, however strange and unexpected, there can never be any doubt, for the discourse that articulates the existential analysis—that is, at the level of the "existenzial"—that the call is a house call that *Dasein* pays upon itself. Indeed, within the economy of *Being and Time* this is precisely the *interest* of the call. For it is this call that enables the argument to proceed from the analysis of being-to-death, which establishes the *general possibility* of an authentic existence, to the demonstration that such a possibility is also a *specific demand* that *Dasein* makes of itself. From the standpoint of the existential analysis, the call *bears witness* (*bezeugt*), *attests* to this demand (p. 311). The significance and value of this testimony can thus be presented as unequivocal insofar as the transaction takes place within *Dasein* itself, between *Dasein* and its Self. Through this call, *Dasein* bears witness to its proper calling, to the propriety and the property of its notness. If the call thus testifies to the indebtedness and responsibility of a being that only can *be* in accepting (and excluding) and supporting what it is not, there is never any doubt that the debts thus incurred are *Dasein's own*.

It is this *claim* that provides the background—or is it the foreground?—of the decidedly inauthentic refusal to accept the collect call from one Martin, Martine, or martini Heidegger. Instead of assuming a debt that would ultimately prove to be his own, the narrator calculates, maneuvers, seeks to negotiate—and decides, "very quickly to refuse." The call, he tells the operator, is only "a joke." What he might have added, was that it probably was not for him in the first place. For if the caller gave his, her, or its name, that of the called is not mentioned, not at least in the story we are told.

Which is why, *perhaps*, the call of *La carte postale*, in contrast to that of *Being and Time*, was not to be accepted, but only *assumed* in and as a *story*. For what was lacking was the name, the proper name. And yet, that name was also *there*, all the time. Where? *Da:*

> Naturellement je ne l'ai jamais accepté, ni toi, ce n'etait pas possible, mais je le veux encore. . . . J'accepte, ce sera désormais ma signature, mais que cela ne t'inquiète pas, ne t'inquiète de rien. Je ne te voudrai jamais aucun mal, entends bien ce mot en toutes lettres, c'est mon nom, que *j'accepte,* et tu pourras compter, y compter comme sur les clartés capitales, de toi j'accepte tout. [*Carte postale*, p. 31]

> Naturally I never accepted it, nor you, it wasn't possible, but I still want it. . . . *I accept,* henceforth this will be my signature, but don't let that worry you, don't worry about anything. I will never wish you any harm, take this word literally, it's my name, that *I accept,* and you can count . . . on it. . . . from you I accept everything.[6]

NOTES

1. In the original French: "Freud en prend tellement à son aise dans une situation aussi embarrassante, il décline la dette avec une assurance si empressée, une légèreté si imperturbable qu'on se demande: s'agit-il de sa propre dette? Ou de la dette d'un autre? Et si la dette était toujours d'un autre? Comment se sentir et ne pas

se sentir à la fois, d'avance, acquitté et coupable de la dette d'un autre quand celui-ci, en soi logé par l'effet d'une singulière topique, revient à soi selon une filiation dont tout reste à penser? Comment spéculer sur la dette d'un autre à soi revenant?"

2. In the original French: "Si l'on tient à surnommer Oedipe la figure du *fort: da,* telle que nous l'avons vue fonctionner l'autre fois, c'est en y *remarquant* une matrice nébuleuse et plus qu'abyssale de l'un seulement de ses effets ou si vous préférez de ses rejetons. C'est comme si on la tirait, cette matrice nébuleuse à fusions ou fissions en chaine, à permutations et commutations sans fond, à disséminations sans retour, par un seul de ses fils. *Il est vrai que cette tentation (un seul de ses fils pour former le trait) n'est pas une limitation contingente dont on puisse se dispenser de rendre compte.* Car c'est comme si l'on voulait faire revenir à l'un de ses fils, autrement dit à la mere matricielle, à une mere qui ne serait que ce qu'elle est."

3. *Protokolle der Wiener Psychoanalytischen Vereinigung,* vol. 1 (Frankfurt: S. Fischer, 1976), p. 338. In regard to Freud's relation to philosophy and philosophers, one can consult with great profit the studies of Paul-Laurent Assoun, including: *Freud, la philosophie et les philosophes* (Paris: P.U.F., 1976), *Freud et Nietzsche* (Paris: P.U.F., 1980), *Introduction à l'épistémologie freudienne* (Paris: Payot, 1981).

4. Concerning the minimal "exteriority" and distance required by the strategy of deconstruction, see *Of Grammatology:* "I wished to reach the point of a certain exteriority in relation to the totality of the age of logocentrism. Starting from this point of exteriority, a certain deconstruction of that totality which is also a traced path, of that orb which is also orbitary, might be broached" (pp. 161–62).

5. The distinction between hypothesis and assumption—*Annahme*—is by no means new to the history of philosophy. It is, for instance, at the core of Hans Vaihinger's *Philosophy of the As-If,* first published in 1911. Vaihinger, who discusses *Annahmen* within the framework of a general theory of *fictions,* himself refers to Alexis von Meinong and Heinrich Maier as convergent theorists of *Annahmen.* This aspect of Freud's theoretical practice thereby discloses its affinities with certain contemporary philosophical versions of Neo-Kantianism, a point that has been explored by Paul-Laurent Assoun.

6. But the circle would not be complete were I not to point out, here at the end and in passing, that not only is the proper name of the "sender" inscribed there, in the *Envois,* but also the very term I have suggested was missing, and which seems to denote the exact opposite of that 'name': *Annahme verweigert!* (acceptance [or assumption] refused). For indeed, this term was *there,* all the time. Where? On the very first page of the very first envoi, which begins as follows: "Yes, you were right, henceforth, today, now, at every instant, at this very point on the card, we are only a minuscule remnant 'left unclaimed, rejected, disclaimed, refused' [*laissé-pour-compte*]: of what we said to each other, of what—don't forget—we made of each other, did to each other, wrote to each other. . . . 'Left unclaimed'—I would have preferred to say of what we *destined,* solely, for each other" (pp. 11–12).

The phrase *laissé-pour-compte* is thus the first explicit citation or quotation of the book. It designates the "we" of the *Envois*—from the perspective of the "I"—as unclaimed vestige, remnant of what "we" "said," "did," "wrote," but above all, *sent to, destined* for each other. And yet, we will not be entirely surprised any longer to discover that it is in another place—another text—that this destiny plays itself out, a play in which the "left-over" is both assumed and refused, assumed-as-refused.

This, then, is the beginning (itself a repetition and reproduction) of: Derrida, *Die Postkarte, Von Sokrates bis an Freud und jenseits* (Berlin, 1982): "Ja, Du hattest recht, wir sind künftig, heute, jetzt, in jedem Augenblick, an diesem Punkt hier auf der Karte nichts als ein winziges Überbleibsel, dessen 'Annahme verweigert' wurde: . . . . 'Annahme verweigert' würde ich lieber von dem sagen, was wir uns einer dem anderen, einzig, geschickt haben" (p. 13).
  Einzig . . . geschickt.

REFERENCES

Derrida, J. *Of Grammatology*. Translated by G.C. Spivak. Baltimore: Johns Hopkins University Press, 1976.
————. *La carte postale*. Paris: Flammarion, 1980.
Freud, S. *Standard Edition of the Complete Psychological Works*. London: Hogarth, 1953–74.
  The Interpretation of Dreams (1900–01), vols. 4, 5.
  Totem and Taboo (1913), vol. 13.
  Beyond the Pleasure Principle (1920), vol. 18.
  An Autobiographical Study (1925), vol. 20.
Heidegger, M. *Being and Time*. Translated by J. Macquarrie and E. Robinson. New York: Harper & Row, 1962.
Nietzsche, F. *On the Genealogy of Morals*. Translated by W. Kaufmann and R.J. Hollingdale. New York: Random House, 1967.
————. *Beyond Good and Evil*. Translated by W. Kaufmann and R.J. Hollingdale. New York: Random House, 1967.
————. *Ecce Homo*. New York: Random House, 1967.
Sterne, L. *Tristram Shandy*. New York: Norton, 1979.

3   The Double Game:
An Introduction

ALAN BASS

Tantrum, paralysis.

How to write about Derrida and Freud? About translating Derrida and becoming an analyst? About transference to the professor and transference to the analyst? About resistance to translating and resistance to analysis, which itself is so often compared to translation? Is there any resource of style that Derrida has not tapped before me, more rigorously, more powerfully? (Transference is resistance, the analyst says here. You are using your feelings about Derrida to rationalize not working.) Will the practice of analysis be at all affected by the deconstructive readings of analytic theory? (You are accrediting the metaphysical oppositions of theory and practice, of "text" and "reality," and all the values they imply, the deconstructive reader says here. There is no discipline exempt from metaphysics, and no discipline without a complex relation to its own language.) What remains is the power to say, do it yourself. If you wish to, read Derrida, find out what he has to say about psychoanalysis. And if you wish to, continue to rationalize away your own emotional conflicts from the vantage of an alleged superiority to the "naïve" metaphysical assumptions of psychoanalysis.

Tantrum, paralysis: the dismissal of both audiences, analysts and academics, instead of writing to them.

Instead, then, the fragment of a pseudo-autobiographical account of the relations between psychoanalysis and deconstruction. I am an analyst, having trained for that career after training for an academic one, and I have translated four books by Derrida. Most of the translating was done during the course of my analytic training (and therefore of my analysis). Throughout, the topic I will pursue is the relation between Derrida's concept of undecidability, of irreducible doubleness, and resistance to the analytic process, particularly the analyst's resistances. And how this became clear to me in my attempts to put Derrida into English while becoming an analyst. But I must emphasize how pseudonymous this account will be. One of the great common lessons of psychoanalysis and deconstruction is the generative power of what is left out. So be it. I will fall well within the bounds of the timid and the conventional in what follows.

I went to France for the first time during my junior year of college, as have so many others. Before leaving, I had been admonished by my department chairman not to do anything crazy, "like studying structuralism," if I wished to receive "full credit" for my year abroad. Of course, studying structuralism was exactly what I had intended to do all along. This was also my first trip outside the United States. Never again will I experience such a thrilling sense of excitement in daily life as I did those first months in Paris. And, not by chance—I found out retrospectively—the family I was assigned to live with for the year included a senior student in philosophy at the Ecole Normale Supérieure. Looking back at the incredible *joie de vivre* I felt during those months, I can also recognize a classic example of the peculiar relation between geography and the superego. Away from familiar surroundings depression lifts magically, energies are released, and the "manic defense" against inner conflicts takes over. I had felt depressed enough the year before to seek help at the college counseling service, my first stab at therapy. In my mind at the time, therapy had a peculiar meaning: everyone was doing it, so I would not. But I was also truly unhappy. Painful states that had dominated me since childhood erupted into periods of frightening misery during that second year of college. So I went to the counseling service. The therapist I was assigned to—a graduate student in psychology?—suggested that I not go abroad the next year, and that I enter analysis. End of therapy.

Thus my euphoric year in France. I immersed myself in "structuralism," studied music, wrote plays, worked for a theater troupe, made friends. Daniel, the *normalien* in whose apartment I was living, helped by recommending books to read, and indicated that his teacher at the Ecole Normale, Jacques Derrida, was also someone to know about. Daniel passed along his copy of the acts of a colloquium on *Genesis and Structure* that contained Derrida's small essay on Husserl entitled " 'Genesis and Structure' and Phenomenology." I will never forget my first attempts to read it: compared to this Lévi-Strauss and Foucault were writing popular novels. All that I got from this first attempt was a vivid memory of the red circles on the book cover. Six years later it was the last piece of *Writing and Difference* that I translated—even though it is in the middle of the book—and I cited it in my introduction. I still think that for anyone not familiar with Husserl the essay is mainly impenetrable, and its first paragraph is monstrous. However, it also contains passages on the way logos, reasoned discourse as we know it, differs from itself in attempting to reappropriate itself, and on writing as the dangerous moment of this difference, passages that I find completely admirable for their programmatic statement of much that was to come in Derrida's works. The essay was written in 1959.

During my very turbulent senior year of college (1969–70) I continued to attempt to understand what Derrida was about. It began to dawn upon me that here was a philosopher who saw Western thought as violent and repressive. In a rather confused way I linked this to the violence and repression that were such an overriding concern in the spring of 1970. But more attractive still, I was beginning to understand that the counterviolence Derrida wished to oppose to Western thought was related to the study of literature. Justification at last! Someone was saying that I could spend my time reading and studying and still be doing something radical. I applied to the graduate program in Comparative Literature at Johns Hopkins in order to study with Derrida. A fellowship, and the chance to begin working with Derrida in Paris were offered, and I accepted.

But not without misgivings, misgivings as confused as my initial understanding of Derrida. I had many rationalizations for these misgivings, but none make sense viewed retrospectively. In essence, I had formed a powerful transference to Derrida by reading him. Doubtless this is a typical experience for young intellectuals, but it has to be analyzed and taken into account in any theoretical discussion. And as always, Derrida precedes me here. He hints at a generalization of this idea in the opening paragraphs of "Cogito and the History of Madness" (1978), where he speaks of his own unhappy "disciple's" consciousness in entering into a dialogue with Foucault, a former "master." He expanded this analysis in the description of the "family scene" that takes place behind "Plato's pharmacy" (1981a). And most recently he has made a decisive contribution to the psychoanalytic debate over the death drive by analyzing it in terms of the legacy of Freud's transferences and the transference of Freud's legacy; see "Speculer—sur 'Freud' " in *La carte postale*. But this rather calm retrospective understanding is meant to contrast with the passions evoked by these experiences. For Derrida is a writer of passion and violence.

And so my transference developed, principally by reading *De la grammatologie*, "La pharmacie de Platon," and "La double séance" during my first semester of graduate school. Rousseau, Plato, Mallarmé. Although this is starting to be well-trod territory, I can only repeat what others have written. I was astonished, moved, excited by what I learned from *De la grammatologie* (1967, 1976). First there was the idea that our thought as such is logocentric (although Derrida now speaks of phallologocentrism)—that is, it always values speech over writing because speech is "closer" to truth and presence. And then that speech itself is a form of "writing": although speech presumably has the closest potential relation to truth and presence, the fact that it *is* made of signs implies the "preexistence" of representation, of the potentially untrue and nonpresent, a radical possibility of otherness, the otherness that makes speech, truth, and presence possible, simultaneously dividing them from any purely vocal, true, or present origin. This is Derrida's expanded notion of writing and textuality. Thus I learned that Derrida was proposing a deconstruction of thought as we know it, to be guided by the illogical, contradictory statements that any body of thought contains when it deals with its own vehicles of expression. Since these vehicles are the danger to truth, due to their being inherently deceptive, they are to be kept in a secondary position; and yet they are totally necessary. In *Of Grammatology* this led to the stunning analysis of Rousseau. Who before Derrida would have thought of relating Rousseau's condemnation of masturbation to this condemnation of writing, both being "dangerous supplements"? And who would have thought that the double meaning of *supplément*—that which is both missing and extra—would turn out to be symptomatic of the disturbing and disruptive notions of doubleness that our thought as such always attempts to set aside? And that it is no accident that the concepts used to describe writing always have such a contradictory, double meaning? Writing and masturbation, the inevitable evils always to be condemned as surplus, and yet always to be fallen back upon in the eternally vain attempt to make good what is missing.

This analysis made it easier to understand why Derrida considers it decisive for Western thought that Plato should have conceptualized writing as *pharmakon*—both remedy and poison. For me, and I wish to emphasize myself here, the most compelling moments of "Plato's Pharmacy" are the ones that link writing as *pharmakon* to *The Interpretation of Dreams*. I offer this as a personal favorite among Derrida's analyses, precisely because of the reference to Freud, and because of the expansion of philosophical and psychoanalytic thinking it implies. It was this analysis that first alerted me to the profound influence of Freud on Derrida, an aspect of his work that became increasingly important to me as my understanding of it grew.

I begin with Derrida's assertion that when Plato attacks the Sophists, it is not because of their insistence on memorization, but because of their "substitution of the mnemonic device for live memory"

(1981a, p. 108). Live memory is *mneme*; Plato condemns *hypomnesis*—the mechanical devices substituted for truth, living memory. Plato *"dreams* of . . . a memory with no sign. That is, with no supplement. A *mneme* with no *hypomnesis* no *pharmakon"* (p. 109; Derrida's emphasis). Why does Plato—and the rest of philosophy with him—consider the substitute to be mechanical, dead, dangerous, poisonous? Precisely because it is a substitute, because it implies the possibility of mistaking the original for the reproduction. If the sign were not repeatable, if speech could not be reproduced, there would be no discourse on truth, true *mneme* could not function. But the repetition and reproduction intrinsic to the sign are the very things in opposition to which the unique, living truth is always defined. "Memory therefore always already needs signs in order to recall the non-present, with which it is necessarily in relation. . . . Memory is thus contaminated by its first substitute: *hypomnesis"* (p. 109). Further, since the substitute is always defined as what is *outside* the living truth, the necessity of the substitute *also* implies that what is normally considered radically *outside* the truth has always been *inside* it, dividing truth from itself: "The 'outside' does not begin at the point where what we now call the psychic and the physical meet, but at the point where *mneme,* instead of being present to itself in its life as a movement of truth, is supplanted by the archive, evicted by a sign of re-memoration or of com-memoration. The space of writing, space *as* writing, is opened up by the violent movement of this surrogation, in the difference between *mneme* and *hypomnesis.* The outside is already *within* the work of memory. The evil slips in within the relation of memory to itself" (p. 109).

The dangerous situation that programs philosophy, then, is that its founding concepts—truth, presence—are self-contradictory. They are the origin to which thought always attempts to return, yet they imply something nonoriginary—nontrue, nonpresent, unalive—in order to be conceptualized at all. This is why philosophy always stumbles when it attempts to think about writing, and always blindly recurs to double-meaning concepts whose doubleness can in no way be synthesized or unified. Writing, the sign of the sign, the signifier of the signifier, is always conceived as that which is external to truth, and yet as that which already haunts the innermost recesses of truth as the possibility of repeating it.

Continuing Derrida's analysis:

> Just as Rousseau and Saussure will do in response to the same necessity, yet without discovering *other* relations between the intimate and the alien, Plato maintains *both* the exteriority of writing *and* its power of maleficent penetration, its ability to affect or infect what lies deepest inside. The

pharmakon is that dangerous supplement that breaks into the very thing that would have liked to do without it, yet lets itself *at once* be breached, roughed up, fulfilled, and replaced, completed by the very trace through which the present increases itself in the act of disappearing.

If, instead of meditating on the structure that makes such supplementarity possible, if above all instead of meditating on the reduction by which "Plato-Rousseau-Saussure" try in vain to master it with an odd kind of "reasoning," one were to content oneself with pointing to the "logical contradiction," one would have to recognize here an instance of that kind of "kettle-logic" to which Freud turns in the *Traumdeutung* in order to illustrate the logic of dreams. In his attempt to arrange everything in his favor, the defendant piles up contradictory arguments: 1. The kettle I am returning to you is brand new; 2. The holes were already in it when you lent it to me; 3. You never lent me a kettle, anyway. Analogously: 1. Writing is rigorously exterior and inferior to living memory and speech, which are therefore undamaged by it. 2. Writing is harmful to them because it puts them to sleep and infects their very life which would otherwise remain intact. 3. Anyway, if one has resorted to *hypomnesis* and writing at all, it is not for their intrinsic value, but because living memory is finite, it already has holes in it before writing ever comes to leave its traces. Writing has no effect on memory.

The opposition between *mneme* and *hypomnesis* would thus preside over the meaning of writing. This opposition will appear to us to form a system with all the great structural oppositions of Platonism. What is played out at the boundary line between these two concepts is consequently something like the major decision of philosophy, the one through which it institutes itself, maintains itself, and contains its adverse foundation. [pp. 110–11; translation slightly modified]

Thus, despite all of philosophy's protests to the contrary, its "adverse foundation" is "analogous" to the logic of dreams. Philosophy treats writing *defensively* because the question of writing makes philosophy *anxious,* compels philosophy to betray the logical thinking that is supposed to be its crowning achievement. How far-reaching is the analogy to psychoanalysis, to the "logic" of dreams that is so different from ordinary logic? At this point, we should turn to "Freud and the Scene of Writing," which was actually written and published before "Plato's Pharmacy," and which discusses the analogy to psychoanalysis. However, I will continue to follow the order of my own readings, which went right from "Plato's Pharmacy" to "The Double Session" (whose title has an obvious analytic import).[1] The psychoanalytic analogy is deepened throughout "The Double Session," although at the time I misunderstood in a way that Derrida had already warned against in "Freud and the Scene of Writing." At the time, though, I was becoming as (over) enthusiastic about Derrida's persistent use of psychoanalytic concepts as I was about his radicalism concerning thought in general. How typical this is in retrospect! (From "Marx" to "Freud," from the demonstration to the couch. . . .)

So: from *Of Grammatology* the double meaning of the supplement; from "Plato's Pharmacy" the double meaning of the *pharmakon*. Both were disengaged from what philosophy says despite itself (defensively, anxiously) about writing. In "The Double Session" Derrida reads the double meaning of Mallarmé's *hymen*—both virginity and consummation—as a literary practice that challenges the philosophy inherent in all literary criticism. Criticism, as Derrida often points out, derives from the Greek *krinein,* to *decide.* All criticism, thus far, has been programmed by the metaphysical *decision* to value truth, presence, meaning. Mallarmé's *hymen,* for Derrida, practices the "logic" of undecidability that the double meanings of the supplement and the *pharmakon* betray. For as long as criticism attempts to *decide* on the truth or meaning of a text, it will operate the way, for example, Plato and Rousseau do when they come across the paradoxes of writing: they will unwittingly follow the hyper- or hypo-logic exemplified by the dream or the borrower of the kettle. Whether undecidable doubleness is practiced (as in Mallarmé), or inevitably revealed (as in philosophy in general) is not an accident however: " 'Undecidability' is not caused here by some enigmatic equivocality, some inexhaustible ambivalence of a word in a 'natural' language, and still less by some '*Gegensinn der Urworte*' (Abel) [32]" (1981a, p. 220). And note 32 reads: "We are referring less to the text in which Freud is directly inspired by Abel (1910) than to *Das Unheimliche* (1919), of which we are here, in sum, proposing a rereading. We find ourselves constantly being brought back to this text by the paradoxes of the double and of repetition, the blurring of the boundary lines between 'imagination' and 'reality,' between the 'symbol' and the 'thing it symbolizes' . . . , the references to Hoffman and the literature of the fantastic, the considerations on the *double meaning* of words: 'Thus *heimlich* is a word the meaning of which develops towards an ambivalence, until it finally coincides with its opposite, *unheimlich* . . .' " (1981a, p. 220).

"The Double Session," then, is also a rereading of a text of Freud's. Not the 1910 paper "The Antithetical Meaning of Primal Words," but the 1919 paper "The 'Uncanny.' " Why again the reference to Freud, the analytic analogy? I will give a lapidary answer that will take some time to explain: because of the difference between Hegel and Freud on the question of contradiction. Pages 220–21 of "The Double Session" spell out the crucial aspects of this difference, and why Derrida should refer to it in his analysis of Mallarmé.

Derrida begins with a caution in the sentence that immediately follows the one on undecidability just cited. Recall, though, that the footnote on "The 'Uncanny' " is between the "undecidability" one and this one: "In dealing here with *hymen*, it is not a matter of repeating what Hegel undertook to do with German words like *Aufhebung, Urteil, Meinen, Beispiel,* etc., marveling over the lucky accident that installs a natural language within the element of speculative dialectics." What is Derrida warning against here? Why the reference to Hegel right after the footnote on the double meaning of *unheimlich*?

Hegel, for Derrida, is the thinker against whom everything must be checked. As the ultimate speculator, the most encyclopedic of thinkers, there is almost nothing that has escaped him. Indeed, for Derrida, Hegel is the thinker whose aim, precisely, was to let nothing escape him, to reappropriate everything for the profit of metaphysics. And Hegel, too, reflected on the role of words with double meanings in his thought. As Derrida indicates here, for Hegel it is a wonderful coincidence that his language, German, the language in which speculative dialectics is to be brought to its highest pitch, should be so rich in words that themselves are "dialectical," words that combine opposite meanings, words that contradict themselves. Thus, if Derrida is claiming to depart from metaphysical thinking, and if he is doing so with special attention to words that contradict themselves, he has to differentiate his analysis of self-contradictory words from Hegel's. With reference to Freud.

Speculative dialectics aims to master, to unify, and to reappropriate contradiction. Truth is reached by negation and reconciliation. This is why Hegel finds it so felicitous that a natural language should provide him with words he can privilege in order to express this process. This is where Derrida differentiates his practice from Hegel's. With reference to Freud:

> What counts here is not the lexical richness, the semantic infiniteness of a word or concept, its depth or breadth, the sedimentation that has produced inside it two contradictory layers of signification. . . . What counts here is the formal or syntactical *praxis* that composes and decomposes it. . . . what holds for *"hymen"* also holds, *mutatis mutandis,* for all other signs which like *pharmakon, supplement, différance,* and others, have a double, contradictory, undecidable value that always derives from their syntax, whether the latter is in a sense "internal," articulating and combining under the same yoke, *huph'hen,* two incompatible meanings, or "external," dependent on the code in which the word is made to function. But the syntactical composition and decomposition of a sign renders this alternative between internal and external inoperative. One is simply dealing with greater or lesser syntactical units at work, and with economic differences in condensation. Without reducing all these to the same, quite

the contrary, it is possible to recognize a certain serial law in these points of indefinite pivoting: *they mark the spots of what can never be mediated, mastered . . . or dialecticized. . . . Is it by chance that all these play effects, these "words" that escape philosophical mastery, should have, in widely differing historical contexts, a very singular relation to writing? . . . Without any dialectical Aufhebung, without any time off, they belong in a sense both to consciousness and to the unconscious, which Freud tells us can tolerate or remain insensitive to contradiction.* [1981a, p. 221; emphasis added in last three sentences]

Elsewhere (and here I *am* skipping ahead for the sake of explication), Derrida has put it thus: "the 'undecidable,' which is not contradiction in the Hegelian form of contradiction, situates, in a rigorously Freudian sense, the *unconscious* of philosophical contradiction, the unconscious which ignores contradiction to the extent that contradiction belongs to the logic of speech, discourse, consciousness, presence, truth, etc." (1981b, p. 101, n. 13).

What Derrida is saying in these two citations branches out in many directions. The idea is that Freud's description of the unconscious as ignoring contradiction, as the "illogic" that leaves opposites unresolved, represents a profound challenge to the metaphysical thinking that construes contradiction only in terms of resolution, in terms of *deciding* in the name of truth. This is why an essay on Mallarmé is also a rereading of an essay of Freud's. Mallarmé, for Derrida, practices the *hymen,* sees literature as a practice of suspending decision, of articulating doubleness. In "The 'Uncanny,' " Freud, perhaps despite himself, also comes to remark upon a literary practice of irreducible doubleness. Such practices leave one suspended *between* truth and nontruth, and "between-ness" is what Derrida is emphasizing as concerns writing and the unconscious. Between-ness—the suspended decision—is intolerably anxiety-provoking for thought as we know it. Speech, consciousness, presence, and truth, as we have said several times now, form a system of values that *must* disavow "writing" and "the unconscious," the functions of irreducible doubleness that are what Derrida called in "Plato's Pharmacy" philosophy's "adverse foundation."

Which makes "Freud and the Scene of Writing" necessary at this point, both because—as I indicated above—it had already cautioned against overextending Derrida's psychoanalytic analogies, *and* because it had provided the basis for them. In the introductory section to his essay, Derrida quite simply says: "Despite appearances, the deconstruction of logocentrism is not a psychoanalysis of philosophy" (1978, p. 196). (Again, "logocentrism" is Derrida's shorthand for metaphysics as such, in its valuation of speech, consciousness, truth, presence. "Deconstruction" is the term Derrida has coined to describe his enterprise: it entails the rigorous analysis of the hierarchy of metaphysical values, and then the elaboration of "concepts" that do not practice the logic programmed by these values.) Quite usefully, Derrida then goes on to list the appearances that make deconstruction look like a psychoanalysis of philosophy: "the analysis of a historical repression and suppression of writing since Plato. This repression constitutes the origin of philosophy as *epistēmē* [knowledge], and of truth as the unity of *logos* [reason, discourse] and *phonē* [voice]" (1978, p. 196). Thus, Derrida acknowledges that what he is doing *appears* to be a "psychoanalysis of philosophy" because he is concerned with necessary and inevitable repression: philosophy would not be what it is without the repression of writing. "Repression, not forgetting; repression, not exclusion," he goes on. "Repression, as Freud says, neither repels, nor flees, nor excludes an exterior force; it contains an interior representation, laying out within itself a space of repression. Here, that which represents a force in the form of the writing interior to speech and essential to it has been contained outside speech" (1978, pp. 196–97).

Derrida takes his analogy to repression even further, listing another aspect of deconstruction that makes it *appear* to be a psychoanalysis of philosophy: "The *symptomatic* form of the return of the repressed; the metaphor of writing which haunts European discourse, and the systematic contradictions of the onto-theological exclusion of the trace. The repression of writing as the repression of that which threatens presence and the mastering of absence" (1978, p. 197). This is an explicit comparison to the theory of symptom formation: when the repressed returns, as it inevitably does, the system defends itself by distorting the repressed, even at the price of self-contradiction. (Recall the contradictory statements of Plato and Rousseau about writing.) Again the question arises: how far does the analogy extend? Is philosophy a "neurosis" or "psychosis" of thought? Is deconstruction "like" psychoanalysis in its attempts to undo the "pathological defenses" ("systematic contradictions") eventuated by intolerable "anxiety" ("that which *threatens* presence . . . ")?

This is where Derrida begins his precautions. First, he makes a general one, concerning thought as the system of logocentric values: "Logo-phonocentrism is not a philosophical or historical error which the history of philosophy, of the West, that is, of the world, would have rushed into pathologically, but is rather a necessary, and necessarily finite, movement and structure . . . the European form of the metaphysical or onto-theological project, the privileged manifestation, with worldwide dominance, of dissimulation, of general censorship of the text in general" (1978, p. 197).

This is a general principle: nothing simply escapes metaphysics. Only the most detailed analysis of a given text permits one to understand how that text both obeys metaphysical constraints and challenges them.

This holds for Freud as well as for any other thinker, and thus Derrida's next paragraph, containing the specific precaution:

> An attempt to justify a theoretical reticence to utilize Freudian concepts, otherwise than in quotation marks: all these concepts, without exception, belong to the history of metaphysics, that is, to the system of logocentric repression which was organized in order to exclude or to lower (to put outside or below), the body of the written trace as a didactic and technical metaphor, as servile matter or excrement.
>
> For example, logocentric repression is not comprehensible on the basis of the Freudian concept of repression; on the contrary, logocentric repression permits an understanding of how an original and individual repression became possible within the horizon of a culture and a historical structure of belonging.
>
> . . . Certainly, Freudian discourse—in its syntax, or, if you will, its labor—is not to be confused with . . . necessarily metaphysical and traditional concepts. Certainly it is not exhausted by belonging to them. Witness the precautions and the "nominalism" with which Freud manipulates what he calls conventions and conceptual hypotheses. . . .
>
> The necessity of an immense labor of deconstruction of the metaphysical concepts and phrases that are condensed and sedimented within Freud's precautions. [1978, pp. 197–98]

Thus, although the kind of reading of Freud that Derrida proposes is not—despite appearances—a "psychoanalytic" one, it continually cites psychoanalytic concepts, while disengaging the part of metaphysics within them. Since the metaphor of writing is the symptomatic form of the return of the (philosophically) repressed, Derrida's first major text on psychoanalysis is on the metaphor of writing in Freud. Returning to my "autobiographical" perspective, I wish to note that "Freud and the Scene of Writing" was my introduction to any critical perspective on Freud's works as a whole, and a curious perspective it is. By this time, I was well-enough instructed to know that in examining the treatment of writing in a given corpus, Derrida aims at readings that reorganize, and sometimes undermine, all previous understandings of that corpus. To read Plato or Rousseau from the vantage of the role of writing in their thought produces a change of perspective that can only be compared— again the analytic analogy—to the change of perspective produced by the understanding of unconscious forces in oneself. Derrida is asking us to tolerate a reading of Freud that accounts for the way Freud's thought—like every other—is fissured by the return of the philosophically "unconscious." And as one might anticipate, Freud's relation to the (*symptomatic*) way the metaphor of writing imposes itself upon him

is not quite that of philosophy's. As Derrida writes: "From Plato and
Aristotle on, scriptural images have regularly been used to *illustrate* the
relationship between reason and experience, perception and memory.
But a certain confidence has never stopped taking its assurance from the
well-known and familiar term: writing. The gesture sketched out by
Freud interrupts that assurance and opens up a new kind of question
about metaphor, writing, and spacing in general" (1978, p. 199).

Derrida's reading of Freud guided by the metaphor of writing
comes up with this surprising fact: from the beginning to the end of his
career, Freud refined his conception of psychic content and structure
according to metaphors of traces and machines. These metaphors finally
fell into place, with the two combined, in the "Note upon the Mystic
Writing-Pad." As Derrida says, this 1925 text answers precisely the questions raised in the "Project" of 1895. Here, though, I am less interested
in the specifics of how the mystic writing-pad fulfills the conditions set
down in the "Project"—one simply has to read "Freud and the Scene of
Writing" to understand this—than in the kinds of questions this discovery—and again, did anyone notice this before Derrida?—leads to. Here
they are:

> We shall not have to ask if a writing apparatus—for example, the one
> described in "Note on the Mystic Writing Pad"—is a *good* metaphor for
> representing the working of the psyche, but rather what apparatus we
> must create in order to represent psychical writing; and we shall have to ask
> what the imitation, projected and liberated in a machine, of something
> like psychical writing might mean. And not if the psyche is indeed a kind
> of text, but: what is a text, and what must the psyche be if it can be repre-
> sented by a text? For if there is neither machine nor text without psychical
> origin, there is no domain of the psychic without text. Finally, what must
> be the relationship between psyche, writing, and spacing for such a meta-
> phoric transition to be possible, not only, nor primarily, within theoretical
> discourse, but within the history of psyche, text, and technology? [1978,
> p. 199]

It was this series of questions that helped me to understand the
importance of the *machine* for Derrida. Writing is always treated by
philosophy as a *technique,* as part of the technology of communication,
which always means the communication of truth and meaning. According to the traditional view, technology has no life of its own, and is to be
kept below and apart from the living truth. Like writing. It is no accident, then, that the machine—the dead mechanism which endlessly
produces the same thing—should be as unthinkable for philosophy as
writing. And it is no less accidental that the "unconscious," which
ignores contradiction, suspending decision, should be represented by a

writing machine. These are conceptions that cannot be governed by traditional metaphysical thinking. Where traditional thinking does make its claim again, however, is in the relegation of the mechanical metaphor to the status of a representation external to what is represented, here "the unconscious." This is what philosophy has always done, since Plato disqualified *hypomnēsis* (see above) "according" to the logic of the kettle:

> A pure representation, a machine, never runs by itself. Such at least is the limitation which Freud recognizes in his analogy with the Mystic Pad. . . . his gesture at this point is extremely Platonic. Only the writing of the soul, said the *Phaedrus,* only the psychical trace is able to reproduce and to represent itself spontaneously. Our reading had skipped over the following remark by Freud: "There must come a point at which the analogy between an auxiliary apparatus of this kind and the organ which is its prototype will cease to apply. It is true, too, that once the writing has been erased, the Mystic Pad cannot 'reproduce' it from within; it would be a mystic pad indeed if, like our memory, it could accomplish that". . . . Freud, like Plato, thus continues to oppose hypomnemic writing and *en tei psychei,* itself woven of traces. . . . Henceforth, the Mystic Pad, separated from psychical responsibility, a representation abandoned to itself, still participates in Cartesian space and mechanics: *natural* wax, exteriority of the *memory aid.* [1978, p. 227]

The deconstructive reading asserts here that the machine is no less exterior to the psyche than writing is to speech. To jump ahead to a paper not yet written, I would like to suggest where one might begin to find an answer to Derrida's question about what kind of apparatus must be created in order to represent not only psychical writing, but psychoanalysis itself. I think that one would have to pursue two mechanical metaphors from Freud's paper "The Dynamics of Transference" (1912). (The title itself, of course, being one of Freud's most familiar mechanical metaphors.) In this paper Freud compares transference both to a *vehicle* and to a *stereotype plate* (the solid mold of a plate of type that can be used over and over; again the scriptural and mechanical metaphors combined). What kind of apparatus, then? An unthinkable one, of course—perhaps a sort of vehicular printing press.

In charting these first encounters with Derrida on Freud, I am leaving aside the encounters with Hegel and Heidegger that were just as important at the time—my years in graduate school. Here, though, I come to another transference phenomenon, one that took me much time to understand. For Derrida, as discussed briefly above, Hegel is the most encyclopedic speculator, with whom the encounter never ends: "Misconstrued, treated lightly, Hegelianism only extends its historical domination, finally unfolding its immense enveloping resources without obstacle" (1978, p. 251). There is an adversary relation to Hegel: Derrida is indeed attempting to set obstacles in the path of Hegel's immense enveloping resources, but without treating Hegelianism lightly. Thus, Derrida's scrupulous differentiation of his own emphasis on words with double meanings from Hegel's.

But Derrida has predecessors in this enterprise, and he does not hesitate to name them:

> The privilege granted to consciousness . . . signifies the privilege granted to the present. . . . This privilege is the ether of metaphysics, the element of our thought that is caught in the language of metaphysics. One can delimit such a closure today only by soliciting this value of presence that Heidegger has shown to be the onto-theological [i.e., the most general, *onto-*, and the highest, *theo-*] determination of Being. . . . by means of an interrogation whose status must be completely exceptional, we are also examining the absolute privilege of this form or epoch of presence in general that is consciousness as meaning in self-presence. . . . Before so radically and purposely being the gesture of Heidegger, this was also the gesture of Nietzsche and of Freud, both of whom, as is well known, and sometimes in such similar fashion, put into question consciousness in its assured certainty of itself. [1982, pp. 16–17]

Heidegger, Nietzsche, Freud: the three predecessors who began the systematic questioning of presence and consciousness, yet also repeated in their own ways the metaphysical views of writing and machines. Each has to be read scrupulously, carefully, endlessly. However, while the deconstructive reading of Freud was what fascinated me the most, it was the reading of Heidegger that produced the strongest emotional reaction. For the passionate enthusiasm that Derrida provoked in me had to have its underside: there is no idealization without hatred.

What happened is that for a certain time I became convinced that there were no fundamental differences between Derrida and Heidegger.[2] This was a private crisis, one that I kept more quiet than my personal crisis of wanting to leave academia. In terms of what Derrida calls the family scene of philosophy, with its obvious psychoanalytic basis, this crisis might be analyzed thus: one undermines the authority of the father by relegating him to the status of brother. It is as if I were reproaching Derrida in this way: you, in your relation to Heidegger, are no more than I in my relation to you. Heidegger is your father, as you are mine. Now, this touches upon another of Derrida's key points, to wit, that it is *also* no accident that "writing," since Plato, has always been assigned to the role of the bastard, the illegitimate child whose paternity is unclear. The implication is that all of Derrida's discourse actively works to prevent *his* becoming a philosophical father. When the student's or reader's wish for a father is left unanalyzed, the stance prohibiting paternity and clear lines of filiation provokes frustration and rage. If one could prove that deconstruction *does* have a legitimate father, then one both undermines the entire enterprise and maintains the hope of being a legitimate son.

I mention all this because I think that my reaction not only was one of the typical reactions of serious readers of Derrida, but also is instructive as concerns the relations between psychoanalysis and deconstruction, and why Heidegger plays such a critical role in Derrida's reading of Freud. First, a prolonged confrontation between Heidegger and Derrida led me—painfully—to admit to myself that I was wrong. Despite his avowed debt to Heidegger, there is no way to disavow what Derrida has shown in numerous texts: throughout Heidegger's works there is a persistent valuation of the voice, of propriation, of authenticity that is in conflict with his own project of destroying metaphysics. Deconstruction, in its affirmation of the text, of dispersal, of the doubleness that undermines all authenticity, is no more the *legitimate* child of the destruction of metaphysics than it is of psychoanalysis. (The use of the neuter "child," and not "son," is deliberate here.) Since both Heidegger and Freud, in their own ways, made fundamental contributions to the questioning of presence and consciousness, and yet both repeated certain exclusions of textuality in the name of presence and/or consciousness, Derrida can only be said to be the mutant offspring of some unimaginable union between these two predecessors. (This is one of the themes of the *Envois* in *La carte postale,* 1980.) In fact, to my knowledge there is no text of Derrida's on Freud that does not bring Heidegger into play. I have found that analysts often have trouble tolerating this.

Further, while I was slowly working this out, I had both completed a first draft of the translation of *Writing and Difference* and decided to begin analytic training. Imagine what happens when the difficulties of translation intertwine with powerful feelings of idealization and hatred, with self-glorification and the urge to attack. To put it briefly, the translation is neither faithful nor faithless, but both in that it too literally and too *quickly* transcribes one language into another. After setting aside the first draft of *Writing and Difference* and then rereading it, I had the awful experience of realizing that it was not in English. As I began to rework *Writing and Difference* I noticed that I was spending more and more time checking myself in dictionaries, looking up words and usages (particularly prepositions) whose English equivalents I thought I had been sure of. "Never assume, look it up," became my rule of thumb. As banal as this sounds, I think it is the index of an important "clinical" problem.

For as I began to understand my own wish to undermine Derrida via Heidegger (and thereby, paradoxically to create the possibility of legitimate affiliation to Derrida), I was also beginning to understand what was so difficult about analysis. Adjusting to the day-in, day-out routine of "saying what comes to mind" without having it interpreted was proving to be extremely difficult. Why was this so for me, and why is it so for every "patient"? Although there are many answers to this question in the analytic literature, I would like to propose one that derives from my own peculiar experience of being in analysis while translating the works of the "illegitimate offspring" of Heidegger and Freud whose enterprise frustrates every attempt to turn him into a father. Freud, I recall, consistently compared analysis to a process of translation. To press the analogy further, I would also recall that there is no translation without recourse to dictionaries, and I would posit that the more extensive the recourse to dictionaries, the better the translation. The analytic persistence on asking what comes to mind, instead of interpreting, puts the patient in the position of the dictionary, to be consulted endlessly before the translation is made. The resistance to asking what comes to mind before receiving an interpretation, is not much different from translating without spending endless hours "looking it up." In fact, I would put this axiomatically: every mistranslation, every failure to consult the "dictionary," is the archive of unanalyzed transferences. And vice versa: unanalyzed transference works the way a mistranslation does when it remains unnoticed and becomes canonic, accruing to itself a set of interpretations.

For example, there is a text of Derrida's in which he alludes to Pascal's familiar expression *le roseau pensant*—the thinking reed. The translator rendered *roseau* here as "rosebush," a clear failure to check his translation against the dictionary. Imagine, now, what would happen if someone were to comment on Derrida's use of "rosebush" as a metaphor. What would be most interesting would be to examine the interplay of the mistranslation, the commentary it engenders, and the translator's transferences. Such an examination would have to extend in every direction, crossing the borders between the personal and the theoretical.[3] And of course, this is the inevitable and necessary "danger" built into the analytic situation. Is there any analysis in which the analyst does not somewhere interpret too soon, due to his own transferences, and in which this interpretation does not become canonic, thus compelling the analyst to undertake the kind of examination I have just indicated? And would there be analysis without this danger?

Thus, I am suggesting that what is most difficult about analysis and translation is the suspension of decision in order to "look it up" or "say what comes to mind." This provides the chance (Derrida's topic in this

volume) for the inevitable mistranslation and its analysis. Resistance to
either process is the attempt to cut off the chance for this process, *abolir
le hasard* in Mallarmé's famous phrase. How many times have I heard
patients respond, after I have asked "What comes to mind?" for the nth
time, "What do you think I am? A movie/television/radio/book?"
(And I would like to note that I have heard this kind of response from
patients in all the traditional diagnostic categories.) The patient's choice
of metaphor here is no more accidental than the metaphor of writing
that "haunts European discourse" from Plato onward, and that is always
treated according to the logic of the kettle. For by resisting saying what
comes to mind, because it makes him into a mere form of entertaining
telecommunication (movie, television, radio, book, etc.), the patient is
also attempting to cut off the chance for his mistranslation—whatever
transference feeling is related to the current resistance. Which at the
same time—still according to the kettle logic—repeats the mistranslation—transference—but in its devalued form: the textual metaphor in
relation to anxiety and defense. If the patient's gesture is typically Platonic—"being in the position of having to repeat myself over and over is
frustrating and frightening, and makes me feel that you are relegating
me to the status of nothing more than a text from which *you* get pleasure at will"—the analyst's response must be a "deconstructive" one, a
response that affirms the chance for transference, affirms the necessary
play of mistranslation, affirms the delay of interpretation in favor of
"looking it up," affirms the doubleness without which there is no analysis.

   For just as striking to me as patients' use of the textual metaphor are
the reflections on doubleness by those analysts who have taken Freud
most seriously. This affirmation of doubleness cuts across "theoretical"
lines, and is to be found among those who consider themselves expo-
nents of ego psychology, of object-relations theory, or of "classical" drive
theory. I would call it the essence of psychoanalysis if I had not learned
from Derrida that the concept of essence is designed to denigrate the
play of doubleness. Thus, I will call the affirmation of doubleness the
metaphor that imposes itself upon any conception of the analytic situation, and will say that this metaphor is no more secondary and exterior to
such concepts as transference and resistance, ego and id, than writing is
to speech. Two citations, my emphasis:

   The transference is resistance and is the "resisted," i.e., the patient
   repeats infantile defenses (which are the "transference resistances") to
   avoid rendering conscious childhood situations of anxiety and pain which
   he is about to re-experience in the transference. . . . The *double nature* of
   the transference, its manifest and its latent content, resistance and the
   resisted, should always be kept in mind. [Racker, 1968, pp. 50, 53]

We have to play a *double game* with the patient's instinctual impulses, on the one hand encouraging them to express themselves, and, on the other, steadily refusing them gratification. . . . what concerns us is not simply the enforcement of the fundamental rule of analysis for its own sake but the conflict to which this gives rise. It is only when observation is focused now on the id and now on the ego and the direction of interest is *twofold*, extending to both sides of the human being whom we have before us, that we can speak of psychoanalysis. [A. Freud, 1966, pp. 13, 15]

How is the analyst to keep in mind the double nature of transference, to play the double game with the ego and the id? By being "as it were, *two* people—himself *in abeyance* and himself as an extra function to his patient" (Greenacre, 1981, p. 33). In abeyance and extra: an exact duplication of supplementarity as Rousseau condemns it and Derrida affirms it. The analyst's resistance to being two people, to being supplementary, can be understood, I think, in terms of the kettle logic that treats "writing" as a necessary evil, always to be kept in a secondary, nonthreatening position. As much as the analysis of mistranslation, the analysis of the analyst's supplementarity must confound the division between the "personal" and the "theoretical," in order to give the analyst's mistranslations their chance. This has ever been the aim of the analyst's analysis; I am also suggesting that this process *also* belongs to the deconstruction of metaphysics, to the affirmation of irreducible doubleness in the face of all the anxiety and defensiveness doubleness will always provoke. How prepared are we to think of resistance and the resisted not as opposed to each other, but as doubles of each other, to think of the ego and the id, secondary and primary processes, as the same?

Thus, I am also suggesting that just as writing and the machine are intrinsic to speech and presence, something like the passions of translating are intrinsic to becoming an analyst. Where does translation of the professor stop and transference to the analyst begin? Is there a way to think of transference and translation as the same, following the etymological metaphors that give transference, translation, and metaphor the same derivation, and that similarly yoke them under the same word in German: *Ubertragung*? This question always breaks down the division between the theoretical and the personal, and it is very much part of the "prehistory" of psychoanalysis. In conclusion, then, a passage from Jones's biography on Freud's translations and transferences in the years 1886–91. My emphasis:

he had embarked on the translation of four large volumes, two of Charcot's and two of Bernheim's. He *was not content merely* to translate them, *however faithfully,* but added important prefaces to two of them. The first one was Charcot's *Neue Vorlesungen,* 1886, the preface having been written in the previous July; it was a volume of 357 pages. The second one, also a considerable volume of 414 pages, appeared in the following year; it was the first of the Bernheim books. There was then an *interval* of four years, when two books appeared *almost simultaneously.* One was the second Bernheim book, *Hypnotismus, Suggestion und Psychotherapie* (380 pages). He furnished no preface for this one; by then his interest had moved from direct suggestion in therapy to the deeper matters of psychopathology he had begun to investigate. The last book, Charcot's *Leçons du Mardi,* delivered in the session of 1887–1888, appeared in parts during the years 1892–1894 under the title, *Poliklinische Vortrage* (Clinical Lectures); it has 492 closely printed pages. This book Freud did not merely translate; he edited it. He wrote a preface, and added sixty-two footnotes which brought the literary references up to date and contained many of the *translator's personal opinions*—sometimes in criticism of Charcot's. Some of these footnotes are of great interest in adumbrating Freud's earliest ideas in psychopathology, but he learned later that Charcot had been displeased at what he considered his translator's arbitrary behavior since *no permission had been asked.* [1953, p. 228]

What permission can give the chance to a mistranslating machine, a vehicular printing press?

NOTES

   1. At the time, in fact, I did not even have a copy of "La double séance." I have opened this footnote in order to thank Prof. J. H. Miller for loaning me a photocopy of his copy of "La double séance." Was I supposed to return it? I don't know; but I still have that copy. And I wish to add this: Derrida had inscribed Miller's copy of "La double séance," in its *Tel Quel* version. In many ways, having this copy of Derrida's writing and signature was a powerful impetus to my rapidly developing transference. And elliptically I add a citation from Derrida's recent article on Freud and telepathy: *il n'a que de la téléanalyse*—there is only tele-analysis (1981, p. 11).
   2. Later I learned how frequently this transferential reaction to Derrida occurs. See *Positions,* 1981b, p. 55 and p. 103, n. 28.
   3. I have attempted this kind of analysis of Freud's maintenance of a mistranslation in his Leonardo study, a mistake that produced the kind of situation just described. See my article "On the History of a Mistranslation and the Psychoanalytic Movement" (Bass, 1982).

REFERENCES

Bass, A. "On the History of a Mistranslation and the Psychoanalytic Movement." In *Difference in Translation*. Edited by J. Graham. Ithaca: Cornell University Press, 1984.

Derrida, J. *Of Grammatology* (1967). Translated by G. Spivak. Baltimore: Johns Hopkins University Press, 1976.

————. *Writing and Difference*. Translated by A. Bass. Chicago: University of Chicago Press, 1978.

————. *La carte postale*. Paris: Flammarion, 1980.

————. "Telepathie." *Furor* 2 (1981): 5–41.

————. *Dissemination*. Translated by B. Johnson. Chicago: University of Chicago Press, 1981a.

————. *Positions*. Translated by A. Bass. Chicago: University of Chicago Press, 1981b.

————. *Margins of Philosophy*. Translated by A. Bass. Chicago: University of Chicago Press, 1982.

Freud, A. *The Ego and the Mechanisms of Defense*. New York: International Universities Press, 1966.

Freud, S. *Standard Edition of the Complete Psychological Works*. London: Hogarth, 1953–74.

"Project for a Scientific Psychology" (1895), vol. 1.

"The Dynamics of Transference" (1912), vol. 12.

"A Note upon the 'Mystic Writing-Pad' " (1925), vol. 19.

Greenacre, P. "Reconstruction: Its Nature and Therapeutic Value," *Journal of the American Psychoanalytic Association* 29 (1981): 27–46.

Jones, E. *The Life and Work of Sigmund Freud*, vol. 1. New York: Basic Books, 1953.

Racker, H. *Transference and Counter-Transference*. New York: International Universities Press, 1968.

4   Atoms Again:
The Deaths
of Individualism

WILLIAM KERRIGAN

Derrida is a champion of unboundedness, welcoming unmeaning into his sense and indistinctness into his concepts. With a rhetorical agility unmatched in Nietzsche himself, he plays out the arduous gambit of refusing to have lost everything by affirming the nothing left, venturing that the "willed forgetting" at the roots of his Nietzschean discourse is neither denial nor self-deceit. What does he mean? Where is he coming from or going to? What is his position? Not to lie, not to play false, while continuing to speak and to play. Because the new demands of his peculiar (and, I think, unusually scrupulous) intellectual integrity require him to occupy and vacate positions simultaneously, Derrida is as fascinated as we are by the master question of where he is—by self-regard. The moment of self-regard in Derrida is not technically narcissistic, like the "autoaffection" he diagnoses in the writing of Rousseau, nor only another strategy for plucking himself from the fate of closure. It is primarily an old-fashioned display of discipline, warning intrigued readers that the price of this seemingly uninhibited, happily self-defiling thought is the necessity of being patient with unrelieved suspense and vigilant about not relieving it prematurely. Suspense, unboundedness, indeterminacy: one of their abiding images is the monster, and one of their abiding myths, Chaos. This, too, Derrida regards. Ending "Structure, Sign, and Play" with "a glance toward those who, in a society from which I do not exclude myself, turn their eyes away when faced by the as yet unnameable which is proclaiming itself and which can do so, as is necessary whenever a birth is in the offing, only under the species of the nonspecies, in the formless, mute, infant, and terrifying form of monstrosity" (1978, p. 293), Derrida from inside his text places himself among those outsiders who would turn away from the monstrous birth this very same text compels us, in suspense, to await.

But the bearer of unnameable monsters also puts on a familiar face for us. Derrida regularly plays the historian. ". . . as is necessary": one of his characteristic gestures is the discovery of "why"—of the law, the rule, the rigorous necessity that made the twinning of two issues, the range of meanings in a single word, or the suppresssion of a certain idea in the context of another idea, inevitable. What has happened has happened. History at its simplest, as chronicle, retraces the past. History of the sort Derrida practices, which seeks to uncover the necessitating rule, retraces in a double sense the "always already" of the past, forcing what has happened to happen all over again. Not the least of Derrida's ardors is to confront us with the extremity of chance and the extremity of fate.

Haphazardly, ineluctably, the two extremes have always tended to produce each other. Once we determine that it must exist, chance becomes our fate, and fate, once we determine that it must exist, invariably trails with it the question of how it has chanced to be. I would like to plot out a recurrent drama in the history of the interplay between fate and chance over the last three or four centuries—mostly in the weak sense of simply observing it, but leaving open the possibility that there may be evidence of a rule here, lending, if not a necessity, then a likelihood, an uncanny familiarity, a strong historical continuity to the "terrifying form of monstrosity" Derrida is now delivering.

Writing for this volume, he associates his project of deconstruction with the wayward and oppressed tradition of classical atomism. While not, as we will see, inconsistent with the usual genealogy that derives his themes from Marx, Nietzsche, Freud, Husserl, and Heidegger, this new linkage betrays a notable swerve in his historical self-regard. From the time of Descartes and Gassendi, it is true, atomism has figured prominently in French culture; Gaston Bachelard wrote a brilliant little book on the subject in 1931, and the revisionist history of science now being blocked out by Michel Serres promises to make Lucretius one of the commanding figures of Western thought. Perhaps I have mistaken for a genuine hint another instance of how Derrida's moving finger, having writ, moves on, leaving abandoned intellectual homes in its wake. But passages such as the conclusion to "Structure, Sign, and Play" suggest that a key aspect of Derrida's accomplishment is to have reformulated for our period the traditions of chaos mythology, and in the field of intellectual history atomism is surely the most active and various element in the

recent history of this mythology. Reflecting on the functions and trans-
formations of atomism has helped me to understand my conflictual
responses to Derrida's texts and their influence, and in the hope that my
own clarification may be useful to others, I will sketch in some of the
vicissitudes of the atom in Western culture.

We begin late in the Renaissance. This period generated a plot of
intellectual and affective self-analysis that subsequent periods, Romanticism in particular, have reasserted in an increasingly radical manner. At a
later point in the argument we will loop back briefly to the classical world
in whose image the Renaissance became itself.

THE ATOMS OF BURCKHARDT

Jacob Burckhardt is to Renaissance studies approximately what
Freud is to psychoanalysis. Despite cavils and qualifications, he continues to define the horizons of the discipline—what it is that Renaissance studies has been constituted to talk about. In this famous passage
he addresses a major difference between medieval and Renaissance man:

> Medieval man was conscious of himself only as a member of a race, people,
> party, family, or corporation—only through some general category. In Italy
> this veil first melted into air. . . . Man became a spiritual individual, and
> recognized himself as such. [1958, vol. 1, p. 143]

The Renaissance in Italy is marked by a new cult of the individual apart
from determining categories—individual in the Latin sense of *individ-
uum,* the indivisible core of assertive human energy that precedes and in
Italy comes to resist all the contingent predicates we fall into by virtue of
class, occupation, and so on. Renaissance artists learned how to convey
the depth and weight and gravity of this individual; Renaissance human-
ists developed genres of praise in order to ensure his recognition and
immortality, and among themselves used praise as a form of money able
to measure, apart from the inflations of the patronage market, the true
worth of this individual. To confirm that Burckhardt's insight was current during the period itself, scholars often refer to the creation myths of
Pico and Vives, in which man has by nature no fixed nature, enjoying
instead an unchained being, free to act *toward* his own self-determina-
tion rather than, like other creatures, condemned to act *out* an essence
or *quidditas* given him from the beginning. But the voices of the late
Renaissance in England were not silent on this matter, and they were
arguably wiser than the earlier ones.

George Herbert's "The Pulley" is very much a poem in the
Pico-Vives tradition. "Strength first made a way": what could be more

Burckhardtian, more of the Renaissance, than this? Strength is the first gift of God to man, prior to beauty and (surprisingly) to wisdom, which lags behind in third place. But man is not given "rest," which is to say, a fixity or essential identity, a being in which to rest. Thus it is that by the end of the poem human strength has lapsed into weariness. Man creates for himself only exhaustion, and finds his missing gift only when thrown exhausted onto the breast of God: this is Pico in another tone. A still more suspicious attitude toward individualism can be heard in a passage usually quoted to exemplify another trend indicative of this period—the new empiricsm. People, Donne observes in his *First Anniversary,* are doubting everything but their individuality. Indeed, they cast the world in doubt in order to secure this sovereign selfhood:

> And new Philosophy cals all in doubt,
> The Element of fire is quite put out;
> The Sunne is lost, and th'earth, and no mans wit
> Can well direct him, where to looke for it.
> And freely men confesse, that this world's spent,
> When in the Planets, and the Firmament
> They seeke so many new; they see that this
> Is crumbled out againe to his Atomis.
> 'Tis all in pieces, all cohaerence gone;
> All just supply, and all Relation;
> Prince, Subject, Father, Sonne, are things forgot,
> For every man alone thinkes he hath got
> To be a Phoenix, and that there can bee
> None of that kinde, of which he is, but hee.
> [ll. 205–18]

One might be tempted to gloss "crumbled out againe to his Atomis" as a reference to the four elements traditionally thought to have been combined in the generation of all other entities. Beyond earth, air, fire, and water, in this conception, it is impossible for the resolution of matter to proceed.[1] However, when Donne shifts from nature to culture, he tells us that *four* relations are forgot ("Prince, Subject, Father, Sonne"), which more than suggests that he has *not* just alluded to the inhibited atomism of four distinct elements, but rather to the more thorough fragmentation posited by Democritus, for whom the kinds of atoms are infinite, or by Epicurus and Lucretius, for whom the kinds are "incomprehensibly large," there being an infinite stock of each kind. Donne might have learned of these speculations from Nicholaus Hill's *Philosophia epicurea, democritiana, theophrastica* (1601), which we know he possessed a copy of (for a useful account of this book, see McColley, 1939). The world of distinct forms, which implies the submission of atomic *individua* to "general categories," is in this passage wittily crumbled out again by the revival of atomic theory, so that men, like cancerous cells, may go their own way, returning society to a chaos of self-begotten phoenixes falling where they will.

The *individua* in matter, the *individua* in culture: Donne's famous metaphor exposes a nerve in intellectual history, where the fortunes of these two entities do indeed run together. For now, I want to note that the darkened vision of these late English responses to individualism—in Herbert, a wearying burden of insufficiency inherent in our lack of original circumscription; in Donne, a scientific *contemptus mundi* in the service of egotistical autonomy—is suggestively closer to that of Burckhardt himself than the wonder-struck, celebratory voices of Pico and Vives. The founder of Renaissance studies arrived at his period with medieval, or as we used to say, not altogether accurately, "classical" values—limits observed, things in their places. "The fundamental vice of this Renaissance character was at the same time a condition of its greatness—namely, excessive individualism" (1958, vol. 2, p. 442). Substituting "atomist cosmos" for "Renaissance character" in Burckhardt's sentence, we can see immediately that the Renaissance very nearly rendered this judgment upon itself. If the period begins in the literary and artistic celebration of the "condition of its greatness," it ends with a new way, given authority by a science that was itself claiming the authority once allowed to literature and art, of contemplating its "fundamental vice."

Donne was right in intuiting that atomic materialism sponsors, after a fashion, social atomism. But the secret alliance posited in his metaphor would not be explored openly for another two centuries in the work of Marx and Nietzsche. During the Renaissance proper, the revival of atomic materialism was experienced viscerally as an assault on the substantiality and expectations, the *earnings* of the human individual. Bachelard (1975, pp. 1–3) has contended that physical atomism displays two apparently contradictory traits. It is categorical: in this vocabulary one manipulates the ultimate foundation, striking through phenomena to the synthetic regularities beneath, behind, or within them. Simultaneously it is analytic, violent, iconoclastic ("crumbled out againe to his Atomis"), threatening to diminish, and for some serious purposes (constructing a picture of reality, contemplating origins and ends, assessing one's place in the design of things) even to usurp the phenomenal world. The most emotional expression of this second function in the Renaissance concerns the anticipation of death. Selfhood, whatever it be and wherever it is found, sits on, or in, or is somehow coordinated with, a body; the intersection of selfhood and corporeality has come to be known in psychoanalysis, largely through the work of Paul Schilder

(1950), as the "body image." This self-representation—the fantasy assertion of individualism, of the bounded and integral self—underwent some striking changes at the end of the Renaissance.

What is the unity of a person? In Christian culture the answer to this question is believed to be manifest at the moment of death, when the subtle knot that makes us man comes undone, releasing the parts of us. At his play's last scene, Donne writes in Holy Sonnet VI, he would have the three parts of his cunning little world return to their native sectors in the world at large—flesh to earth, soul to heaven, sins to hell, "that all may have their right," their birthright (cf. Arthur Gorges's "Some wil commend and prayse their mistres crisped hayre"). Death is an *analysis* of human being, its resolution into constituent elements. It has often been remarked by psychoanalytic commentators that the ortho- dox model of this resolution, the bipartition of body and soul, is anal. Spit, snot, wax, piss, shit: when inside the human body these things generally excite no disapproval, but when expelled seem to enter a new phenomenal zone wherein they stand forth as objects of scorn or revul- sion. In the end the body, which alive could shelter these substances from disgust, becomes their ultimate representative; the Christian body is at last an outside, voided by the living soul. But in order to take account of a central attitude toward the corpse in Christian culture, and to appreci- ate in these terms the affective power of late Renaissance atomism, the commonplace psychoanalytic view must be importantly modified.

Let us take the example of Ben Jonson. His anal character has often been noted, and managed to express itself, not surprisingly, in the lan- guage of the new atomics. Donne's copy of Hill's *Philosophia epicurea* belonged originally to Jonson, whose name he scratched out and wrote over (see Keynes, 1958, p. 216); Jonson names Hill in his scatological brief epic "The Famous Voyage," incorporating atomism and death into a joke about flatulence:

> Here, sev'rall ghosts did flit
> About the shore, of farts, but late departed,
> White, black, blew, greene, and in more formes out-started,
> Than all those *Atomi* ridiculous,
> Whereof old DEMOCRITE, and HILL NICHOLAS,
> One said, the other swore, the world consists.
> [Vol. 8, p. 86; see also vol. 1, p. 145]

The dissolution of the body into flitting atoms was good matter for humorous ridicule. But in his graver epitaphs Jonson drew consolation from a vision of death contrary to the implications of atomism. *Requies- cat in pace.* Diseased no more, free from the addictions of appetite, the flesh will finally come to rest. This traditional quiet merges in the Renaissance with stoic and epicurean consolations for death. Thus, in Jonson's epitaph on his son, it is not only that the soul has escaped the world's rage, but also that the body has escaped the flesh's rage. "Rest in soft peace. . . ." And in the epitaph on his daughter, the division of death gives her soul a mother in heaven and, in the final image of a child tucked into bed, her body a mother in the grave: "Which cover lightly, gentle earth." The corpse so conceived is not a last reminder that life produces filth, the foul and lethal end of nourishment. This peaceful body is the soul's uncanny double, the enemy converted at last and awaiting reunion at the end of time.

Atomism offends all of the desires implicit in a graveyard—the wish to honor the dead, memorialize them, shelter them, and not least to preserve their individuality by separating them from others among the dead. One might think here of Shakespeare's epitaph, which is quite likely authentic:

> Good friend, for Jesus' sake forbear,
> To dig the dust enclosed here.
> Blest be the man that spares these stones,
> And curst be he that moves my bones.

It is hard to imagine a modern poet wasting his last comment on such a futile and nonmetaphorical defense of his turf, but this is probably authentic in part because the sentiment was so conventional. Sextons of cramped yards were not above reusing their plots, and no site, after all, could be guaranteed in perpetuity. Perhaps, as Sir Thomas Browne thought, it was pomposity to desire otherwise; this man was as willing to be cremated like the pagans as to be interred in the Christian manner. Few rose to his lofty detachment. Anxiety over the desecration of the grave was widespread in the late Renaissance (which is not to imply that it is absent today—witness the film *Poltergeist*). But what if such defilements were to occur by decree of nature?

The outrage inevitably forthcoming to the idea of the self as individual, which is presupposed in the ego-situated intentionality of every one of our thoughts and feelings, fuels the terrific rhetorical pressure of Donne's final sermon:

> But for us that die now and sleepe in the state of the dead, we must al passe this *posthume* death, this *death* after *death*, nay this death after buriall, this *dissolution* after *dissolution*, this death of *corruption* and *putrifaction*, of *vermiculation* and *incineration*, of *dissolution* and *dispersion* in and from the grave, when these bodies that have beene the *chil-*

dren of *royall parents*, and the *parents* of *royall children*, must say with
Job, Corruption thou art my father, and *to the Worme thou art my mother
and my sister. Miserable riddle*, when the *same worme* must bee *my
mother*, and *my sister*, and *my selfe. Miserable incest*, when I must bee
maried to my *mother* and my *sister*, and bee both *father* and *mother* to my
owne mother and *sister*, *beget* and *beare* that *worme* which is all that
miserable penury; when my *mouth* shall be *filled* with *dust*, and the
worme shall *feed*, and *feed sweetly* upon me, when the ambitious man
shall have *no satisfaction*, *if* the *poorest alive* tread upon him, nor the
poorest receive any *contentment* in being made *equall* to *Princes*, for they
shall bee equall but *in dust*. [*Complete Poetry and Selected Prose*,
pp. 584–85]

Obeying a convention as old as the hills, Donne presents death as an
affront to pride, a fate uniting prince and pauper. But he stirs the ashes
of this convention by making the oneness literal, a real mixture. The
deaths after death constitute a negative genealogy. Whereas the dispersions of living seed produce otherness within the family, link family with
family and repopulate the class structures of society, the dispersions of
the graveyard are in effect implosions, undoing familial and social structure by equating all the terms, reducing otherness to indistinctness.
Donne goes on to evoke the two limiting cases of Renaissance individualism—the public greatness of government, the private greatness of self-
government:

That that *Monarch,* who spred over many nations alive, must in his dust lie
in a corner of that *sheete of lead,* and there, but so long as that lead will
laste, and that privat and *retir'd man,* that thought himselfe his owne for
ever, and never came forth, must in his dust of the grave bee published,
and (such are the *revolutions* of the *graves*) bee mingled with the dust of
every high way, and of every dunghill, and swallowed in every puddle and
pond: This is the most inglorious and contemptible *vilification,* the most
deadly and peremptory *nullification* of man, that wee can consider; *God*
seemes to have caried the declaration of his *power* to a great height, when
hee sets the *Prophet Ezechiel* in the *valley of drye bones,* and says, *Sonne
of man can these bones live?* as though it had bene impossible, and yet
they did; The *Lord* layed *Sinewes upon them, and flesh,* and *breathed into
them,* and *they did live*: But in that case there were *bones* to bee *seene,*
something visible, of which it might be said can this thing live? But in this
death of *incineration,* and dispersion of dust, wee see *nothing* that wee call
that mans; If we say, can this dust live? perchance it *cannot,* it may bee the
meere *dust* of the *earth,* which never did live, never shall. It may be the
dust of that mans *worme,* which did live, but shall no more. It may bee
the dust of *another* man, that concernes not him of whom it is askt. This
death of *incineration* and dispersion, is, to naturall *reason,* the most *irre-
coverable death* of all. . . . [pp. 585–86]

Emotions that for centuries had clustered about the incineration of the corpse and the violation of the graves are here generalized to death itself. The atoms of the corpse are a reduced estate, humbling the monarch, but through the slow incineration of dispersion drift anywhere and everywhere, humbling the retired man. *Death's Duell* confronts us with something new and turbulent in the imagery of death—a Christian assimilation of Lucretius. The imagining of death does not rest in an imageless extinction or a static placement of mortal remains, but is rather compelled to behold the utter dispersal or "nullification" of individualism's premiere substance. The Alexander of *Hamlet*'s graveyard scene may eventually stop a bunghole; yet the great man still *is* and still is *somewhere*. In Donne, the *individua* temporarily submissive to the general category of the individual will desert this impermanent unity, and not in a passive way, blown by wind or sundered in the future vicissitudes of a graveyard. Subversive energies lie coiled in the particles that make us possible, and death is their liberation.

Perhaps we find ourselves thinking ahead to Romanticism—to the Lucy poems of Wordsworth, or to the democratic Democritus of *Leaves of Grass*. There can be something exciting and consoling about the return of our substance to the deep cradle of natural process. Donne had no need to discover calm or gratification in the dispersal of his individuality, for this unsparing nullification served ultimately to make the resurrection newly graceful and miraculous; God has tagged and numbered every atom, and in the fullness of time will reconstitute the unique body. In the poetry of Edward Herbert, however, we discern a Renaissance mind edging toward romantic sensibility. "How still these ashes lie, how free from lust," George Herbert counseled his wanton soul in "Church Monuments," but his brother Edward, who visited Gassendi toward the end of his life, recognized that there was no quiet, no lying still, in store for the restless flesh. He was a man, as he says in his own epitaph,

> who was free from either hope or fear,
> To have or loose this ordinary light,
> That when to elements his body turned were,
> He knew that as those elements would fight,
> So his immortal soul should find above,
> With his Creator, Peace, Joy, Truth, and Love.
>   [*Poems*, p. 54]

The traditional stoic calm, the traditional beatitude of the soul—but for the body, an untraditional Empedoclean strife. In his great "Elegy on a Tomb" Herbert unmetaphors a dead beauty with a scientific and philosophical force normally absent from the play of metaphysical wit: her light returns to the sun, her curled hair to the ocean's waves, and the speaker receives no answer, which is the profoundest answer, to his question about where her beauty now resides. Herbert's willingness to hold off the Christian resurrection as he contemplates the afterlife solely within the natural order is a measured step—certainly not a lunge—toward romanticism; and in fact, the quasi-pantheist visions of Romantic poets rarely penetrated beyond the phenomenal realm of grass and flowers, rocks and trees to the wholly unfeeling, nonempathic atomic world that Santayana had in mind when, comparing Lucretius to the romantics, he called the Latin writer "a poet of the source of landscape, a poet of matter" (p. 56). The seventeenth century is marked by many cautious inspections of ideas that had taken a long time to be reborn into European culture and were still felt (as they often are today) to be potentially monstrous.

Atomism took uncertain, discontinuous paths through the Renaissance, staying pretty much outside the university and in the vicinity of alchemy and hermetic medicine (Partington, 1939, pp. 260–61; Whyte, 1961, pp. 44–46). The classical thinkers were distorted from the beginning in Renaissance humanism. Thus Valla's *De voluptate* (1431) embraced the pleasure principle of Epicurean ethics but discarded altogether the physical atomism; Empedocles entered the Renaissance solely through Plotinus, and was therefore no longer the atomist he was for Aristotle (Bercovitch, 1968, pp. 68–71); Ficino threw Lucretius into the fire (after, we should not forget, reading him), a pagan unable to be digested by a Christian syncretism as tolerant as his; and although their sense of pleasure differed sharply from that of Valla, Erasmus and More continued the tradition of finding a Christian philosophy in Epicurean ethics. I have maintained that one reason for this prolonged reluctance lies in the way atomism sets the components of human individuality against that individuality, revolutionizing the imagination of death by denying to the body both rest and distinctness. But the reasons were many: Renaissance conceptions of the body had repercussions throughout the provinces of knowledge. This was a busy center of analogical thought, where ordering metaphors arrived and departed. The context of the cosmic body, for example, expanded and reworked anxieties prompted by atomism in the context of the individual body. The atomist postulate of an initial Chaos ran counter to the doctrine of creation *ex nihilo*. More generally, it weakened the cosmological stature of harmony and individuality: because a world of distinct entities whose fundamental rule, in view of the Chaos that preceded it, must be that their existence is mutually tolerable, comes second and by chance (in Epicurus and Lucretius, if not in Democritus), lucid things may return to the initial disarticulation. Insofar as the atomist cosmos has generated a typical overarching plot, this history tends to move from Chaos to order to Chaos, precisely the opposite of Christian sacred history in its movement from a good beginning to the relative disorder of human history to the good clarity of the end. Epicurean Chaos—Chaos as an end—is the universal death of all individuality save that of the atomic minutiae.

Chaos appears oddly but insistently in Renaissance literature. It is there as it is in the Bible—in metaphors that remember an old horror no longer credible, but indelible nonetheless. In Spenser it wears its ancient Near Eastern face: the monster. When Shakespeare's Othello says, "And when I love her not, Chaos is come again" (III.iii.91–92), he seems to behold in the structure of his life, strangely and maybe inexplicably, the cosmology of Lucretius, where initial Chaos in the figure of Mars is mastered by Venus, sustainer of harmony, who will one day withdraw her gift and abandon the world to the self-consuming fury of Mars; Othello, after killing his love, does indeed end in the passions of the battlefield, murdering himself as once before he "took by th'throat the circumcised dog / and smote him—thus." Milton believed as a point of doctrine that Chaos was not primordial, but the result of God's retirement from a portion of himself. Yet the symbolism of his epic presents us with a gulf that seems ageless, forever mingling infancy with senility. Chaos personified is "the Anarch old / With falt'ring speech and visage incompos'd" (II.988–89)—no clear sign, an expression that will not fix itself. As we look ahead in the history of Chaos mythology, this expressive but unreadable face seems particularly resonant. Lucretius had proclaimed in a famous passage that atoms were to bodies as letters were to words, but the Renaissance atomist, Giordano Bruno, thought it more accurate to say that atoms were to bodies as dots and strokes were to letters (Michel, 1973, p. 81). Potentially, an atomist Chaos could disturb the fundamental distinctness of meaning as profoundly as it could the fundamental distinctness of individuality.

The two were inseparable, as a brief meditation on the skeleton will reveal. It fascinated the Renaissance. During this period, after all, the complex articulations of the body were first figured out. The most extraordinary books produced by the first age of printing were the great Bibles, addressed to the soul, and the great anatomies, picturing the body—a pair that reproduces in the realm of texts the conventional bipartition of Christian death. Opening the *Tabulae Anatomicae* of Casserius, we find two plates of a gigantic, muscular male, seen front and then back, holding a staff. The pictures are repeated on the next two pages, but now the man is a skeleton, and now his staff has become a shovel. This is a moral and theological statement, a vision of old Adam the gardener holding the tool with which, having fallen, he must plant himself; yet it is also a revelation of the deep logic of the human body, of the solid order that informs the insides of us. In the Renaissance one could almost say his skeleton thought, or better, that his skeleton wrote. So many books entitled "An Anatomy": and since we have been dwelling on Donne, we might think here of his "ragged bony name" scratched on the mirror/window of "A Valediction: of my Name in the Window," a signature readily imagined to be a skeleton. The relationship of graphic to skeletal articulation surfaces with arresting clarity in William Davenant's description of Astragon's castle in *Gondibert* (1971, pp. 155–59), which contains two Baconian museums, one devoted to the skeletons of all creatures and therefore called "The Monument of Bodies" (Astragon has somehow managed to collect and display on the wall the complete bones of those two great dinosaurs, Adam and Eve), and a sister room devoted to manuscripts and therefore called "The Monument of Vanished Minds" (Astragon has here gotten hold of the scrolls of Thoth himself, Egypt being the Eden of textuality). Writing is the deposit, the hard core of internal order and unity, left by thought. Once again, this nexus of metaphor (which regularly puts in an appearance in Renaissance discussions of fixed and retrievable meaning) proceeds from the idea of death as a stable placement of the body, or of what gives the body form and coherence. But what if the corpus were not at rest? What if writing were not the deposit of specific and enduring sense capable, like the dry bones in Ezekiel, of being reanimated?

Against these and other resistances, atomism arose to enjoy its many conquests in the seventeenth century. Renaissance thought ends in a blaze of theorizing about the ultimate constituents of matter—the space-encapsulating atoms of Descartes, the void-traversing atoms of Gassendi, the physico-politico geometry of Hobbes, the thing-informing gas (coined from the term "*chaos*") of Van Helmont, the colorless corpuscles of Boyle, the cells of Hook, the monads of Leibniz. This was the theme in common, as Boyle suggested when comparing Descartes and Gassendi: "For they agree with each other and differ from the schools in this grand and fundamental point, that they not only take care to explicate things intelligibly, but that whereas those other philosophers give only a general and superficial account of substantial forms as accounting for the phenomena of nature, which the most ingenious among themselves confess to be incomprehensible, and certain real qualities which knowing men of other persuasions think unintelligible, both the Cartesians and the atomists explicate the same phenomena by *little bodies variously figured and moved*" (emphasis added; quoted in Harrison, 1933, p. 210). It was a partial emergence—an atomism made to play into the hands of God, subjected to pre-established harmonies of one kind or another. The ambitions of Renaissance individualism were not, of course, blown away in the atomism of the seventeenth century. The *kunstwerk* of the magnificent individual born centuries before in Italy managed to continue itself on the new atomist canvas. There were disillusionments to come. But it is well to remember, lest we become smug about our forebears, that the Renaissance concluded itself by delivering to us the first terms, the *individua*, of this corrective disintegration. In the long sweep of intellectual history, the turn to the ultimate constituents of matter at the sundown of the Renaissance produced—in genetics, in the physical sciences generally, and (as we will soon take note) in psychoanalysis—our severest critiques of the sovereign individual at the sunrise of the Renaissance. Moreover, the large pattern of assaulting the individual by positing the subversive, unanswerable character of his particles gives shape, Renaissance shape, to many of the disillusionments to come.

RENAISSANCE FALLOUT

If this historical impression were to become an authentic history I would discuss the several cognate forms of atomism that appear outside the physical sciences in the aftermath of the Renaissance. In literature, for instance, we find an increased emphasis on the sublime moment as a fundamental unit of value detachable from the entirety of the work, and in philosophical empiricism the concept of the sensation employed as the irreducible atom in psychic space. Eventually these issues would take us, as so many others do, to Germany, romanticism, and Kant. The second antinomy in *The Critique of Pure Reason* (pp. 402–9) sets the infinite divisibility of spatial things against the classical notion of the indivisible or "simple" atom—a theme resumed somewhat histrionically in Fichte (*New Exposition of the Science of Knowledge*, pp. 86–90 and passim), who remarked that "To him whose eyes have been opened there is nothing more funny than the ideas which modern philosophies promulgate about space" (p. 88) even as he himself derived "the absolute unity of freedom and being in knowledge" from the divisibility/indivisibility paradoxes implicit in drawing a line. Nicolas of Cusa and Giordano Bruno would have been delighted by such belated confirmations of their ideas. Is this really an aftermath? Is it superfluous that the *Critique* (second edition) was dedicated to Francis Bacon?

Signs of a Renaissance dominate the atmosphere of Romantic Germany. This country had undergone a Reformation rather than a Renaissance, which is a cultural project turned toward and engaged with a lost or defaced purity in the classical past that must now be cleansed, beheld, incorporated, and extended. By the end of the eighteenth century, Germans stood at the forefront of European classical scholarship, Greek studies in particular, and their country was exporting Romantic culture to the rest of Europe in much the way that Italy had once disseminated the Renaissance. German Romanticism was, in a sense, the last of the European Renaissances.

It harbored the afterlife of the Renaissance individual. For this proud fugitive survived the new atomistic sciences of the seventeenth century primarily in philosophy: the metaphysical "subject" as precondition for all determinations of judgment regains the old desire to stand over and above mundane classifications. Discovered by Descartes in a perfect solitude of self-induced ubiquity, this ego preserves for its shadow empire of knowledge the ambitions of Burckhardt's princes by halving the world with atoms. The new individual forfeits character. He forfeits mass and weight, which are transferred to the atoms. But in exchange he secures analytic mastery over *res extensa*. Atoms might be, as Descartes thought, subject to mechanical laws, or they might be, as others hoped, the vital and organic substrate of a universe dedicated to life. But some form of the dualism we tend mistakenly to confine to Descartes, surrendering body to atoms in order to save everything else for spirit, appeared to guard the philosophical ego from any conceivable consequences of the new sciences. The atom had become, in effect, the ego's ally. And what does the philosophical subject wish to be? A supreme atom, an inviolable atom of thought. Thus it is that Kant, when arguing that atomic parts cannot be conceived outside of composite wholes, falls into the groove that Descartes and Leibniz had worn in this argument when he must pause to note that self-consciousness, like the Kantian atoms, is not "an absolutely simple substance" and "must exhibit compositeness in its appearance" (pp. 408–9). Thus it is that the libertines of Sade project, behind a "secondary nature" of rule-bound processes, a "primary nature" of madly colliding atoms (Deleuze, 1971, pp. 24–25). Atoms that had once appeared to outrage individual self-representation became, as if through an intellectual enactment of identification with the frustrator, a repository of self-representation.

Critiques of this hidden collusion occur in the work of two figures who fulfill and conclude major strands of Romantic thought.

In his Jena doctoral dissertation of 1841, *The Difference between the Democritean and the Epicurean Philosophies of Nature*, Karl Marx identified in Epicurus a Hegelian drama of self-consciousness cast as a philosophy of nature. The atoms of Epicurus fall in straight lines until, at a moment attributed to irreducible chance, they swerve, hook together, and constitute a world. The young Marx saw in the swerve or *clinamen* an emblematic refusal of "non-self-sufficiency" (p. 49); as they desert the line of fate, throwing off the tyranny of the general category, the atoms manifest "the form of independence, of individuality" (p. 70). Thus understood, Epicurus neither initiated a new trend in

Greek thought nor recovered from the Pre-Socratics a speculative physics
lost in Plato and Aristotle. He was rather the last Greek philosopher of
the wise man, developing this ancient theme in a manner especially
congenial to the Roman world-view that followed. "This *potestas,* this
declinare is the defiance, the headstrongness of the atom, the *quiddam
in pectore* of the atom" (Marx, p. 475)—self-consciousness stripped
down to a shell of pure resistance. Atomism, communism: it is arresting
that the first ideology critique on the road to communism should be the
exposure of atomist physics as a way of ceding absolute independence to
individual self-consciousness.

One cannot make a similar claim for the primacy of atomism in the
deconstructive project of Nietzsche. His remarks about the subject, if
numerous, are brief and widely scattered. It is not clear whether he
bothered to gain firsthand knowledge of classical physics; much of what
he assumes about the atomist philosophers seems to have been drawn
from Lange's *History of Materialism.* But he, too, recognized the doubling of atom and subject:

> A quantum of force is equivalent to a quantum of drive, will, effect—
> more, it is nothing other than precisely this very driving, willing, effect-
> ing, and only owing to the seduction of language (and of the fundamental
> errors of reason that are petrified in it) which conceives and misconceives
> all effects as conditioned by something that causes effects, by a "subject,"
> can it appear otherwise. For just as the popular mind separates the light-
> ning from its flash and takes the latter for an *action,* for the operation of a
> subject called lightning, so popular morality also separates strength from
> expressions of strength, as if there were a neutral substratum behind the
> strong man, which was *free* to express strength or not to do so. But there is
> no such substratum; there is no "being" behind doing, effecting, becom-
> ing; "the doer" is merely a fiction added to the deed: it posits the same
> event first as cause and then a second time as its effect. Scientists do no
> better when they say "force moves," "force causes," and the like—all its
> coolness, its freedom from emotion notwithstanding, our entire science
> still lies under the misleading influence of language and has not disposed
> of that little changeling, the "subject" (the atom, for example, is such a
> changeling, as is the Kantian "thing-in-itself"). [*The Genealogy of
> Morals,* p. 45]

Like the atom of science, the subject of philosophy hypostasizes becoming and erects a substantial unity, which carries with it concepts such as
"cause" and "responsibility," to master what is really a volatile play of
forces. Nietzsche several times returned to the complementary myths of
atom and subject in his notes for *The Will to Power,* indicting "the false
autonomy of the individual, as atom" (p. 414; see also pp. 297, 338,

374). Nietzsche was a strong misreader of Burckhardt. Attacking both halves of the division of the world into atom and subject accomplished at the end of the Renaissance, he championed an overcoming strength reminiscent of the original energy—the unreflective personal power, innocent as yet of modern science and philosophy—found in Burckhardt's Italian potentates. "Ages are to be assessed according to their *positive forces*—and by this assessment the age of the Renaissance, so prodigal and so fateful, appears as the last *great* age," he wrote in *Twilight of the Idols* (p. 91), confessing in the same book that, exactly like those great forceful Italians, his attitudes toward nobility, his ambitions as a stylist, were Roman, not Greek (pp. 105–8).

Marx, of course, went on to other things, and the atom and the Italian Renaissance may amount to no more than a byway in Nietzsche's work. But in the career of Freud the Renaissance latent in Romanticism stands forth emphatically.

Psychoanalysis begins with the monadic neurons of "Project for a Scientific Psychology" (1895). Freud calls them "material particles" (p. 95), and they are ambitious and Burckhardtian *individua*. For what, to be grossly anthropomorphic, is their purpose? Or what, to be Nietzschean, is their deed? To clear a path, make an impression, leave a trace, and thus to create . . . memory, the locus of fame. Their supreme achievement is the wish, or as Freud would often say, the "immortal," the "indestructible" wish. It was probably the Burckhardt of *History of Greek Culture* that touched Freud most directly, but like the authors of the Renaissance, Freud assumed that being civilized meant, at its most sublime, responding to the classics. How much an imaginative citizen of the Renaissance Freud seems when, on the excursion recalled in "A Disturbance of Memory on the Acropolis" (1936), his desire to leave monuments like these casts him back to the schoolroom—the ongoing scene of the humanist tradition, where he learned the Greek in which he kept a boyhood diary—to the ambitions born in that schoolroom, and finally to the defensive, self-fashioning thought that the Acropolis had not become real until he had visited it! In the same late essay (by chance? at least with an evident rightness: a piece of fortune falling together with other pieces into a design) Freud ruminates on the twin defenses of derealization and depersonalization, which happen to characterize the two main philosophies of the Renaissance—Neoplatonism (the derealization of the external world made systematic, a defense against the internal emergence of gnawing melancholy and disruptive desire) and stoicism (the depersonalization of the internal world made systematic, a defense against the external emergence of a frustrating or intolerable fate). The theory was named after Sophocles, but about whom did Freud write? Shakespeare, who distorted, fragmented, and rearranged the classical plot. He was obsessed with the figure of Moses, but in whose form? Michelangelo's. His only full-length book on art was the *Leonardo*. When he presented psychoanalysis as the latest installment in modern man's disillusionment, the initiator of the process was Copernicus (1916–17, pp. 284–85).

Perhaps the finest—certainly, with regard to the history of our culture, the most evocative—of his many metaphors for the psyche is the layered Rome of *Civilization and its Discontents* (1930, pp. 69–71), which speaks to the "general problem of preservation in the sphere of the mind" (p. 69): to understand in these terms Freud's psychic city one must be at least a citizen of the Renaissance, aware historically of the difference between ancient and modern structures. In no trivial way, I think, psychoanalysis is the latest *translatio imperii*. The last major development of Freud's theory acknowledges the "excessive individualism" implicit in the beginning. When the neurological inscription of the pleasure principle into an immortal memory at last encounters Thanatos, producing an Empedoclean *eris* of unity and dispersal, Valla has met Gassendi, and things are "crumbled out again into their Atomis." The evolution of psychoanalytic theory recapitulates in broad outline the course of the Renaissance from individualism to iconoclastic atomism. But now the subversive decomposition of the final Renaissance death analysis has been elevated to the psyche, obliterating the Cartesian settlement. Held in the play of soul-forces is a great dispersing pressure that would not remember, not register, and thus annihilate the very conditions of individuality.

The iconoclastic triumvirate of Marx, Nietzsche, and Freud turns the romantic individual against himself. They complete what is virtually a death analysis of Romanticism, combing out its constituent elements—with Marx, the urge for social reform; with Nietzsche, the desire to oppose the mind-forged manacles of hierarchical ethics; with Freud, the fascination with the child and with disordered states of consciousness. They find the hyperbole that renders these aims fatal: reform means revolution, and revolution the effacement of the individual; opposition to all the ethics built on hierarchical distinctions means nihilism; the truth of the child means fate as much as it means uncursed innocence—repetition, trauma, a silent death drive that gets seated in us during the painful transitions of early psychic development. Classical Greek thought and Renaissance thought concluded with atoms—a disillusionment, but also a veiled reassertion of the immortality of the individual, passing on the heritage of the beginning. What has been left us in the purged atoms at the death of Romanticism?

About the time of Freud's death we split the atom, and Chaos in its ancient form has come again. Chaos, order, Chaos. We have generated a secular cosmogony beginning everything with a Big Bang; ahead of us we have placed an anxious secular eschaton that might end everything with a nuclear war. In between, where we are, Derrida tries to think without the "subject" and its many attendant fixities. "First," he replies to an interviewer in *Positions* when explaining why his analytic terms are neither words nor concepts, "because these are not *atoms*" (1981, p. 40).

CHAOS, DERRIDA, CHAOS

There could be a birth in the offing, he sometimes reminds us. But it is clear that Derrida wants to think through the end of Romanticism without hurrying us into a brave new period. Though he has shied away from prolonged encounter with Marx, he has offered readings of Nietzsche and Freud attuned to the survival in their work of assumptions, procedures, and expectations that their best insights render untenable. Facing up to the end, getting straight about our losses, is his pervasive theme: the problem of how not to betray the untraditional. He speaks as our disillusioner about previous disillusionments, one who over and over tells us that we must mourn (in writing is death, in reading is death) even as his inventive and exuberant style shows us what graces might be gained in undertaking this rigorous mourning. The losses he would have us face all lead to an individual who lives at home—as atom of consciousness, as exemplar of humanity, as point of origin, as author of his own sense and dispenser of ultimate sense to others—in the "metaphysics of presence."

For Derrida's generation the major alternative to the "Christian or atheist existentialisms" (1982, p. 116) that dominated postwar French thought was a version of intellectual atomics. Structuralism, in dissolving the individual *parole* into phonetic and semic minima, made the classic exchange of submitting to the antiphenomenal severity (we never experience *langue*) of particles in order to recoup this forfeit in explanatory mastery. Derrida's nonconcept of *différance* aims at the splitting of the structuralist atoms: between the *individua* of any differential structure hidden acts of differing will always be deferred. In his book on Husserl, *Speech and Phenomena*, Derrida brought his suspicion of philosophical distinction to the concept of intentional meaning—the representative of authorial ownership, and thus of individualism, in the field of hermeneutic theory. Classically considered as a duplication of speech or consciousness, inferior to these in being subject to uncorrectable misinterpretation but superior in its permanence and amplification, the written text had for centuries provided a "realistic" substitute for the body image. Endlessly vital, able to make over reader after reader in its own image with no loss of potency, the text was an achievement answerable to the earliest desires of the authorial ego. Derrida has, of course, exposed this cherished fantasy, and however unconventional his notion of the text, the deep imagery of his exposure could not be more familiar: death by dispersal. Through citation bits of the text will appear transformed in other texts, and these texts in still other texts. Because writing "can break with every given context, and engender infinitely new contexts in an absolutely nonsaturable fashion" (1982, p. 320), something of the monstrous fecundity of protean atoms belongs to the essence of the text—iterable in the absence of its author and its referents, without original and final context, spineless, redoable.

It is important to understand the fears Derrida engenders. When academics in this country sputter vituperation at the mention of his name, this is not just because he opposes the ways in which academic disciplines conceive of their tasks. His work strikes at the motivational structures that underlie the activities of reading and writing, of being someone to whom texts come and from whom texts issue. Deeper still, his work disturbs the intimate presuppositions of individual existence, disturbs our *distinctness*—and thus activates, for some people in the world today, the emotions waiting in the gulf of Chaos. What order can there be between Chaos and Chaos, lost origins and nonteleological ends? What would it mean for me, the individual, to be unable to distinguish as I do between the said and the not-said, interpretation and mistake, philosophy and literature, this genre and that genre, this context and that context? It is uncertain where the renovation demanded by the possibility of assent to Derrida would end, if indeed it could end.

But like his precursors in the exhibition of Chaos, Derrida is categorical as well. Iconoclasm and explanatory power. Normally the second has been a compensation, a disguised undoing, of the first. Is this so in Derrida? The rule-giving element in Derrida's work seems on the one hand the indelible impression left by Husserl (how kind Derrida is, for a modern French intellectual, to Descartes—see 1978, pp. 31–63). I do not mean to criticize. In fact, this survival seems to me one of the secrets of his strength. Famous Derridean analyses such as the iterability that belongs essentially to all communication and all performance exemplify, in no sense overturn or reinvent, phenomenology's eidetic essences, save that Husserl accents the sameness in reproduction, Derrida the alterity. This rule-giving is also, as I noted at the beginning, historical. Especially in the first part of the *Grammatology*, Derrida appears to be laying down a series of axioms about Western philosophy and suggesting that, based on these, one might make an inventory of the kinds of rhetoric philosophical writing has adopted in order to be philosophical writing. The necessitarian Derrida, rigorous tracer of the chains that bind, has not disappeared altogether from the later work.

So it goes with atoms and periods. . . . The individual survives yet another dispersal. Explanatory power is once again the reward for disillusionment. So maybe this is as it should be—necessary, chancy.

NOTES

1. The editors are noncommital—see *The Poems of John Donne*, ed. H. Grierson, 2 vols. (Oxford: Clarendon Press, 1912), 2: 189; *The Complete Poetry of John Donne*, ed. J. Shawcross (Garden City, N.Y.: Anchor, 1967), p. 279; *The Epithalamions, Anniversaries, and Epicedes of John Donne*, ed. W. Milgate (Oxford: Clarendon Press, 1978), p. 141. Frank Manley, editor of *John Donne: The Anniversaries* (Baltimore: Johns Hopkins University Press, 1963), probably speaks for standard opinion in maintaining that Donne did not really care what he was saying about the world, its origin, and its end, in the atomism passage, but simply wanted to make the general point that things are falling apart (p. 145). Charles Coffin implies that Donne was referring to the conservative atomics of the four irreducible elements in *John Donne and the New Philosophy* (New York: Columbia University Press, 1937), pp. 134, 160–74.

REFERENCES

Bachelard, G. *Les intuitions atomistiques (essai de classification)*. 2d ed. Paris: Librairie philosophique J. Vrin, 1975.
Bercovitch, S. "Empedocles in the English Renaissance." *Studies in Philology* 65 (1968): 67–80.
Burckhardt, J. *The Civilization of the Renaissance in Italy*. 2 vols. Translated by S. Middlemore. New York: Harper, 1958.
———. *History of Greek Culture*. Translated by P. Hilty. New York: Unger, 1963.
Casserius. *Tabulae Anatomicae*. Venice, 1527.
Davenant, W. *Gondibert*. Edited by D. Gladish. Oxford: Clarendon Press, 1971.
Deleuze, G. *Sacher-Masoch: An Interpretation*. Translated by J. McNeil. London: Faber and Faber, 1971.
Derrida, J. *Speech and Phenomena*. Translated by D. Allison. Evanston: Northwestern University Press, 1973.
———. *Of Grammatology*. Translated by G. Spivak. Baltimore: Johns Hopkins University Press, 1976.
———. *Writing and Difference*. Translated by A. Bass. Chicago: University of Chicago Press, 1978.
———. *Positions*. Translated by A. Bass. Chicago: University of Chicago Press, 1981.
———. *Margins of Philosophy*. Translated by A. Bass. Chicago. University of Chicago Press, 1982.
Donne, J. *Complete Poetry and Selected Prose*. Edited by C. Coffin. New York: Random House, 1952.

Fichte, J. *New Exposition of the Science of Knowledge.* Translated by A. E. Kroeger. St. Louis, 1869.

Freud, S. *Standard Edition of the Complete Psychological Works.* London: Hogarth, 1953–74:

"Project for a Scientific Psychology" (1895), vol. 1

Introductory Lectures on Psycho-Analysis (1916–17), vol. 16

Civilization and its Discontents (1930), vol. 21

"A Disturbance of Memory on the Acropolis" (1936), vol. 22

Gorges, A. *The Poems of Sir Arthur Gorges.* Edited by H. Sandison. Oxford: Clarendon Press, 1953.

Harrison, C. "Bacon, Hobbes, Boyle, and the Ancient Atomists." *Harvard Studies and Notes in Philology and Literature* 15 (1933): 191–218.

Herbert, E. *The Poems of Lord Herbert of Cherbury.* Edited by G. Moore Smith. Oxford: Clarendon Press, 1923.

Hill, N. *Philosophia epicurea, democritiana, theophrastica.* Paris, 1601.

Jonson, B. *Ben Jonson.* 11 vols. Edited by C. H. Herford and P. and E. Simpson. Oxford: Clarendon Press, 1932–47.

Kant, I. *Critique of Pure Reason.* Translated by N. K. Smith. New York: St. Martin's, 1965.

Keynes, G. *A Bibliography of Dr John Donne.* Cambridge, Eng.: Cambridge University Press, 1958.

Lange, F. *History of Materialism.* Translated by E. G. Thomas. New York: Harcourt Brace, 1925.

McColley, G. "Nicholas Hill and the *Philosophia Epicurea.*" *Annals of Science* 4 (1939): 390–405.

Marx, K. *Collected Works,* vol. 1. New York: International Publishers, 1975.

Michel, P-H. *The Cosmology of Giordano Bruno.* Translated by R. Maddison, Ithaca, N.Y.: Cornell University Press, 1973.

Nietzsche, F. *Twilight of the Idols* and *The Anti-Christ.* Translated by R. J. Hollingdale. New York: Penguin, 1968.

———. *The Will to Power.* Translated by W. Kaufmann and R. J. Hollingdale. New York: Random House, 1968.

———. *On the Genealogy of Morals* and *Ecce Homo.* Translated by W. Kaufmann and R. J. Hollingdale. New York: Random House, 1969.

Partington, J. "The Origins of the Atomic Theory." *Annals of Science* 4 (1939): 245–82.

Santayana, G. *Three Philosophical Poets,* Garden City, N.Y.: Anchor, n.d.

Schilder, P. *The Image and Appearance of the Human Body.* New York: International Universities Press, 1950.

Whyte, L. *Essay on Atomism: From Democritus to 1960.* Middletown, Conn.: Wesleyan University Press, 1961.

5 Institutional Authority vs. Critical Power, or the Uneasy Relations of Psychoanalysis and Literature

DAVID CARROLL

The psychoanalytical institution, divided as it is into various and often conflicting national and international associations, is a complicated conglomeration of movements, schools, societies, and splinter groups with their own officials, administrations, bylaws, internal and external policies, means of accreditation, educational apparatus, and techniques of analysis. What links them all together in spite of their differences is the name of Freud and the "science" he founded. Each unit, association, school, or splinter group may feel that it alone is carrying on the true legacy of Freud, or even that it has supplemented his teaching, improved it, and progressed in the direction he would have taken had he lived longer; but in doing so, each in the same way pays homage to Freud, the father-founder, and attempts to root its own authority in his. The struggle for such authority links them together as rivals for the same place, unites them in spite of their differences.

Interested in combating the restrictive effects of such an institutionalization of psychoanalysis in the name of Freud and the sterility of the struggles for mastery of the institution resulting from it, Jacques Derrida, in a recently published essay, calls attention to the way Freud himself used the expression, the "foreign policy" of the world psychoanalytical institution, "as if it were a sort of state administering its relations with the rest of the world."[1] Derrida's point is to show how the statelike characteristics Freud attributes to the institution affect both its "foreign and domestic policies," its relations with the nonpsychoanalytical world and the forces at work within itself. In general, the institutional-bureaucratic structure of psychoanalysis has subdued, repressed, and deflected its potentially radical critical powers; the psychoanalytic bureaucracy has legislated that this "state" withdraw as much as possible from the political scene of which it is a part and avoid its political and psychoanalytical responsibilities. For the sake of international unity, even if it is only an abstract unity, a serious price is paid.

In this essay, given first as a talk before a group of psychoanalysts, Derrida presents himself to the group in the role it has in fact assigned to him by inviting him to speak early in the morning of the first day of its colloquium, the role he is only too happy to play: that of the invited guest, the outsider. With no valid or validated psychoanalytical credentials, neither being an analyst nor ever having gone through analysis, he is, as he says, "psychoanalytically irresponsible" (p. 14), a "foreign body": "this foreign body who belongs to no body, who is in no way a member of any of the analytical corporations of this part of the world or the rest of the world. . . . I say 'foreign body' in order to designate that thing that can neither be assimilated nor rejected, neither interiorized nor, at the limit of the border separating inside and outside, foreclosed" (p. 13). The perspective of the foreign body, if it is really a perspective at all, is that of the border or limit, and Derrida's essay concerns itself precisely with limits: the limits of the institution, the limits of political neutrality for the sake of international unity, the serious limits psychoanalysis imposes on itself when it refuses to raise in any serious way the question of the political effects of psychoanalysis and the psychoanalytical sense of the political. Neither inside nor outside, the perspective of the foreign body is not in any sense a privileged perspective transcending both inside and outside. Its force and critical power result from the fact that it can neither be incorporated into the institution and made to serve its ends nor excluded from it in a strategy of self-defense. It persists in affecting the body proper as an other that is within, an opening to the outside that is inside. The foreign body is a pest.

The political-ethical issue that Derrida raises in his essay is that of torture, and he criticizes the International Psychoanalytical Association, in its abstract condemnation of that practice made in the name of the rights of man, for its refusal to name the geographic-political area, Latin America, which he claims is "the only area of the world where there coexist, whether confronting each other or not, an important psychoanalytical society and a society (civil or state) practicing on a large scale a kind of torture that is not limited to its brutally classical and easily identifiable forms. . . . The psychoanalytical medium is permeated by this violence. All intrainstitutional relations, the entire clinical experience, all the relations with civil society and the State are marked by it, either directly or indirectly. This is as much as to say that there is no simple interiority of the analytical medium" (p. 29). Derrida's claim is that psychoanalysis cannot keep the violence of the "political outside" outside because it has always-already penetrated the interior of the institution.

Derrida's text is, as he says, a "call to name Latin America" in order to "measure up to what has been uncovered there, to respond to what menaces psychoanalysis, limits it, defines it, defigures it or unmasks it" (p. 30). It is also a call to think and practice a different form of psychoanalysis, one that questions its internal and external political relations and takes the risks such a questioning would entail, the risks of a radical transformation of the institution itself, as well as a transformation of the political realm to which it is internally and externally related:

> In spite of the multiplication of discourses on this question of "psychoanalysis and politics" for at least the last ten or twelve years, one is forced to admit—and this is even the sign of it—that there does not exist today any political problematic or code of political discourse which has integrated into itself in a rigorous manner the axiomatic of a possible psychoanalysis, if in fact psychoanalysis is possible. My hypothesis is, therefore, that such an integration has not taken place. . . . And the integration I am alluding to would not be a tranquil appropriation; it would not occur without deformation and transformation on both sides. That is why, paradoxically, the less psychoanalysis and ethical political discourses are integrated with each other in the rigorous sense I have just indicated, the easier the integration or appropriation of the apparatus, the one by the other, is, the easier the manipulation of the psychoanalytical realm by political and police forces is, the easier the abuse of psychoanalytical power is, etc. [pp. 20–21]

The administration of this psychoanalytical association may want the association to remain politically pure, neutral, above such political matters, even those as horrible as torture, taking only a weak, abstract stance with regard to them in order to preserve its international character, but the avoidance of or withdrawal from the political (the immediate political situation and the question of the political in general) ends up, Derrida holds, being the surest way to be controlled by the most repressive form of the political, the surest way to take on that form in one's own internal and external relations.

There is obviously no *one* way to respond to the call Derrida makes in this essay, and in his own work there is no one, magisterial path into, through, and beyond psychoanalysis. Psychoanalysis in Derrida's work is treated from different angles and in terms of different problems. At times, its critical, deconstructive powers are called on; at other times or at the same time, its philosophical and political limitations are analyzed and undermined by calling on other critical powers that psychoanalysis cannot master or subdue. Derrida's position on psychoanalysis, then, is in fact not one position at all; it consists of a strategy of occupying various positions both within and without. The foreign body is not the one but many; its place is not fixed but mobile; its ends are disruptive rather than institutional.

One of the paths into, through, and beyond psychoanalysis passes by way of literature, itself a difficult term to define and delimit, a term whose status is positional rather than essential, itself a kind of foreign body to and in psychoanalysis. After evoking the question of torture in Latin America, it might seem scandalous or, even worse, trivial to suggest that something might be learned about the political-institutional limitations of psychoanalysis, about the causes and effects of its refusal to deal with ethical-political problems except in an abstract manner, by looking at its internal and external relations with literature (assuming we know what that term means), its foreign and domestic policy concerning this other that is treated at various times as an ally, at other times as a foe. The torture of other men and women is of such an extreme, outrageous, inhuman nature that it seemingly should make any other question insignificant. Once evoked, it should silence those of us who, because of our positions as professors of literature, would be tempted to continue to write, teach, and debate the nature, function, and status of literature (or philosophy or politics or psychoanalysis or whatever). And yet the problem is not as simple as that, I would argue—perhaps somewhat defensively—convinced in some sense that we are not all, in all instances, wasting our time or totally irresponsible when it comes to political issues. Latin America should certainly be named and denounced and all efforts made to pursue the tack that Derrida suggests in "Géopsychanalyse"; everything possible should be done in this country to put pressure on our own government, which is certainly more directly involved in what is taking place in Latin America than any international psychoanalytical association, to stop supplying the money, the support, the military and police equipment and training that help perpetuate the horrible situation there. If the psychoanalytical medium is, as Derrida claims, marked by this violence, how much more must our own society be marked by it, given our responsibility for it?

But does this mean that there are no problems to be dealt with other than the immediate, pressing problems of the present? The dangers of ignoring the present are obvious and serious and I am certainly not suggesting such a course. But there is another danger, just as serious in the long run, and that is of being so totally caught in the immediacy of the present that there are *only* political solutions offered for social problems, with political defined here in the most narrow, economically deterministic sense, a situation in which everything ends up being determined by the political without the political itself ever being seriously questioned or challenged, or alternative political possibilities pursued. Sartre was certainly not wrong to have said of his own novel *La nausée* that when compared to a starving child, it is of no consequence, but it is also true that a "politically committed" literature or philosophy or psychoanalysis can have limiting, restrictive, politically repressive effects, not only on literature, but, more importantly, on the development of ethical-political alternatives. There is no literature (or any other form of discourse) that is not directly and indirectly, internally and externally, involved with political questions, and the responsibilities that go with such an involvement can be ignored but not avoided. At the same time, the direct and massive determination of all sociocultural phenomena by the political, whatever its form, should be resisted, the authority of the political challenged and undermined, for in such a situation, the political would be dogmatic and even totalitarian rather than liberating.

There are two sides, then, to Derrida's call to name Latin America. There is the pressing necessity to respond to the immediate political situation there, to protest, cry out against the situation in which men and women are tortured and killed, and to work for an immediate change in the political-economic structure of such an inhuman form of society. There is also a just-as-pressing but less immediate necessity to investigate critically the grounds of the political in general and to use the critical powers of psychoanalysis to assist in rethinking the relations between psychoanalysis and the political. The pressing aspect of one side of the call does not cancel the just-as-pressing but more deliberate aspect of the other side of the call.

In terms of the relations of psychoanalysis and politics and the development of a critique of the institutional effects of each, to dismiss the question of literature as being frivolous or irrelevant is too hasty a response on at least two grounds: (1) it neglects or underestimates the role of fiction, drama, myth, and so forth, in Freud's own writings and in his writings on *Kultur* in particular; and (2) it assumes that there are simple, direct, immediate solutions to all political-ethical questions and that alternative social-political systems exist or could be imagined to exist in the future that could be called upon to provide solutions for them. In this way all political-ethical problems are resolved before they are even raised, certain forms of institutions protected by not being challenged, and a particular end projected onto history in terms of these institutions in order that history be determined in terms of this end. Literature, or the question of literature, approached in a certain way, might provide, and in Freud to some extent does provide, critical perspectives on these and other political-social problems, and in this sense, the pursuit of the question of literature is not as frivolous a path as it might at first have seemed. The perspectives it provides can only be considered critical, however, if the limitations of literature are themselves questioned and if the concept of literature is itself transformed in the process, if the institutions organized in its name (or in the general name of humanistic values) and pretending to speak of it and from within it with authority, are themselves challenged and combated.

The best known and undoubtedly the most discussed of Freud's texts on *Kultur* is *Civilization and its Discontents*. Certainly any attempt to apply the findings and techniques of psychoanalysis to society as a whole must confront this text; any attempt to formulate a particularly psychoanalytical conception of politics must deal with it. Interestingly enough, this text concludes by questioning its own authority in sociopolitical matters and by seriously doubting the effectiveness of its analysis of the "dis-ease" of civilization as well as the possibility of a cure based on this analysis. The first difficulty is that in moving from the individual subject, *the subject* of psychoanalysis in Freud's own words, to the group subject, there is no norm to which the group can be compared: "In an individual neurosis we take as our starting-point the contrast that distinguishes the patient from his environment, which is assumed to be 'normal.' For a group all of whose members are affected by one and the same disorder no such background could exist; it would have to be found elsewhere" (*S.E.* 21: 144). In the case of the group, the environment of the individual is the object of analysis, the background is the foreground, and normality is no longer a given. And to take this a step further, further than Freud wants to take it, since *Civilization and its Discontents* seriously puts into question the "normality" of the social environment, one can only wonder why the contrast between it and the individual can be considered to be proof of his or her neurosis rather than a sign of his or her "health." Surprisingly enough, the antipsychoanalytical stance of a Laing or a Deleuze and Guattari could be rooted in Freud in this instance, for how can a patient be considered sick if society, the norm with which he or she is judged, is itself sick? If the efficacity of psychoanalysis is in question in terms of the social group, then by extension it must also be considered questionable with respect to the individual subject because its starting point is highly problematical—the normal cannot be taken as normal. Freud is of course unwilling to go this far. So that the authority of psychoanalysis to bring about a cure will not be undermined in all instances, he draws a line between individual subject and group subject (a line he nevertheless frequently crosses), falling back on the "success" psychoanalysis has already had in curing individual neuroses as his support.

The second limitation of psychoanalysis when it comes to the analysis and "cure" of *Kultur* has to do with the lack of authority of the psychoanalyst and of psychoanalysis as a movement and institution within the very society being analyzed, its inability to impose its cure on it. The analyst cannot speak as if he were untouched by the society he puts on the couch, as if he occupied a transcendent position above it rather than being subject to the forces at work within it that contribute to its neurosis. Within it, he hasn't the political authority to act: "And as regards the therapeutic application of our knowledge, what would be the use of the most correct analysis of social neuroses, since no one possesses authority to impose such a therapy upon the group?" (*S.E.* 21: 144).[2] One of the problems with society, then, is the lack of legitimate authority; no institution, no political system, no political party, and certainly no public figure seems to possess it. How could such authority be possessed if society itself is "dis-eased" and inclined to reject such authority? According to what norms could the validity of psychoanalytical investigations of the discontents of society be recognized? How could the critical power of psychoanalysis be legitimized? How could its authority be enforced and by what or by whom? Without such legitimacy and authority, psychoanalysis is destined to remain speculative rather than scientific when it comes to matters of *Kultur*, unsure of its own critical powers and powerless to effect a cure on society.

Such authority and legitimacy could not be delegated by the social unit as a whole either, for no political system possesses such legitimacy to delegate, even if governments and other political institutions do possess the force necessary to impose their will on people. Freud evokes both the communist and capitalist systems (the Soviet Union and the United States) in order to criticize them both and show their shortcomings and illegitimacy. The communist model, like the Christian model he has already discussed and rejected, is based on the illusion, says Freud, that by nature "man is wholly good and is well-disposed to his neighbour," and further, therefore, that the primary cause of hostility is private property, which, when abolished, would end "ill-will and hostility" (*S.E.*, 21: 113). No matter how much of a simplification and caricature of communism this might be, Freud raises a problem that is nevertheless quite serious and complex and which cannot be dismissed: that not even with the unity of the masses brought about by the end of the class structure, not even with the abolishment of private property supported by a process of identification of the individual with the universal proletarian subject, not even with this utopian situation will we have the end of the "differences in power and influence which are misused by aggressiveness, nor have we altered anything in its nature. Aggressiveness was not created by property. It reigned almost without limit in primitive times, when property was still very scanty, and it already shows itself in the nursery almost before property has given up its primal, anal form" (p. 113). Conflicts of power existed before the institution of private property and will continue after it is abolished, and this means that legitimate authority cannot be guaranteed by the communist system. As in any other political system, authority is claimed only after a struggle among contending forces and factions, each of whose goal is to impose its own will on people and install or institutionalize itself at their expense.

At the other end of the political spectrum—or is it not more of a mirror image of the communist system and thus at the same end?—is America, which Freud will criticize because of "the danger of a state of things which might be termed 'the psychological poverty of groups.' This danger is most threatening where the bonds of a society are chiefly constituted by the identification of its members with one another, while individuals of the leader type do not acquire the importance that should fall to them in the formation of a group" (pp. 115–16).[3] Here no leader (no legitimate authority) emerges from the group because the group is self-contained, all its members identifying with one another (with themselves), and all values debased, all authority by definition illegitimate. These competing social systems cannot, then, provide the context in which legitimate authority could emerge and be recognized, for neither puts an end to or rises above the petty but lethal struggles for power that define them, delimit them, and determine that social unrest is perpetuated within them.

Freud, however, is not willing to give up the search for legitimate authority, and one of the places to which he frequently turns, when society itself comes up short, is to the "poets," as if psychoanalysis could use their authority in matters where its own and that of society as a whole were both suspect. There is, I am sure, no need here to evoke the numerous instances in Freud's work where he derives the authority of psychoanalysis from that of the poets, where he admits that psychoanalysis only belatedly discovered truths that the "poets already knew." No need either to mention the frequent references to myth, drama, fiction, poetry, and the like as models for the process of analysis itself. All this is well-known and has been frequently commented on. In the case of *Civilization and its Discontents*, however, it might be fruitful to pursue the question of Freud's reliance on the authority of a certain literature in terms of the problem of the institutional limitations of psychoanalysis. It is a literary figure, Romain Rolland, who is used to introduce the problem of the "oceanic feeling," the first element of and even pretext for the complicated, discontinuous narrative and argument that are developed in this text. Perhaps the most interesting aspect of Rolland's role in the text is the way Freud introduces him (originally without naming him; he is identified only in a footnote added in 1931):

> It is impossible to escape the impression that people commonly use false standards of measurement—that they seek power, success and wealth for themselves and admire them in others, and that they underestimate what is of true value in life. . . . There are a few men from whom their contemporaries do not withhold admiration, although their greatness rests on attributes and achievements which are completely foreign to the aims and ideals of the multitude. . . . One of these exceptional few calls himself my friend in his letters to me. [p. 64]

Rolland, a man of letters, sends letters to Freud and calls him his friend, setting up a bond, a community, an international friendship society between them and between literature and psychoanalysis as well. This pact has very definite benefits for Freud and psychoanalysis, for Rolland is an example (one of very few) of a man who is admired by the multitude for the "right reasons" and not for reasons of wealth, success, or power; he seems to hold the precarious position of an authority who is placed by the multitude above the multitude, who is respected by them without sharing their petty, "dis-eased" values, a figure, one would imagine, who would have the authority to transform society's false standards and even effect a cure for its neuroses and discontents—and perhaps even pass this authority on to his friends. In an environment of illegitimacy, his authority is legitimate. Can there be any doubt that such a "great man" is a model for the kind of authority psychoanalysis would like to have, that he is a figure whom Freud admires and of whom he is jealous and whose place he would like to occupy or at least share as a friend?

Throughout this text and throughout his entire work for that matter, Freud follows the lead of poets; he tries to achieve "scientifically" what they have achieved "through their imagination." At key moments of this and other texts, their work fills in the spaces that science and his own experience leave blank: from the "oceanic feeling" that Freud "cannot discover" in himself to the ultimate question of the origin of society that no one has or could have convincing evidence of. At beginnings and ends of chapters, at crucial moments of his argument and narrative, when science, logic, reason, and experience all come up short, myth and literature (the realm of the "poets") are called upon, not so much to resolve the problems that the above-mentioned disciplines and discourses are unable to resolve, but rather to make it possible to continue to speculate, to offer hypotheses, to "suppose" (p. 99) things to be a certain way when because of either inconclusive or contradictory evidence one cannot "know" exactly how they are or should be. In other words, the poets make it possible to take positions (perhaps in an "athetic way"),[4] no matter how tenuous and uncertain, no matter how often the positions have to be changed, on questions that no philosophical, scientific, or political system has succeeded in answering or will be able to answer in the future—unless psychoanalysis itself with the aid of the poets and on the basis of speculations that it cannot defend, will be able to succeed where other disciplines and sciences have come up short.

In *Civilization and its Discontents*, it is Fontane, Voltaire, Rabelais, Heine, Plautus, Twain, Shakespeare, and especially Goethe, to name only some of the "literary" references in the text, who are the supports of Freud's speculations. Whether it be Heine, who as "a great imaginative writer may permit himself to give expression—jokingly, at all events—to psychological truths that are severely proscribed" (p. 110), as psychoanalysis after him also does, or Goethe, who in his *Faust* provides Freud with "a quite exceptionally convincing identification of the principle of evil with the destructive instinct" (p. 120), or in *Wilhelm Meister* with a "moving arraignment of the 'Heavenly Powers'" (p. 133), their function is to already be at the origin and end of the difficult journey Freud is taking us on and for which he apologizes "for not having been a more skilful guide and for not having spared them [his readers] empty stretches of road and troublesome *détours*. There is no doubt that it could have been done better" (p. 134). Without the poets, the journey would truly be endless and there would be no "sigh of relief" possible: "And we may well heave a sigh of relief at the thought that it is nevertheless vouchsafed to a few to salvage without effort from the whirlpool of their own feelings the deepest truths, towards which the rest of us have to find our way through tormenting uncertainty and with restless groping" (p. 133).[5] In this sense, then, literature and the truths revealed in it, are the destination, the end, the telos of psychoanalysis, especially as it applies itself to problems of *Kultur*.[6] Effortlessly, from the depths of their own feelings, poets express the truths that the psychoanalyst can only hope some day to stumble onto.

When Freud at the end of *Civilization and its Discontents* states that psychoanalysis lacks the authority to impose its cure on society for its neuroses, it certainly comes as no surprise, then, given the way Freud has continually deferred to the poets in the course of the essay and placed the authority of psychoanalysis under theirs. The question of whether the poets really possess the authority Freud projects onto them and whether, even if they did, this authority would be transferable to him and through him to the movement he founded, is one of the many questions left unanswered at the end of the essay and one of the factors contributing to what I would call his critical pessimism concerning the future of civilization and the efficacity of psychoanalysis.[7] That Freud desires such authority and recognition for himself and his movement, as long as it is the legitimate kind he ascribes to Rolland, seems to me undeniable: his modesty in these matters is undoubtedly one of the tactics he uses to posit a relationship between psychoanalysis and the truth, the universal truth that before psychoanalysis only the poets were able to express. What is interesting here is that by Freud's own admission, psychoanalysis does not quite arrive at its destination in the truth (in literature), that the detours never quite come back to the direct path giving immediate access to the truth, that the path through literature never quite returns to psychoanalysis, thus forcing psychoanalysis to remain tentative, speculative, and unscientific when it comes to *Kultur*.

This is undoubtedly an uncomfortable position for any "science" to find itself in; and even if it is a way of approaching the truth, a more direct path, one that is entirely psychoanalytical in form and content (assuming that something like a psychoanalytical specificity could be determined), would have provided a better defense of psychoanalysis. The problem is that it simply was not available for the study of *Kultur*, and given the particular nature of this object of study and the place of psychoanalysis within the very object it analyzes, were such a path to be taken it would undoubtedly miss its mark. The hypotheses, speculations, suppositions, detours, and misdirections characteristic of this text and others are all necessary and inevitable. The real problem is not just whether the usurpation of the authority of literature is ever successfully realized, or even whether the truth that is initially projected outside, in this other realm, is ever brought inside psychoanalysis and made its own; it is also and more importantly the problem of the grounds on which the authority of literature itself can be posited, how it can be claimed to express and master the truth. Freud may use a certain literature to situate all philosophical, political, and even psychoanalytical authority, to provide him with a critical perspective on their claims to capture the truth and on the question of authority in general; but the authority of literature itself is for the most part left uninvestigated and unchallenged. The critical process, then, stops here, in literature, for psychoanalysis needs some authority to remain legitimate if it is ever to insinuate itself into a place of legitimate authority and be able to use the power that goes with such a position.

Jacques Lacan, in his analysis of Poe's "The Purloined Letter" (1966), as part of his rectification and return to the letter of the Freudian text and thus its truth, finds it convenient to leave Freud's text and deal with a "literary fiction" in order all the better to return to Freud. He is in this sense in practically the same position as Freud in relation to literary texts; but, coming after Freud, he seems to have an advantage over Freud. For Poe's "fiction" is treated by Lacan as an illustration of a truth that now can be called "Freudian," and thus Lacan is in the position of claiming that the journey from psychoanalysis through literature back to psychoanalysis can and must be completed, thus realizing also the usurpation of literature's authority over psychoanalysis by making literature serve its ends. In spite of Barbara Johnson's ingenious effort to do so (1977), [8] it seems impossible to deny this aspect of Lacan's text, its identification with "Freudian truth" and its demonstration of the authority of psychoanalysis over literature through a masterful reading of this literary text (and the problem of mastery and rivalry contained within it). Lacan's project is clearly to return this text to Freud.

It is precisely the authority of Lacanian psychoanalysis and his projection and assumption of Freud's authority that Jacques Derrida questions in "Le facteur de la vérité."[9] In doing so, it might at first seem that Derrida accomplishes his deconstruction of Lacan's position by simply reversing the position of the powers in play in Lacan's reading, that is, by granting to Poe's text and to literature in general priority, and the "strength," the power to resist psychoanalysis (and any other theory)—a power no theory has the force to neutralize and one that makes all theory subservient to it. Derrida does use a certain literature to undermine the authority of psychoanalysis, and especially Lacanian psychoanalysis, but this reversal is only a moment of a more complicated critical strategy and not an end in itself. The trump cards Derrida uses in this struggle may be cards that are often associated with literature, but they are not necessarily only literature's to use. The question that should be asked is what happens to literature in this confrontation with Lacan? Does it come out of the power struggle intact and with no wounds? Is literature really the origin of Derrida's critique of Lacan and the ultimate end toward which his critique is oriented? Does its authority over psychoanalysis and over itself go unchallenged in Derrida's text? Many would implicitly or explicitly claim this in order either to defend Derrida's critique on "literary grounds" or to dismiss it for being too "literary," but in both instances, the readings of Derrida are, I would argue, seriously limited.

Derrida begins his essay by focusing on psychoanalysis's claims to universality, evident in the manner in which it projects and therefore finds itself, that is, finds confirmation of itself everywhere, without ever investigating the effects on it of the contexts in which it finds itself. These are precisely the effects Derrida proposes to analyze:

> Where then? Where does psychoanalysis, already, always, find itself?
> That in which it is found, if it is found, let us call it text. Not only for the purpose of recalling that the theoretical and practical inscription of psychoanalysis (in the text as "language," "writing," "culture," "my-

thology," "history of religion, of philosophy, literature, science, medicine," etc., in the text as a "historical," "economic," "political" realm, a field of "drives," etc., in the heterogeneous and conflictual fabric of difference, defined elsewhere as *general text*—and without boundaries) must have effects that have to be taken into account. But also for the purpose of defining the space of a particular question. ["The Purveyor of Truth," pp. 31–32; translation modified]

Literature, then, is just one of the fields in question, one of the texts in which psychoanalysis is inscribed. It is neither the original, nor the dominant, nor the most extensive field, nor the field of all fields. The "general text without boundaries" far exceeds it and precedes it, thus making literature's boundaries, those it assigns itself or those assigned to it, appear relative and secondary.

Derrida's concept of the text, if it is a concept, clearly cannot be confined to any one field, discipline, or border. The various forces at work in any text, even those forces that are claimed to originate there and only there, cannot be contained within the boundaries of a single text, no matter what authority is called upon and what force is used to ensure that boundaries are not crossed. In another essay, Derrida refers to the transformation of the concept of the text in recent years in order to stress the inadequacy of the boundaries traditionally used to delimit it—

all those boundaries that form the running border of what used to be called a text, of what we once thought this word could identify, i.e., the supposed end and beginning of a work, the unity of a corpus, the title, the margins, the signatures, the referential realm outside the frame, and so forth. What has happened, if it has happened, is a sort of overrun [*débordement*] that spoils all these boundaries and divisions and forces us to extend the accredited concept, the dominant notion of a "text," of what I still call a "text," for strategic reasons, in part—a "text" that is henceforth no longer a finished corpus of writing, some content enclosed in a book or its margins, but a differential network, a fabric of traces referring endlessly to something other than itself, to other differential traces. Thus the text overruns all the limits assigned to it so far . . . all the limits, everything that was to be set up in opposition to writing (speech, life, the world, the real, history, and what not, every field of reference—to body or mind, conscious or unconscious, politics, economics, and so forth). [1979a, pp. 83–84]

No single field or border could possibly encompass or enclose such an "overrun"; no authority could ever be powerful enough to neutralize and effectively control any of the borders, and most certainly not all of them.

Derrida finds evidence of a repeated neutralization of its textual (literary, but also historical, philosophical, political, etc.) contexts in the posturing and self-positing of psychoanalysis: and in order to dramatize the effects of such neutralization, he chooses an extreme situation to analyze—but is it that extreme given Lacan's choice of Poe's text and Freud's choice of similar texts to serve as examples of psychoanalytical truth? Perhaps such texts even await psychoanalysis in order to entrap it, are not so much chosen as dictating choice? The "extreme situation" in question is the one in which a literary text not only stages psychoanalytical truth for the benefit of psychoanalysis, but stages also the process of analysis used by psychoanalysis (and any other theory bent on discovering or positing the truth) to decipher it. In such a situation, literature is one step ahead of psychoanalysis:

> What happens in the psychoanalytical deciphering of a text when the deciphered (text) already explains itself? When it reveals a great deal more than the deciphering text (a debt acknowledged more than once by Freud)? And above all when it inscribes in itself *in addition* the scene of deciphering? When it deploys more force in its staging and derives (diverts) the analytical process down to its last word, for example, the truth?. . . . But the truth, is it an example? ["The Purveyor of Truth," p. 32; translation modified]

The force and authority of such literary texts—but are they simply literary?—seems absolute; they have on their side the powers of self-reflexivity and some would even say self-deconstruction. Nothing can be done to them that they have not already done to themselves: no truth can be found in them that they have not already explicitly staged in order to be found, whose discovery they have not already thematized and dramatized. The self-reflexive text lays a trap for everyone and everything, for all theoretical discourses that attempt to penetrate, decipher, enclose, and master it. The self-reflexive staging process is primary, and everything else is dependent on it. Psychoanalysis can only find here what the text, seemingly in full control of itself and its powers, lets it find, and it can only find it in the way the text lets it find it. The authority of the literary text is in these cases a function of its mastery of the staging process itself; it is the mastery of self-reflexivity.

Lacan and Freud, by choosing such texts (or by being chosen by such texts) to serve as examples of psychoanalytical truth, reveal more than they want to reveal—that is, that psychoanalysis does not in all instances dominate the contexts in which it projects and finds itself, that its contexts have a certain authority over it. But is Derrida claiming more than this in his critique of Lacan? Is he not making in his turn claims about the force and thus the authority of a certain form of literature capable of such a staging, about the authority of literature defined as the self-reflexive staging of itself? Is the sense and truth of literature the staging process itself and therefore a truth that has priority over and that encompasses all others? Such a position is very popular today, but is it Derrida's?

When literature situates within itself the analytical scene of deciphering, the search for meaning or truth, it says and does more than search and discover the truth itself. It makes the search and discovery of the truth part of a much more complicated and longer historical-intertextual process that no historical moment and no text encloses or controls, even a radically self-reflexive text. The situation, then, can no more be considered "literary" than "historical" or "philosophical." Each is only a part of a much larger process: "This overrun does not express the mastery of an author, or, even less, the meaning of fiction. It would rather be the regular effect of an energetic framework. Truth would play a certain part of it: extracted, by the philosopher or the analyst [or, I would add, the literary theorist], from within a more powerful functioning" ("The Purveyor of Truth," p. 33, translation modified). Literary theory or practice, when it attempts to make literature into the master of such a process, when it equates the process with literature and finds itself and its truth in it—perhaps through a theory of the *mise en abyme* or deconstruction as literature—performs the same reduction that the analyst or philosopher does here. It extracts from within a complicated intertextual and intercontextual play and conflict of forces a part of that play and one of the forces and resolves the conflict in the name of literature, thus greatly reducing its critical power, scope, and impact. This is to replace one truth with another and to transform a critical strategy with a potentially wide impact into a narrow defense of literature.

In discussing Freud's analysis of dreams of nudity in *The Interpretation of Dreams,* Derrida shows how the mode of analysis used by Freud—the penetration of the veils or disguises of various fictions in order to discover the truth in its unveiled state, the reduction of the texts to their "naked truth, but also to truth as nakedness" (p. 34)—has already been thematized and performed (employed on itself) by the fictions being analyzed, in this case *The Emperor's New Clothes:*

> If we take into account the more than metaphorical equation of veil, text, and fabric, Andersen's tale has the text as its theme. More precisely, the determination of the text as a veil within the space of truth, the reduction of the text to a movement of *aletheia.* Freud's text is staged when he explains to us that the text, e.g., that of the fairy tale, is an *Einkleidung* of the nakedness of the dream of nakedness. What Freud states about secondary revision (Freud's explaining text) is already staged and represented

in advance in the explained text (Andersen's fairy tale). This text, *too*, described the scene of analysis, the position of the analyst, the forms of his discourse, the metaphorico-conceptual structures of what he seeks and what he finds. One text is located (finds itself) in the other.

Is there, then, no difference between the two texts? Yes, of course, there are many, many differences. But their co-implication is undoubtedly more complex than one would think. [pp. 37–38; translation modified]

Derrida is calling attention here to the complex interconnections of the two texts, not the simple enframing of one by the other. Fiction and truth, literature and psychoanalysis, may not be the same thing, as Derrida says, but they are not ultimately separable the one from the other either. If this is so, this is not only a comment about the truth and the various discourses and disciplines that claim to capture or unveil it, but it also says something about fiction. It says that fiction is never a simple antidote for the truth, that fiction does not exist only in itself, in a field or context over which it has ultimate authority, and, therefore, that fiction cannot be considered the privileged form of discourse simply because it admits its own "fictiveness" and the illusory nature of the truth as it stages itself and the truth. The above postulates, in fact, are all strategies of self-representation aimed at instituting fiction (or literature) as a truth, aimed at staging the truth of fiction as *the truth*.

The overlapping of the two realms, the overrun of one into the other, indicates that the frame of each is open, that neither fiction nor psychoanalysis has complete authority over the other or over itself. Fiction has the relative advantage in Derrida's argument and strategy because it can be used to situate and undermine psychoanalysis's claims to the truth, but the advantage *is relative* and cannot be used to privilege literature in all instances and in all contexts. If "psychoanalysis finds itself—all that it finds—in the text it deciphers," if it finds "more than itself" in the text (p. 39), then the same must be said for all forms of fiction and all theories of literature that make similar claims for literature, that posit or construct a literature that finds itself, in itself, everywhere. Are there any grounds left for such a concept of literature, for such a self-positing of itself and its truth? I would argue that there are not, and that the impossibility of answering the following questions decisively undermines the assumptions and foundations of both literature and psychoanalysis, and that this is the point of Derrida's critique of Lacan. "For truth to inhabit fiction, is this to make fiction true or truth fictive? Is that an alternative? a true or a fictive one?" (p. 41; translation completely modified). If such questions cannot be answered, no institution—psychoanalytical or literary—can claim to have priority and authority when it comes to the relations of fiction and psychoanalysis.

The abyssal situation in which truth and fiction are each implicated in the other, with neither totally grounding or enframing the other, cannot then be claimed to be the essence of literature. To decide that the "overrun" is in each instance a literary overrun, that it always serves the interests of literature, that its force and critical powers are literary, is no different than to decide that the truth—whether defined by psychoanalysis or philosophy or history—is master of fiction. In each case it is the decision that stops the interaction, that puts an end to the dynamic and conflictual exchange and transformation of the various forces and institutions in play and vying for prominence and even domination. This is precisely the situation when literature is seen as the antidote to representation and truth and equated with the process of the *mise en abyme*. The *mise en abyme* is the means by which a certain formalist literary tradition is perpetuated; it defines a position of power that can be occupied by literary authorities. As Derrida indicates, one should be extremely cautious of its use: "I have never wished to overuse the abyss, nor above all the abyss structure [*mise en abyme*]. I have no strong belief in it, I distrust the confidence that it, at bottom, inspires, and I find it too representational to go far enough, not to *avoid* the very thing into which it pretends to plunge us" ("Coming into One's Own," p. 120). The question that must be asked of literature defined as a *mise en abyme* is the one Derrida asks in this essay: "What does the appearance here of a certain *mise en abyme* open on, and close around?" (p. 120). In other words, what forces are subdued by being enclosed in such a structure and for whose benefit? Whose power and authority are being protected and at what cost to opposing forces?

There seems to be no interpretative situation in which power is not in play, in which some force or other is not called upon to confront, neutralize, overcome other forces in order to protect the integrity and authority of the institutions making use of the so-called dominant forces. The purpose of Derrida's insistence on the general narrator in Poe's "The Purloined Letter" (and in Poe's other stories), on the telling of the story as much as on the story told, is not, then, to protect the integrity of literature from a powerful usurper (as if it needed protection and hadn't already programmed its own defenses and as if the usurper were an alien invader and not already inside)—not to "save the text," then, but rather to emphasize the psychoanalytical, political, and philosophical, as well as literary, effects of the narrator, the effects of his position on the events narrated and how they are narrated. Derrida's purpose is to show how Lacan's unveiling of Freudian truth proceeds by means of a neutralization of the narrative function and a refusal to take into account the effects of the contexts of the truth on the truth found there—a neutralization that Derrida claims is not neutral, not only as concerns Poe's text but more importantly as concerns the relation of psychoanalysis to truth.

Lacan's neutralization of the narrator is directly linked to his positing of a transcendent position of psychoanalysis (no matter how complicated and contradictory this positing might be), to the establishment of Lacanian psychoanalysis as the legitimate Freudian institution, as *the authority* on Freudian truth. This is the position from which Lacan speaks when he distinguishes between truth and falsity; between other psychoanalysts who are dupes and illegitimate heirs of Freud and himself and certain of those (the true, legitimate members) of the École Freudienne who share his position and accept his authority and that of his version of Freud; between, as Derrida puts it, "you-psychoanalysts" and "we-psychoanalysts" ("The Purveyor of Truth," p. 74). The true masters are those who know how to avoid the false, imaginary allure of simple mastery and to neutralize and transcend (obfuscate, one could say) their own interests as well as the conflict of forces and interests constituting the cultural-political fields and contexts in which they are located (locate themselves). Neutralization is the only way to achieve mastery, and all institutions and schools work this way: by neutralizing oppositional forces they pretend to speak with a unified voice from a position of authority that is as suspect as it is powerful and lethal when allowed to function unopposed.

As Derrida argues in "Scribble (writing-power)" (1979b), the battles that occur within and among contending institutions, schools, departments, disciplines, ideologies, and so forth, cannot be resolved by calling on some higher authority, whether it be political, philosophical, or literary. To have the key to such a resolution of conflict and difference is to enclose the conflict within a very limited frame:

> There is not *one* power, *the* power of *the* mark. This singular would still lead to some mystification: fostering the belief that one can do otherwise than to oppose powers to powers and writings to other writings, or again that the unity of *power* (and of *knowledge*) is always itself, the same, wherever it is and whatever force it represents. But there are *powers, knowledges*, in every instance interlinked and linked to marking forces in a general agonistics. . . . Whoever situates and settles it at once, limits his movement within a strict margin. ["Scribble," p. 144]

There are thus no simple political, philosophical, psychoanalytical, or literary solutions to these power struggles;[10] but just as they cannot be confined to what is popularly known as the "political arena" (a very reduced form of the political) without seriously reducing the complexity, scope, and diversity of the political, they also cannot be confined to any other arena or institution without seriously reductive consequences. Such

struggles cannot be dismissed either, as Derrida argues, by being considered the irrelevant, petty squabbles of intellectuals: "Hence, *struggles*
for *powers* set *various* writings up against one another [*les* lutes pour *les*
pouvoirs opposent *des* écritures]. Let us not shrug our shoulders too
hastily, pretending to believe that war would thus be confined within the
field of literati, in the library or the bookshop. . . . But it is true that the
political question of literati, of intellectuals, in the ideological apparatus, of the places and stockages of writing, of caste-phenomena, of
'priests' and the hoarding of codes, of archival matters—that all this
should concern us" ("Scribble," p. 118). Only the most naïve would
want to claim that the conflicts and disputes found within the pages of
literary or psychoanalytical journals—or in interdisciplinary journals concerned with the relations of psychoanalysis and literature or even with
the relations of psychiatry and the humanities—concern only these limited fields and the scholars working in the institutions and schools
attempting to impose their authority on them and on their external and
internal relations with other fields.

There has been in this country a confinement of Derrida's work, at
least until fairly recently, to literature departments and literary questions, and this has had the effect—the very one Derrida analyzes in
"Scribble"—of underplaying or even suppressing its political-historical
implications and its critique of institutions. It is the literati themselves
who seem to want to "confine the war to the library or bookshop," and
for reasons that can be easily understood: their authority is more secure
there than elsewhere. There is probably no aspect of Derrida's work that
has been more seriously distorted or "misunderstood" than his strategic
use of literature; but as in all such cases, the "misunderstanding" is
itself motivated, controlled by certain forces and benefiting certain
schools and institutions in a way that should be possible to describe. The
misunderstanding or redirection of the critical force of Derrida's work
has taken the following shape: it equates deconstruction with a certain
form of literature and literary criticism, and, more precisely, with the
self-reflexivity, self-referentiality, and, some have even claimed, the self-
deconstructive powers of the literary text. It thus attributes to literature
the power to deconstruct all nonliterary, referential, naïvely representational discourses, the power to enscribe them within itself and thus
undermine their power and authority.[11] In this form, deconstruction is
simply the latest (is it even the latest anymore?) of a series of concepts
and strategies used by the literary establishment to protect its interests
and authority.

But this literary institutionalization of Derrida should not surprise
anyone, for if he is, as he says, a "foreign body" for the psychoanalytical
institution, having absolutely no psychoanalytical credentials, he could
not claim exactly the same "irresponsibility" when it comes to his rela-

tion to literary institutions, at least in this country. Even though trained (having gone through *philosophical* analysis?), licensed, and practicing as a philosopher in France, his literary credentials were obviously considered to be distinguished (and legitimate) enough for him to receive a position as a professor of comparative literature at Yale, at the very top of the university hierarchy. If the metaphor of the foreign body is still to work here, and I think that it can be made to, Derrida's incorporation in-comp.-lit. must remain "in-comp-lete" (as he, in a lecture on the problem of translation, pronounced the name of his department at Yale with an intentionally exaggerated French accent); and this, even though he has been digested, transformed, and made part of the institution, at least from the institution's point of view.[12] Perhaps the best way to resist the effects of the foreign body is to open oneself to it in order to overcome its alterity, in order to make it as much as possible one's own, so that its potentially threatening foreignness will be neutralized as much as possible with the effects on oneself kept to a minimum.

This Yale institutionalization of Derrida has given us a "Yale Derrida, literary critic," a "Yale School of Deconstructive Criticism" formed in his name, and a collective volume of essays, *Deconstruction and Criticism*, edited by Geoffrey Hartman. Thus, when Derrida in the above volume questions the institutionalization of deconstruction by emphasizing the subversive political effects he feels it should have on the institution, when he calls attention to the critique of the structure of the university explicitly present in the notion of translation he develops in his essay, he is questioning the institution much more from within than from without (is he really as "irresponsible" when it comes to psychoanalysis as he claims?): from within the volume serving to publicize the "Yale School," from within (as a permanent and responsible visitor rather than an irresponsible outsider) the institution whose authority dominates the study of literature in this country.[13] The questions he asks about his place and role there—in the volume, in the United States, at Yale, in-comp.-lit., and so forth—are serious and touch on the foundations of the institution, the teaching of literature in it, and the legacy of Derrideanism in this country, for there is now a legacy (actually several legacies) of sorts. "If the question of teaching (not only the teaching of literature and the humanities) runs throughout this book, if my participation is possible only with a supplementary interpretation by the translators (active, interested, inscribed in a politico-institutional field of drives and so forth), if we are not to pass over all these stakes and interests (what happens in this respect in the universities of the Western world, the United States, at Yale, from department to department? How is one to step in? What is the key here for decoding? What am I doing here? What are they making me do?) . . . then we must pause to consider translation" ("LIVING ON," pp. 98–100). What he is saying and doing may not coincide exactly with what "they" are making him say and do, and this noncoincidence is crucial if the critical power of his work is not to be appropriated by the institution. The "Yale translation" of Derrida into a literary critic is a "key" to be unlocked as part of the process of decoding if forces other than the "literary" are to be uncovered in Derrida's work. This is not to say that the "Yale Derrida" is without interest or critical force; it is just that "he" or "it" is of very limited force because it continually defers to the authority of literature and closes itself off to other forces and possibilities. If there is a "Yale key," it is, as Derrida says, "like all keys, it locks and unlocks, opens and closes" ("LIVING ON:" p. 146). Not wanting to deny what it opens onto, I would also want to stress how limiting it would be to remain Yale-locked-in.

What do "they" make him say and do? How do "they" make him be read, translated, and interpreted? The "they" here must of course include Derrida himself, if he is not "irresponsible" in all this; and as a member of the Yale faculty in-comp.-lit., a member of the "Yale School," whether willingly or not, whether sharing its ends or not, he is certainly, at least in part, responsible.[14] If we are to believe the preface to *Deconstruction and Criticism* written by Geoffrey Hartman, one of the links between the various participants in the volume and members of the "Yale School" is their belief in "the importance—or force—of litera- ture," a "shared problem" that commits them to the following ques- tions: "What does that force consist in, how does it show itself? Can a theory be developed that is descriptive and explanatory enough to illu- minate rather than pester works of art?" (p. vii). To place theory, criti- cism, and interpretation in the servile role of "illuminating" the work of art is hardly to assign them a radical, critical place; it is a position that the most traditional humanist could agree with and applaud. If the purpose of deconstruction is to do this, one can only wonder what all the fuss has been about, why so many have polemicized so strongly and so often against it as a threat to the very notion of humanistic studies. One can certainly understand how a department of comp. lit. and how the humanities in general benefit from such a position, how their authority, derived as it is from the canon of "great works," is sustained by it.

For Hartman, speaking here for what he feels unites the members of the volume rather than for what separates them—that is, in a certain sense giving us the charter of the school—the force of literature has something to do with "the priority of language to meaning," and there- fore with "figurative language, its excess over any assigned meaning, or put more generally, the strength of the signifier vis-à-vis a signified (the 'meaning') that tries to enclose it" (p. vii). If Hartman is a valid spokes- person for the group, the "Yale critics" put themselves squarely on the side of what for them is the more powerful force (why back an under-dog?), literature, a literature defined in terms of its recognition and exploitation of the "strength of the signifier."[15] In this play of forces, literature is assured victory over a weaker opponent that never succeeds in enclosing it and that is repeatedly forced to retreat when confronted with the indisputable fact of the "priority of language." To use a phrase Derrida applies to Lacan, it is this "ideality of the signifier" that keeps literature from being "pestered" too much by other contending "extra-literary" forces and discourses, that assures its victory over all opponents. The assumption is that the signifier and figurative language in general are essentially literary, that they serve this master and its ends, that they guarantee its authority. When literature is treated in this way, its illumi-nating truths are protected, and all pests, all foreign bodies, are either locked out or locked in—it amounts to the same thing.

Its power and authority established, Hartman does not want to lock literature up too tightly, for it would be foolish to keep such a force hidden and under wraps. Why not use it? Thus in the same preface he argues that the total separation of literature from other disciplines, here philosophy, benefits neither literature nor philosophy: "The separation of philosophy from literary study has not worked to the benefit of either. Without the pressure of philosophy on literary texts, or the reciprocal pressure of literary analysis on philosophical writing, each discipline becomes impoverished. If there is a danger of a confusion of realms, it is a danger worth experiencing" (p. ix). Once one has defined literature the way Hartman has, however, there is no "confusion" possible, because any intermixing of philosophy and literature will be considered to be a sign of literature's power over philosophy. In other words, all "confusion" is "literary confusion."

But if the pressure were really reciprocal and the two forces, if not always and in all contexts equal, at least coexisted within the same general field with no transcendental status or absolute priority given to either of them, then the conflict of languages, disciplines, strategies, and practices—as well as the "confusion" resulting from such conflict—would neither in the first nor the last instance be a sign of the superiority and priority of literature. The limitation of Hartman's defense of inter-disciplinary pressure is that it is made from a very particular site: from a position of authority within literature. His call for reciprocity has a very particular end in mind for both literature and philosophy, an end that leaves literature intact and philosophy subservient to it. For Hartman, deconstructive criticism (deconstruction-as-criticism) is simply a rigorous form of close reading whose purpose is to illuminate the truth of litera-ture without pestering it in any way, to reveal again what literature has always revealed (what the poets, or at least the poems, always knew!):

"Deconstructive criticism does not present itself as a novel enterprise. There is, perhaps, more of a relentless focus on certain questions, and a new rigor when it comes to the discipline of close reading. Yet to suggest that meaning and language do not coincide, and to draw from that noncoincidence a peculiar strength, is merely to restate what literature has always revealed" (p. viii). Hartman thus gives to the brightest luminaries of the "Yale School" the assignment of keeping such "revelations" from being pestered and obscured, of protecting literature and "saving the text" by putting pressure on all discourse (even literary discourse) for the benefit in the last instance of literature and its truth. It is literature's power and authority that he depends on for this critical task; for him, the critical process always terminates in literature.

Institutions and schools exist to occupy positions of power, to neutralize dissent, and to domesticate all oppositional forces and foreign bodies; their authority depends on it. It is not surprising, then, that a department of literature (at Yale or anywhere else) would attempt to assimilate critical discourses and strategies that were potentially threatening, an assimilation that would undoubtedly transform it somewhat, but would much more radically limit the critical powers of such discourses and strategies. When Hartman, for example, refers to deconstruction and psychoanalysis in exactly the same terms in different contexts, in terms that the literary establishment understands and accepts, the ends of such assimilations are clearly visible. As we have seen, he refers to deconstruction as a form of criticism that provides a "new rigor when it comes to the discipline of close reading"; in his preface to *Psychoanalysis and the Question of the Text,* he states that "ideally, psychoanalysis should provide a closer mode of close reading" (p. xiv). One can only respond by asking, "ideally" for whom or for what? And one can only wonder how close to the text a closer form of close reading can get before it is blinded by the very text it holds close before its eyes, before it is too close to see anything but itself (literature) in the text, blinding itself because of this proximity to all relations with other, extraliterary forces and languages, to all problems of context that cannot be seen from such a close(d) perspective. Being too close is even more of a problem than being too far away, especially when the result is to close literature in on itself, to blind oneself to what is extraliterary within literature.

If the critical powers of literature and psychoanalysis, whatever their potential might be, are not to be domesticated, assimilated into literary, psychoanalytical, or political institutions (a redundancy, for all institutions are political), that is, made subservient to some authority or other, or rather, if the domestication that has already taken place and will continue to take place is to be combated and undermined, then the authority of the schools and institutions that benefit from such strategies of assimilation must insistently be confronted, from within as well as from without, by "foreign bodies" that refuse to be assimilated and with critical strategies that are based on an awareness that the total break with institutions is much easier declared than effectively carried out. Like Freud at the end of *Civilization and its Discontents,* one should be critical and even "pessimistic" perhaps about the authority of any critical power or strategy associated with it, not because things are hopeless and will inevitably get worse (this is not what Freud is saying either), but because a healthy pessimism concerning authority, especially concerning one's own, is necessary in order to resist the inevitable attempts to institutionalize all potentially critical and disruptive forces, to harness and subdue them, making them work for rather than against the institutions whose authority their critical powers should work to undermine. Where the relations between two powers have come too easy, there the institution has succeeded in having its way. It is only when the external and internal relations between powers remain uneasy that a "critical integration" becomes possible, resulting in the transformation of each of the powers in an open process that does not terminate in either of them.

NOTES

1. "Géopsychanalyse—'and all the rest of the world,'" in *Géopsychanalyse: Les souterains de l'institution* (1981), p. 13. All references to this text will be to my own translation.

2. See two of Philippe Lacoue-Labarthe and Jean-Luc Nancy's recent essays, "La panique politique" (1979) and "Le peuple juif ne rêve pas" (1981), for a critical analysis of psychoanalysis in terms of the "problem *of the political,* that is to say, that in terms of which the political becomes problematical" ("La panique," p. 35; my translation). For their analysis of *Civilization and its Discontents,* to which my own is indebted, especially in terms of the problem of psychoanalysis's lack of authority in matters of *Kultur,* see "La panique," pp. 37–38, and "Le peuple juif," pp. 73–76. Their analysis in the two essays is guided by the following *prise de position:* that both "rigor and a politics of the left" demand the undoing of any "submission to the political or to psychoanalysis, or to both of them" ("La panique," p. 34). For another critical rethinking of the political that intersects at various points with that of Derrida and Lacoue-Labarthe and Nancy and owes much to a certain Freud, see the work of Jean-François Lyotard, especially *Discours, Figure* (1978), *Dérive à partir de Marx et Freud* (1973), and all of his recent work from *La condition postmoderne* (1979) and *Au juste* (1979) to the present.

3. Freud's critique of America takes the form of a denial: "The present cultural state of America would give us a good opportunity for studying the damage to civilization which is thus to be feared. But I shall avoid the temptation of entering upon a critique of American civilization; I do not wish to give an impression of wanting myself to employ American methods" (*S.E.* 21: 116).

4. This is a reference to Derrida's "Spéculer—sur 'Freud,' " in *La carte postale* (1980). Parts of this essay have been translated in two different journals. The first part as "Speculations—on Freud" (with the quotation marks around Freud omitted), in *Oxford Literary Review*, vol. 3, no. 2, and the second part as "Coming into One's Own," in *Psychoanalysis and the Question of the Text* (1978). All references to these sections will be to these translations; all other references to this text are my own translations. Derrida's project in "Speculations" is to respond to the following questions concerning *Beyond the Pleasure Principle:* "How must this text proceed, with what step [*pas*] above all, in order one day—today, against so many readings that are as partial as they are canonical, that is to say, academic—for us to become sensitive to the essential impossibility of stopping at a thesis, at a conclusion posed in the scientific or philosophical mode, or in the theoretical mode in general?" In moving "beyond the pleasure principle," the authority of psychoanalysis itself is in question, but Derrida cautions against identifying the "athetic" processes he emphasizes in Freud's text with fiction or literature: "This textual process that cannot be dominated by any instance as such (especially not by the theoretical instance in its scientific or philosophical mode), I shall not be in too much of a hurry to call it 'fictional' or even worse 'literary' " ("Speculations—on Freud," p. 79, translation modified and completed).

5. As Derrida points out in "Coming into One's Own," Freud refused to be considered an artist or a poet (the thesis of Havelock Ellis) and continually defended the scientific status of psychoanalysis and the results that would outlive him and his name (p. 142).

6. René Girard, in his own very different attempt to go beyond psychoanalysis and situate it in relation to what for him is the fundamental cultural-religious truth (mimetic desire), a truth that he believes psychoanalysis, philosophy, and literary criticism all distort, relies heavily on the authority of "great literature" for support. From the "vérité romanesque" of *Mensonge romantique et vérité romanesque* (1961)—translated as *Deceit, Desire, and the Novel* (1965)—through his most recent work, literature is *a*, if not *the* privileged realm of the truth. It is "the great works . . . from Greek theater to Dostoevski and Proust, passing through Cervantes and Shakespeare," that present a "unified theory of desire, and therefore a systemization of delirium" ("Delirium as System," in *To Double Business Bound* [1978], p. 89). For Girard, literature continually demystifies psychoanalysis, literary theory, and philosophy, but never the reverse: "We have on occasion observed Sophocles demystifying psychoanalysis, but we shall never see psychoanalysis demystifying Sophocles. In fact, psychoanalytical thought has never really come to grips with Sophocles"—in *Violence and the Sacred* (1979), p. 206. Girard in this way puts himself in the same position as Freud in relation to literature and the truth it is supposed to contain (even if the truth in each case is different), but he takes this position in order to situate and undermine Freud's authority in these matters and make literature and its authority work for him and against Freud.

7. Lacoue-Labarthe and Nancy argue that the so-called pessimism of *Civilization and its Discontents* is an indication of the internal and external limits of psychoanalysis in relation to political power and political power in relation to psychoanalysis and of a desire to move beyond these limits: "How could psychoanalysis confer authority on itself? How could authority be psychoanalyzed? The political

certainly meets its own limit here because the complete and perhaps inextricable question, in any case, the *limit* question, would be the following: how could psychoanalysis have power (therapeutic power, but is there any other kind?) if power is not psychoanalyzed? And how could power be psychoanalyzed if psychoanalysis, in approaching power, were forced to go beyond itself?" ("La panique politique," p. 37).

8. In spite of Barbara Johnson's recuperation of Lacan, her discussion of the "power struggle" between Derrida and Lacan in terms of Poe's text is especially interesting, as is her analysis of Derrida's strategic use of literature against Lacan. She very accurately shows that Derrida's critique of Lacan is not a defense of literature.

9. This essay first appeared in *Poétique*, no. 21 (1975), and was republished in *La carte postale*. It has been translated quite freely as "The Purveyor of Truth," in *Yale French Studies*, no. 52 (1975). I have had to modify almost all the references to this translation.

10. Near the end of "Spéculer—sur 'Freud,'" Derrida argues, "Posts are always posts of power. Power is exercised by means of posts of power. . . . In its auto-heterology, the drive of postal power is more original than the PP [pleasure principle] and independent of it. . . . Beyond the pleasure principle—power. That is to say, posts [the postal system]. . . . There is power only if there is a principle or a principle of principle. The transcendental or metaconceptual function belongs to the order of power. There is then only the *différance* of power. From which [the] posts are derived" (*La carte postale*, p. 432; my translation).

11. See Rodolphe Gasché's "Deconstruction as Criticism" (1979) for a critique of the equation of deconstruction with literary criticism and, more specifically, with a formalist literary tradition. Gasché argues that such a simplification and distortion of the philosophical sense of deconstruction has the following effects: "A second evidence predominant in deconstructive criticism is the conviction that everything is literature, text or writing. This evidence of Newer Criticism only radicalizes the purely aesthetic or a-historical vista of its academic antecedents. It also continues the conservative function of traditional criticism by neutralizing and blurring the capital differences and critical functions between different kinds of discourses. In the case of the so-called deconstructive criticism, this evidence originates in an illicit application of the Derridean notion of *écriture* to all forms of discourses" (p. 179). In this essay and in " 'Setzung' and 'Übersetzung': Notes on Paul de Man" (1981), Gasché challenges the idea that deconstruction can be linked to any notion of self-reflexivity, for "in the first place it represents a critique of reflexivity and specularity" ("Deconstruction as Criticism," p. 183). Gasché's analyses are indispensable, and his critique of deconstructive criticism right on the mark. I part company with him only in that I have less confidence in "the philosopher" than he does.

12. This does not mean that the members of the institution are unanimous in their acceptance of Derrida's "presence" and agree on the beneficial effects resulting from it. There is undoubtedly conflict within comp. lit. and among various departments concerning it. The "Yale School" is not all of Yale; it just speaks at times as if it were. There are obviously other forces at work within Yale trying to neutralize the effects of the authority of the "Yale School" for their own ends—forces, even, that are not as progressive and as open to critical discourse as the "Yale School" is. In terms of these forces the "Yale School" should be defended and supported.

13. The first six volumes of *Psychiatry and the Humanities* were published by Yale University Press. The great majority of Derrida's texts that I refer to in this essay have been published under the auspices of Yale, either directly in *Yale French Studies* or in collections edited and prefaced by a member of the "Yale School." This does not necessarily mean that everything published in these journals and collections serves the interests of the "School"; it does mean, however, that the Yale effect on these works should not be ignored.

14. Even if no one wanted to take on the responsibility for the "Yale School" or willingly accept being a member of it, the effect of the "School" would continue to be felt. In fact, once charted, it seems that there are as many interested in leaving it or staying on its fringes as there are in joining it. For example, Hartman, author of the preface to *Deconstruction and Criticism*, claims that Hartman and Bloom, professors at Yale and contributors to the volume, are not really deconstructionists in the way the other contributors are and therefore, I suppose, are not really full-time members of the "Yale School": "Derrida, de Man, and Miller are certainly boa-deconstructors, merciless and consequent. . . . But Bloom and Hartman are barely deconstructionists. They even write against it on occasion" (p. ix). (This third-person reference to himself is interesting, and one can only wonder if this Hartman, the one who writes the preface and decides that Hartman is not really a true deconstructionist, is a deconstructionist or not. If he weren't, how could he decide if the other Hartman were in or out?) In " 'Setzung' and 'Übersetzung,' " Gasché not only takes Derrida out of the school because he is "a true philosopher" and not a literary critic, but also liberates de Man. The only member that no one seems to want to remove is Miller, the member who has probably most frequently used the term deconstruction and acknowledged the existence of the "Yale School."

15. Shoshana Felman in *La folie et la chose littéraire* (1978) is willing to accept a place in the "Yale School" whose "dominant member and principal theoretician," according to her, is Paul de Man; and she is willing to accept membership even if the term itself originated in the mass media and obscures the differences among its members (see pp. 21–27). Her definition of the charter of the "School" is similar to Hartman's; it is a school whose members are all concerned with "the place of rhetoric in a theory of literary language, or rather, the place of literature in a theory of rhetoric" (p. 21; my translation). It is unclear whether she would place Derrida in the "School" or not, but her own work does belong there inasmuch as literature is a privileged realm for her, the only realm in which madness continues to speak its truth in its own voice.

REFERENCES

Derrida, J. "Le facteur de la vérité." *Poétique* no. 21, 1975. Republished in *La carte postale* (1980). Translated as "The Purveyor of Truth." *Yale French Studies,* no. 52, 1975.

————. "LIVING ON: Border Lines." In *Deconstruction and Criticism.* New York: Seabury Press,1979a.

————. "Scribble (writing power)." *Yale French Studies,* no. 58, 1979b.

————. "Spéculer—sur 'Freud.' " In *La carte postale.* Paris: Flammarion, 1980. First part translated as "Speculations—on Freud." *Oxford Literary Review* 3, no.

2, 1978. Second part translated as "Coming into One's Own." In *Psychoanalysis and the Question of the Text*. Edited by G. Hartman. Baltimore: Johns Hopkins University Press, 1978.

———. *Géopsychanalyse: Les souterains de l'institution*. Paris: Confrontation, 1981.

Felman, S. *La folie et la chose littéraire*. Paris: Seuil, 1978.

Freud, S. *The Standard Edition of the Complete Psychological Works*. London: Hogarth, 1953–74.

Civilization and its Discontents (1930), vol. 21.

Gasché, R. "Deconstruction as Criticism." *Glyph*, no. 6, 1979.

———. " 'Setzung' and 'Übersetzung': Notes on Paul de Man." *Diacritics* 11, no. 4 (Winter 1981).

Girard, R. *Mensonge romantique et vérité romanesque*. Paris: Grasset, 1961. Translated as *Deceit, Desire, and the Novel*. Baltimore: Johns Hopkins University Press, 1965.

———. "Delirium as System." In *To Double Business Bound*. Baltimore: Johns Hopkins University Press, 1978.

———. *Violence and the Sacred*. Baltimore: Johns Hopkins University Press, 1977.

Johnson, B. "The Frame of Reference: Poe, Lacan, Derrida." *Yale French Studies*, nos. 55–56, 1977. Also in *Psychoanalysis and the Question of the Text*. Edited by G. Hartman. Baltimore: Johns Hopkins University Press, 1978.

Lacan, J. "Le séminaire sur 'La lettre volée.' " In *Ecrits*. Paris: Seuil, 1966. Translated in *Yale French Studies*, no. 48, 1972.

Lacoue-Labarthe, P., and Nancy, J.-L. "La panique politique." *Cahiers confrontation*, no. 2. Paris: Aubier, 1979.

———. "Le peuple juif ne rêve pas." In *La psychanalyse est-elle une histoire juive?* Paris: Seuil, 1981.

Lyotard, J.-F. *Dérive à partir de Marx et Freud*. Paris: 1018, 1973.

———. *Discours, Figure*. Paris: Klincksieck, 1978.

———. *La condition postmoderne*. Paris: Minuit, 1979.

———. *Au juste*. Paris: Christian Bourgois, 1979.

6 Thomas Hardy, Jacques Derrida, and the "Dislocation of Souls"

J. HILLIS MILLER

My focus is a poem by Thomas Hardy, "The Torn Letter." As a way into this admirable poem, a passage from Kafka's *Letters to Milena* and a recent essay by Jacques Derrida will provide a line of communication. First Kafka:

> The easy possibility of letter-writing must—seen merely theoretically— have brought into the world a terrible dislocation [*Zerrüttung*] of souls. It is, in fact, an intercourse with ghosts, and not only with the ghost of the recipient but also with one's own ghost which develops between the lines of the letter one is writing and even more so in a series of letters where one letter corroborates the other and can refer to it as a witness. How on earth did anyone get the idea that people can communicate with one another by letter! Of a distant person one can think, and of a person who is near one can catch hold—all else goes beyond human strength. Writing letters, however, means to denude oneself before the ghosts, something for which they greedily wait. Written kisses don't reach their destination, rather they are drunk on the way by the ghosts. It is on this ample nourishment that they multiply so enormously. . . . The ghosts won't starve, but we will perish.[1]

Thinking and holding are here opposed to writing. The former belongs to "the real world" of persons, bodies, and minds, of distance and proximity. If a person is near, one can touch him, hold him, kiss him (or her). If a person is distant one can think of that person. Such thinking relates one real "soul" to another. It is as genuine a "means of communication" as touch. The souls or selves pre-exist the thinking that joins them, as much as two bodies pre-exist their kiss. Writing is another matter. Nothing is easier than writing—a letter, for example. The writing of a poem, a story, a novel, is no more than an extension of the terrible power of dislocation involved in the simplest "gesture" of writing a note to a friend. The dislocation is precisely a "dislocation of souls." Writing is a dislocation in the sense that it moves the soul itself of the writer, as well as of the recipient, beyond or outside of itself, over there, somewhere else. Far from being a form of communication, the writing of a letter dispossesses both the writer and the receiver of themselves. Writing creates a new phantom written self and a phantom receiver of that writing. There is correspondence all right, but it is between two entirely phantasmagorial or fantastic persons, ghosts raised by the hand that writes. Writing calls phantoms into being, just as the ghosts of the dead appear to Odysseus, to Aeneas, or to Hardy in his poem "In Front of the Landscape." In this case, however, the ghosts are also of the witnesses of those ghosts. The writer raises his own phantom and that of his correspondent. Kafka's ghosts, in his "commerce with phantoms," drink not blood but written kisses. They flourish and multiply on such food, while the one who writes the kisses and the correspondent they do not reach die of hunger, eaten up by the very act through which they attempt to nourish one another at a distance.

Now Derrida: Some remarkable paragraphs in "Télépathie" (1981) seem almost to have been written with "second sight," that is, with prophetic foreknowledge that I would need to cite them here to support my reading of Hardy. In this essay Derrida speculates on the performative power a letter (in the epistolary sense) may have in order to bring into existence an appropriate recipient. If a letter happens to fall into my hands I may become the person that letter needs as its receiver, even though that new self is discontinuous with the self I have been up till now. Derrida's argument is peripherally attached as an appendage to his polemic, in "Le facteur de la vérité" (in La carte postale, 1980), against Jacques Lacan's idea that a letter always reaches its destination. For Derrida, in "Télépathie," a letter reaches its destination all right, but not because the proper recipient, the self to which the letter corresponds, is waiting there for it, already in full-formed existence as a self. No, the letter creates the self appropriate to itself. It creates it by performing (in the strict Austinian sense of performative [see Austin, 1967], though with a twist) the utmost violence on the already existing self of the hapless person who accidentally reads the letter. The "twist" lies in the fact that the performative power of the letter is not foreseen or intended. This is contrary to the strict concept of a performative utterance as defined by Austin, but it may be that Austin, here as in other aspects of his theory, was unsuccessfully attempting to limit the terrible and always to some degree unpredictable power of a performative utterance:

> Why, [asks Derrida] do the theoreticians of the performative or of the pragmatic interest themselves so little, to my knowledge, in the effects of written things, notably in letters? What do they fear? If there is something performative in the letter, how is it that a letter can produce all sorts of these ends, foreseeable and unforeseeable, and in fact even produce its recipient? All of this, to be sure, according to a properly performative causality, if there is such a thing, and which is purely performative, not at all according to another sequence extrinsic to the act of writing. I admit that I do not fully know what I want to say by that; the unforeseen should not be able to be part of the performative structure in the strict sense, and yet. . . . ["Télépathie," p. 9; my translation]

As an example of this strange coercive and yet unpredictable power of the written word, Derrida has suggested on the previous page that someone might determine his whole life according to the "program" of a letter or of a postcard that he accidentally intercepts, a missive not even intended for him. The recipient becomes the self the letter invites him to be (but there is no "him" before he receives the letter), just as poor Boldwood, in Thomas Hardy's novel *Far from the Madding Crowd*, becomes the bold lover Bathsheba's valentine seems to tell him he is:

> I do not [says Derrida] make the hypothesis of a letter which would be the external occasion, in some way, of an encounter between two identifiable subjects—and which would be already determined. No, rather of a letter which after the fact seems to have been projected toward some unknown recipient at the moment it was written, predestined receiver unknown to himself or to herself, if that can be said, and who determines himself or herself, as you know so well how to do, on receipt of the letter; this is therefore an entirely different thing from the transfer of a message. Its content and its end no longer precede it. Here it is then: you identify yourself and you engage your life according to the program of the letter, or perhaps better still of a postcard, a letter open, divisible, at once transparent and encrypted. . . . Then you say: it is I, uniquely I who can receive this letter, not that it is meant especially for me, on the contrary, but I receive as a present the happenstance to which this card exposes itself. It chooses me. And I choose that it should choose me by chance, I wish to cross its trajectory, I wish to encounter myself there, I am able to do it and I wish to do it—its transit or its transfer. In short, by a gentle and yet terrifying choice you say: "It was I." . . . Others would conclude: a letter thus *finds* its recipient, he or she. No, one cannot say of the recipient that he exists before the letter. ["Télépathie," pp. 7–8; my translation]

It almost seems, as I have said, that these sentences were written
with a kind of retrospective prevision of their appropriateness as a commentary on Hardy's "The Torn Letter," or as if "The Torn Letter" had
been written with foresight of Jacques Derrida's meditations on July 9,
1979, though so far as I know Derrida had not then and has not yet read
Hardy's poem. Even so, Hardy's poem, which is a "letter" in the first
person written to an unnamed "you," has found its proper recipient at
last in the unwitting Derrida. Derrida has become its reader without
even knowing it. He has been programmed by the poem to write an
interpretation of it before, beside, or after the letter, so to speak, in
displacement from any conscious encounter with it. He has become the
person the poem-letter invites him to be, in a confirmation of his theories of which he is unaware.

Here is Hardy's poem:

The Torn Letter

I

I tore your letter into strips
        No bigger than the airy feathers
        That ducks preen out in changing weathers
Upon the shifting ripple-tips.

II

In darkness on my bed alone
        I seemed to see you in a vision,
        And hear you say: "Why this derision
Of one drawn to you, though unknown?"

III

Yes, eve's quick need had run its course,
        The night had cooled my hasty madness;
        I suffered a regretful sadness
Which deepened into real remorse.

IV

I thought what pensive patient days
        A soul must know of grain so tender,
        How much of good must grace the sender
Of such sweet words in such bright phrase.

V

Uprising then, as things unpriced
        I sought each fragment, patched and mended;

The midnight whitened ere I had ended
And gathered words I had sacrificed.

VI

But some, alas, of those I threw
    Were past my search, destroyed for ever:
    They were your name and place; and never
Did I regain those clues to you.

VII

I learnt I had missed, by rash unheed,
    My track; that, so the Will decided,
    In life, death, we should be divided,
And at the sense I ached indeed.

VIII

That ache for you, born long ago,
    Throbs on: I never could outgrow it.
    What a revenge, did you but know it!
But that, thank God, you do not know.

[Hardy, 1976, pp. 313–14]

"The Torn Letter" contains several characteristic Hardyan ironic turns away from the straightforward notion that a letter may have a performative power to determine the self of its recipient. Derrida has the general idea of the letter-poem from Thomas Hardy right, but the message seems to have got garbled or overlaid with static and interference on the way. Some parts are twisted a bit or missing entirely, perhaps because somewhere along the line they have been switched or translated from Hardy's pungent and acerb English into Derrida's idiomatic French. In the latter, for example, the recipient of a letter is called its "destinataire," with suggestions that the receiver is predestined, a latent fatality or doomed end point of the message. These overtones are missing in the equivalent English words, such as those I have used in my translation of "Derrida's" ideas back into English.

"The Torn Letter" is spoken or written by someone who has received a letter from an unknown admirer, apparently a woman. Before concluding that the speaker-writer is "Hardy" it must be remembered that Hardy claims most of his poems are "personative," spoken or written by imaginary personages. The poem is addressed to the sender of the letter, but, paradoxically, the poem is posited on the assumption that she will never receive his message and therefore cannot learn how much her letter had made him suffer: "But that, thank God, you do not know." If the poem is thought of as spoken or perhaps as silently thought, then the woman will indeed never know. In fact it is written down (or how else could we be reading it?). The poem itself, in its physical existence, contradicts its own affirmation. It is always possible, perhaps even inevitable, that the poem will fall into the woman's hands and tell her what he says he thanks God she cannot know. If her "revenge" on him for destroying her letter is the permanent ache of a remorse for not having kept it and answered it, his revenge on her is to let her know this in the act of saying she does not and cannot know. The poem is a version of that sort of mind-twisting locution, discussed elsewhere by Derrida,[2] which imposes disobedience to its own command: "Do not read this," or "Burn this without reading it."

Ashamed or embarrassed at receiving such a letter from a stranger (though the reader is never told just what she said), the speaker-writer of the poem has turned her letter into strips, tiny unreadable fragments "No bigger than the airy feathers / That ducks preen out in changing weathers / Upon the shifting ripple-tips." The "I" has divided and subdivided the letter until its bits are mere useless objects like molted feathers. The scraps are no longer able to carry legible words or to communicate any message. The letter has been reduced to detached letters or fragments of words. The fragments are no longer able to form part of a whole and to "fly," so to speak, in the sense of rising above the matter on which the message is written into the airy freedom of meaning. Unlike Farmer Boldwood, the "I" here has such a violent resistance to receiving the letter, responding to it, becoming subject to its performative power, turning into the person it would by perlocution make him be, that he tries to destroy the letter and all its latent power. He wants to turn it back into senseless matter. This is a striking example of part at least of what Derrida may mean by the "divisibility" of the letter. Derrida has in mind a letter's detachment from any single conscious emitting mind or self. He means also a letter's readiness to divide itself indiscriminately at the receiving end and to branch out to exert its power over any number of recipients, "destinataires." For Derrida, and for Hardy too, a letter or a poem is divisible, and divided, at its origin, in itself, and at its end. In "The Torn Letter" the initial emphasis is on its physical divisibility. The letter by no means has the "organic unity" that used to be attributed to the single text. It can be turned into a thousand tiny pieces.

It will surprise no reader of Hardy to discover that neither this theoretical divisibility, nor the fact that the "I" turns theory into practice and fragments the letter, inhibits one bit its implacable performative power. To the contrary. The message is somehow distributed throughout the whole "signifying chain," like the proper name repeated beneath the text in one of Saussure's "hypograms."[3] The message can operate through any fragment of it, as a single cell contains the DNA message for reconstructing the whole organism of which it is a minute part, or as, in one of the more grotesque experiments of modern biology, one worm may learn behavior from another worm that has been pulverized and fed to the first worm. The genetic code or imprint passes by ingestion.

The "I" regrets his rash act. His "regretful sadness" at his "derision" "of one drawn to him though unknown" deepens "into real remorse" as the night wears on. He seems to see the writer of the letter "in a vision," reproaching him. The letter has invoked this vision. It has raised the ghost or hallucination of the lady. It has operated as a prosopopoeia, a speech to the absent or dead. Or perhaps it would be better to say that the act of tearing the letter to pieces, reducing the letter to dead letters, so to speak, has made it act as a magic invocation, as a man might be haunted by the ghost of the woman he had killed, or as "Hardy," in another poem, "In Front of the Landscape," is haunted by the phantoms of those he has betrayed. The poet rises up, collects the fragments of the letter, and pieces them together again.

The "Hardyan twist" is that the speaker cannot find all the pieces of the torn letter. Those lost are the ones with the lady's name and address. The speaker's act, with a reversal of the sexes, is like that of Isis gathering up the fragments of the body of the Osiris she has murdered. In both cases something is missing, the phallus of Osiris in one case, the lady's identification in the other, head source of meaning in both cases. Once again, as in that strange myth, the story Hardy tells is of the dispersal, fragmentation, defacing, depersonification, or even unmanning of the self, since in the end the reader of the poem, as I shall argue, becomes not the speaker, receiver of the letter, but the unattainable woman to whom the poem is spoken. The speaker cannot, after all, write back to the lady. He cannot initiate a correspondence and a relationship in which he would, in spite of his initial resistance to doing so, become the self the letter invited him to be:

> I learnt I had missed, by rash unheed,
> My track; that, so the Will decided,
> In life, death, we should be divided,
> And at the sense I ached indeed.

The Will here is of course the Immanent Will, that unconscious energy within what is which, in Hardy's phrase, "stirs and urges everything."[4] The Will is Hardy's name for the fact that things happen as they do happen. This volition is will as force, not will as conscious intent. Its "decisions" are the decisions of fortuity, the fact, for example, that the poet could not find the scraps with the woman's name and address. This means that the track he should have followed, the destiny that waited for him, remains untrodden. The divisibility of the letter means that he must remain divided from the correspondent, by a "decision" that is another form of division, separating this possibility from that one, this track from that.

"I had missed, by rash unheed, / My track"—the phrasing is odd. On the one hand, the track was truly his. It was fated for him by the Will. The track pre-exists his taking it, and with the track the self appropriate to it also exists. This track is his destiny. How can a man avoid his destiny, even by the "rash unheed" of not responding to the woman's call? On the other hand, "the Will decided" that he should not, as punishment for his rash unheed, take the track that was nevertheless destined for him. It is as if he were two separate persons, or two superposed persons, the one who took the track and the one who did not take it, as in Borges's "The Garden of the Forking Paths."

Though the divisibility of the letter did not mean that its power could be destroyed, that power was partially inhibited, and so another form of division takes place, the poet's permanent division from the lady. On the other hand, the paradox of the poem, another wry ironic turn, is that by missing his track he only follows it more surely and securely. He becomes more deeply and more permanently marked by the letter just because he has lost the name and address of its sender and so cannot answer it back, follow out the track it lays out. The letter is detached from the real name and self of its sender and liberated to have an anonymous or universal power to make new selves and join them. Again as in Saussure's hypograms, what is "proper" to the letter is not a proper name and place attached to it on the outside but a power distributed throughout its minutest parts, its letters, a power to bring into existence the phantom selves of both sender and destined receiver. The fact that the letter lacks the proper name and address is just what gives it its power of the dislocation of souls. This might be defined by saying that although the torn and then reconstructed letter operates as an apostrophe or prosopopoeia, the ghost that is invoked is that dislocated new self of the reader of the letter, the self the letter personified into existence, if such a transitive use of the word may be made. It is as though the letter were being written on my mind, inscribed there, thus giving that blank page a personality it did not have.

Had the speaker answered the letter the episode would have run its course, as always happens in Hardy. Warmth, intimacy, love perhaps, would have been followed by coolness, betrayal, the wrenching apart of a final division. For Hardy it is always the case that "Love lives on propinquity, but dies of contact" (F. E. Hardy, 1965, p. 220). If he had followed the track he would ultimately have gone off the track and ceased forever to be the self the letter commands him to be. As it is the ache remains: "That ache for you, born long ago, / Throbs on: I never could outgrow it." For Hardy, the only relation to another person that can last is one that is in some way inhibited, prevented from moving on from propinquity to contact. In this case, the ache remains, like an unhealed and unhealable wound. One part of the "I" does become and remain the self the letter "performs" into existence. I say "one part" because, as Derrida affirms, "all is not recipient [*destinataire*] in a recipient, a part only which accommodates itself to the rest" ("Télépathie," pp. 9–10; my translation). For Hardy, as for Derrida, or as for Nietzsche in paragraph 490 of *The Will to Power*,[5] the divisibility of the self is not only along the diachronic track, but synchronically, in the moment. At any given time the "self" is a commonwealth of many citizens. The self is the locus of many different selves dwelling uneasily with one another. Each struggles to dominate the others and to become the sole ruler, the single self within the domain of the self. For the speaker-writer in "The Torn Letter," one of those selves will remain the self who would have answered the unknown woman's letter.

One more thing must be said of the significance of the missing name and address in "The Torn Letter." The fact that he cannot attach the letter to a proper name and to a specific place puts the "I" of the poem in the same situation as the reader of this or of many other poems by Hardy. The reader is told precious little of the stories at which Hardy's poems hint. He is given a fragment only, usually lacking names, dates, and places. The poem is cut off from what came before and from what came after. It is the bare sketch of an episode. Vital facts are missing that would allow the reader to attach the poem with certainty to Hardy's biography or to actual places on a map of Dorset. Far from reducing the poems' power to haunt their readers, to stick in the mind and lodge there permanently, as an ache or throb the reader can never outgrow, the absence of these specifications multiplies the poems' powers over the reader a hundredfold. The poems produce something like that tantalizing sense that there is a proper name one cannot quite remember. This incompletion gives the poems their power to dwell within the reader, like a ghost, or like an unrealized self, or like a parasite within its host. Each of Hardy's poems is an unsolved and unsolvable mystery. It is a track the reader cannot take or reach the end of, and so he remains fascinated by it. One part of the reader, too, becomes, by the law of multiple simultaneous selves, permanently the self the poem performatively creates.

As Derrida observes, it is not necessary for a letter that brings a new self into existence in me to contain detailed instructions about what that self should be. Far from it. The performative power of the letter works best if it remains a sketch, like Hardy's poems. If, as Derrida says, "you identify yourself and engage your life according to the program of the letter," it is also the case that "the program says nothing, it announces or enunciates nothing at all, not the least content, it does not even present itself as a program. One cannot even say that it 'works' as a program, in the sense of appearing like one, but without looking like one, it *works,* it programs" ("Télépathie," p. 8; my translation). "The Torn Letter" is a striking confirmation of this. Just because the poem is so bereft of details, like the torn letter itself, it is able to perform its magic on any reader who happens to read it. It is as if he had accidentally come upon a letter intended for someone else. Reading the poem, I, you, or anyone becomes its addressee, since it has no name or specified destination. Hardy is forced to communicate with his lost correspondent by sending out a general letter to the world and publishing it in a book of poems, just as radio telescopists send out messages beamed into outer space in hopes they may be intercepted by some intelligent beings, somewhere: "Is anybody there?"

The reader of "The Torn Letter" becomes not so much, through a familiar kind of negative capability, the self of the speaker-writer of the poem, the "I" who has received the letter and is haunted by it, as, by a far stranger form of metamorphosis, the "you" to whom the poem is spoken or written. The reader becomes the woman who has caused the "I" so much ache. The poem becomes a letter in its turn, a letter missing the name and address of its destined receiver, and so anyone who happens to read it is put in the place of that unnamed receiver and pro- grammed ever after to be, a part of him or her at least, the self that letter-poem calls into being. If letters or postcards perform that fearful dislocation of souls of which Kafka speaks, putting a man beside him- self, as it were, drinking his life in the creation of a phantom self and a phantom correspondent for that self, a phantom who intercepts the most passionate of written kisses so that they never reach their destination, works of literature enact a similar dispossession. A poem, too, may dislo- cate its reader. It may make him someone else somewhere else, perhaps without power ever to go back to himself.

NOTES

1. Kafka, *Letters to Milena* (1954), p. 229, translation slightly altered; for the German, see Kafka, *Briefe an Milena* (1952), pp. 259–60.

2. For example, in "Envois," *La carte postale* (1980).

3. See Starobinski (1971).

4. "The Convergence of the Twain," *Complete Poems* (1976), p. 307.

5. Nietzsche, *The Will to Power* (1968), pp. 270–71; for the German see Nietzsche, *Werke* (1966), pp. 473–74.

REFERENCES

Austin, J. L. *How To Do Things with Words.* Cambridge, Mass.: Harvard University Press, 1967.
Derrida, J. *La carte postale.* Paris: Flammarion, 1980.
———. "Télépathie." *Furor*, February 1981, pp. 5–41.
Hardy, F. E. *The Life of Thomas Hardy: 1840–1928.* London: Macmillan, 1965.
Hardy, T. *The Complete Poems.* Edited by J. Gibson. London: Macmillan, 1976.
Kafka, F. *Letters to Milena.* Edited by W. Hass, translated by T. and J. Stern. New York: Schocken Books, 1954. German edition: *Briefe an Milena.* Edited by W. Haas. New York: Schocken Books, 1952.
Nietzsche, F. W. *The Will to Power.* Translated by W. Kaufmann and R. J. Hollingdale. New York: Vintage Books, 1968. German edition: *Werke*, vol. 3. Edited by K. Schlecta. Munich: Carl Hanser Verlag, 1966.
Starobinski, J. *Les mots sous les mots: Les anagrammes de Ferdinand de Saussure.* Paris: Gallimard, 1971.

7   *Goethezeit*

AVITAL RONELL

Difficile d'imaginer une théorie
de ce qu'ils appellent encore
l'inconscient sans une théorie de
la télépathie.

               Derrida, July 10, 1979

Knochen, Wolken, kurz alles führen Sie
uns höher herbei.

               Hegel to Goethe, February 24, 1821

The recent 150th anniversary of Goethe's death was celebrated with a notable display of "mirth in funeral" by those scholars and critics who are responsible for the renaissance in Goethe scholarship. Like these writers, Freud, too, calculated from the year of Goethe's death, though he would often do so with the aim of getting back to the issue of his birth. In the wake of the anniversary of Goethe's death, we return to the issue of their birth. This difficult, belated birth, which delivered Goethe into the childhood of the modern German language, figures importantly, if ambiguously, in Freud's preoccupations. But if the *Goethezeit*—the time or age of Goethe—has to be newly recounted, this time it will not be without the aid of a well-instructed midwife, the *Hebamme* who was not entirely present at the bedside of the mother tongue. To engage a modern midwife—who, to the chagrin of Goethe's maternal grandfather, was sorely lacking at the scene of birth—is to call upon someone or something whose wisdom was gained from the experience of an equally traumatic birth. For if the psychoanalytic method is to be adopted for the purpose of inducing Goethe's birth at this time, it is not because psychoanalysis has conceived a foolproof method of assuring or controlling birth. Rather, psychoanalysis was born along similar lines of delay and deferral, somewhat like the Mignon of *Wilhelm Meister*, without a proper name or genre and as an androgynous body of uncertain harmony sharing the genetic makeup of art and science.

146

Yet Freud would calculate from the year of his death. On the face of it, there is nothing alarming about such a calculation; so much, in Freud's case, was borne up by death, including the proper name "Psychoanalysis," which he patented, as if by chance, the year of his father's death. Even Freud's birth was calculated by his father, Jacob Freud, from the date of his own father's death. On the same sheet of paper announcing "Schlomo Sigmund" Freud's birth, the father had entered the details of the paternal grandfather's death: Rabbi Schlomo was buried on the eighteenth day of the month of Adar (February 23, 1856). Psychoanalysis would retain this double movement that folds death upon life—*fort* upon *da*—while it would also prop up the number eighteen in order to strengthen the memory of its conception. And Psychoanalysis would utter the name of Goethe when dreaming of the first birth spasms. For the time being, there may be no better way of commemorating the enormous labor pains of these fathers than to reach into the opening of their legacies.

If Goethe occupies a place of honor in the genesis and history of psychoanalysis, then Freud's testimony to this effect could be reasonably expected to suggest the specific terms of Goethe's membership in his large organization. Since the authority that Goethe exercises in Freud is largely of a fantasmatic order, however, it is very likely that any testimony Freud could give on this subject has been altered through secret negotiations he had had with himself, thus making it rather doubtful that what he has to say is strictly on the level. To assert Goethe's fantasmatic strength in these negotiations implies, among other things, that there is a certain probability of miscarriage in Freud's calculations of his unconscious debt to Goethe. Such a debt always falls due to a figure whose loss is as deeply desired as it is regretted; this is perhaps why the calculation of the debt is always linked in Freud to the calculations made from Goethe's death. One way of interpreting those aspects of Goethe's power over psychoanalysis of which Freud himself was not conscious would be to attune one's ears to the telepathic orders that Goethe's phantom transmitted to Freud by a remote-control system. Any gamble on a type of intertextuality that would deal with telepathic channels involves a risk, of course: for example, when one aims to exceed Freud's own calculations, the calculation at which one arrives could amount to a seemingly extravagant reliance on coincidence and chance. However, a case can be made for chance, just as it was made by chance, at least in terms of etymological transmission; that is to say, in this case, the calculation that takes into account some apparent coincidences in order to unmask them might turn out to be inexhaustible, always leaving an outside chance.

While it could never be ascertained on which side he really was, Goethe was often at Freud's side during critical moments. At not so critical moments, he would frequently appear in letters, conversations, and even in analysis sessions. Freud would habitually appeal to Goethe as a citational prop for his scientific investigations. His most frequent appeal for support, despite his predilection for *Iphigenie,* will be to *Faust, Wilhelm Meister, Dichtung und Wahrheit,* or to what he simply terms "Goethe." On three imposing occasions Goethe manifests himself as the primary material for Freud's secondary revisions.

The first of these occasions concerns the case of the guilt-ridden patient who has forsworn his chronic masturbatory habits shortly after his father's death. He tends, however, to renounce his resolve, though "only upon rare and extraordinary occasions" (*S.E.* 10:203). Freud explains, "It [masturbation] was provoked, he told me, when he experienced especially fine moments, or when he read especially fine passages." Freud will disclose only one such passage, and it might be noted in passing that he has taken the precautionary and no doubt welcome measure of including "he told me" within the indirect citation attributed to the patient. That passage, Freud's patient told him, can be found in *Dichtung und Wahrheit,* part 3, book 11.

Now Freud himself returned to that especially fine work in "A Childhood Recollection from *Dichtung und Wahrheit*" (*S.E.* 17) to relish what he had, upon a first reading, merely suspected but which had recently found support in another patient's narration.[1] The issue in question brings Freud to Goethe's opening pages, to the pages that open on Goethe's life. With scrupulous attention to detail, Freud recalls these lines, passing over them without comment in order to arrive at the episode that depicts Goethe throwing the family pottery out the window to a chorus of *"noch mehr!"* ("do it again!"). Freud eventually glides home into an analysis of Goethe's relationship to his mother, basing the specificity of his findings on the beginning of the autobiography. In the first paragraph Goethe was born. However, in the second paragraph he was thought to be stillborn. In fact it took three days for his birth to come about. But Goethe did arrive in the world: he *"kam für tot auf die Welt, und nur durch vielfache Bemühungen, brachte man es dahin, dass ich das Light erblickte"* ("[I] was taken for dead when coming into the world; only after going to great pains, did they manage to have me see the light of day"). Goethe was thus born dead, or taken for dead at birth, and will want to be born again (perhaps for the first time) at his deathbed. For who can avoid overhearing the uncanny bracketing of this bio-graphical closure that begins with a desperate struggle toward light and ends with the legendary cry for *"mehr Licht"* ?

Johann Wolfgang Goethe was given the name of his grandfather, which is to say, of his mother. His mother's family name, which is to say his grandfather's name, was Johann Wolfgang Textor. "This situation," Goethe continues, "placed those around me [*die Meinigen*] in a state of distress but was nonetheless advantageous to my fellow citizens [*Mitbürger*] . . . and helped many of those born after me."² Here we rejoin Freud's analysis, where it turns out that with the exception of his sister, Cornelia, Goethe's brothers and sisters all died. But thanks to Textor's manipulation of the situation, or thanks to the effect that Goethe's first birth-death had on the maternal grandfather, the "fellow citizens" would at least be born without first dying. The grandfather saw to it that the *Hebamme* would, in the future, be more alert to the business of birth. The figure of the *Hebamme* will return to Freud.

Why Freud had, however, forgotten or repressed Textor, who might have furnished the gateway (*Tor*) to his own text—and who, as exemplary dream interpreter endowed with telepathic gifts (p. 40) might have enjoined Freud to read his fortune in this stellar configuration—is a matter for speculation. Did he simply eclipse the sentence or overlook it while transferring the passage onto his own pages? Freud's expressed intention in this essay was to trace the contours of the young Goethe's jealous proximity to his mother, the ramifications of which involved the child's hostility toward her other children, his evanescent siblings. Freud's forgetfulness takes a more radical turn, however, if we recognize that the very scene he resists recurs in his own writing when he himself assumes the role of maternal grandfather to the young Ernst's game of *fort-da*.³ For was not Goethe performing before Textor an original version of *fort-da* with death-life in his mother's bed—little Ernst played the game of absence-presence under his mother's bed—and, quite literally, at the portals of the female cavity? This scene is delivered to the maternal grandfather, be he Freud or Textor, for critical observation. It is the moment signaling the retreat of the paternal name (Textor dissolves into Goethe, Freud into Halberstadt), and Goethe's name, which combines the grandfather's name with that of the father, bears the mark of the nominal *fort-da*. Freud's motivation for playing *fort-da* with the narrated event of Goethe's birth may have something to do with this uncanny likeness. In order to find a home for this growing *Unheimlichkeit*, we could as well begin with Freud's *Italienische Reise*. As we cross the border into Italy, we might wonder whether Freud's omission of Textor also meant to suppress the point he had made in the *Traumdeutung* concerning "an architectural symbolism for the body and the genitals," where it is suggested that "every gateway [*Tor*] stands for one of the bodily orifices [*Körperöffnungen*] ['a hole'] ['*Loch*']" (*Traumdeutung*, p. 352). This takes us rather directly from a female cavity to the mouth of a Venetian canal.

Warum gabst du uns die tiefen
Blicke,

Unsre Zukunft ahndungsvoll zu
    schauen?
                    Goethe

Although it is unusual for Freud to be arrested with anxiety on the
subject of his own work, his letters to Fliess make some reference to the
problem of his writing paralysis. A letter of October 15, 1897, gives focus
to Freud's dream of neurotic impotence. In this dream he has seen the
skull of a small animal, which he associates with "your wish that I find a
skull on the Lido to enlighten me, as Goethe once did." If Freud failed
to discover enlightenment on the Lido, he will eventually discover that
Goethe opposes evil not to God, but to the Libido. However, "the whole
dream was full of the most mortifying allusions to my powerlessness as a
therapist." Elsewhere, at "the climax of my life as a citizen," Freud will
speak of Goethe's psychotherapeutic prowess (Goethe Prize, *S.E.* 21:
207–17). What emerge here, however, in connection with the waning
power of his own therapeutic prowess are the inosculating channels,
which Freud does not pursue, uniting death and Italy with a father
figure. Whether Fliess's wish that Freud be Goethe—that Freud seek
more light, *Goethe's light,* that Freud die in the land of the father's
fatherland—betrays the sadistic calculus with which Fliess may have tried
to total Freud, is not in this reckoning, at least not yet. Rather, it is the
way Freud perceives in Goethe a mortifying portal to his own text that
needs calling to account.

To grasp the degree of mortification that Freud suffers at the hands
of Goethe, Italy, and now Fliess, one must enter the portals of another
text, which Freud called the *Traumdeutung.* This is the work to which
Fliess lends his authority as "first audience," "highest judge," and
"representative Other."[4] A dream comes forth under the heading of
"Another absurd dream that plays with numbers." Its narration runs as
follows:

> One of my acquaintances, Herr M., had been attacked in an essay
> with an unjustifiable degree of violence, as we all thought—by no less a
> person than Goethe. Herr M. was naturally crushed by the attack. He
> complained of it bitterly to some company at table; his veneration for
> Goethe had not been affected, however, by this personal experience. I
> tried to throw a little light on the chronological data, which seemed to me
> improbable. Goethe died in 1832. Since his attack on Herr M. must natu-
> rally have been made earlier than that, Herr M. must have been quite a
> young man at the time. It seemed to be a plausible notion that he was
> eighteen. I was not quite sure, however, what year we were actually in, so
> that my whole calculation melted into obscurity. Incidentally, the attack
> was contained in Goethe's well-known essay on "Nature."
> [*S.E.* 5:662]

This dream will enjoy a rather unique place among Freud's intimate revelations insofar as he will have it published on three occasions between 1900 and 1901 in the *Traumdeutung* as well as in *Über den Traum (On Dreams)*. Before proceeding to Freud's interpretation of this dream, let me make a quick observation on the energy loss or gain from German to English. The Standard Edition, as its title suggests, is the model to which many French and, obviously, a good many Anglo-American writers on Freud refer, so it might be worthwhile to consider what befell the dream as it crossed the frontier into "our" language.

In the first place, Herr M. was "naturally crushed": *vernichtet*, destroyed, exterminated, eradicated; "his veneration for Goethe has not been affected": *nicht gelitten*, did not suffer; "I tried to throw a little light. . . . It seemed to be a plausible notion": here Freud shifts to the present tense, writing *Ich suche mir die zeitlichen Verhältnisse. . . . Es kommt mir plausibel vor*, I am looking for the temporal relations . . . It seems plausible to me that "I was not quite sure what year we were actually in": *Ich weiss aber nicht sicher, welches Jahr wir gegenwärtig schreiben*, I however do not know for sure [in] which year we are at present writing; "the attack": *der Angriff*, onslaught, offensive, from *angreifen*, to seize, grasp, take, or catch hold of, *fig.*, corrode, eat into (as acid), break into, affect (an organ), strain (nerves); related to *Griffel*, stylus (a style or needlelike marking device, in entomology, a small, rigid, bristlelike anal organ).

What sort of calculation was Freud making in this very German dream, and why does it run into obscurity (*Dunkel*, a term often associated with the Unconscious)? Because he is dealing with calculations of a specifically temporal nature, it should be noted that, in the first place, Freud shifts tenses within the narration of the dream. The commentary immediately following the narration of the dream aims "quickly" to "find a means of justifying the nonsense in the dream." Freud justifies the dream content thus: A certain Herr M., whom he had gotten to know among some company at table, had not long before asked him to examine his brother, who was showing signs of mental paresis (*paralytische Geistesstörung*). When seeing the patient, Freud had asked him the year of his birth and made him do several minor calculations so as to test his memory; the patient, "incidentally," passed these tests quite well. At this point Freud recognizes "that I myself behaved like a paretic in the dream (I do not know for sure [in] which year we are writing)." Freud now sums up other recent sources that made their way into the dream: an editor of a medical journal, of whom he is a friend, had just printed a "devastating" critique (*"vernichtende" Kritik*) of the latest book by his friend Fliess. Freud intervened in behalf of Fliess, soliciting a response from the editor who regrets the incident but who cannot promise redress (*Remedur*). Whereupon Freud severs relations with the journal, expressing the hope that "our personal relations would not be affected by the event." The third source of the dream was a recent account given by a woman on the subject of her brother's psychic illness. She had explained to Freud how her brother had broken out in a frenzy with cries of "Nature! Nature!" Doctors attributed this outcry to the young man's intensive reading of "Goethe's striking essay" on this subject and to overwork in his studies—(Freud stops the sentence here in a subsequent version)—of natural philosophy. Freud "preferred to think, however, of the sexual sense in which this word is used even by the less educated people here"; the fact "that the unfortunate young man subsequently mutilated his genitals (*Genitalien*) seemed at least not to disprove me." The young man was eighteen at the time of his outbreak. Freud notes that his friend's book deals with the chronological data of life and shows that the length of Goethe's life was a multiple of a number of days that has a significance in biology. He remembers a sentence from yet another unkind critique of Fliess's book: "One wonders whether the author or the reader himself is mad."

"So it is easy to see that in the dream I was putting myself in my friend's [Fliess's] place (I looked . . . to shed some light . . . temporal relations). I, however, act like a paretic and the dream indulges absurdity. Thus, the dream-thoughts [*Traumgedanken*] were saying ironically: 'naturally, the madman is a fool, and you're the brilliant (*genial*) people who understand it so much better. [The *S.E.* erroneously translates *"Ihr seid"* into "it's *he* (Fliess) who is the crazy fool.] Perhaps, though, it's the other way around [*umgekehrt*]?'" And the other way around, Freud tells us, is generously given in the dream content, insofar as Goethe attacked the young man, "which is absurd," whereas "it is still easy for a young man to attack Goethe, who is immortal [*unsterblich*]"—in the other version Freud replaces the "immortal" with "the great Goethe"—and "insofar as I calculated from the year of Goethe's *death*, whereas I had made the paretic calculate from the year of his *birth*."

Freud has, however, also promised the readers of the *Traumdeutung* "to show that dreams spring only from egotistical motives" (he will later change his mind on this). Thus, he must justify (*rechtfertigen*) that he had made his friend's problem (*Sache*, subject) his own and put himself in the place of his friend who, Freud asserts, takes the place of Herr M. in the dream. But "my critical convictions while I am awake do not suffice. Now, however, the story of the eighteen-year-old and the different interpretations of his outcry, 'Nature!' come into play in terms of the opposition which my claim for a sexual etiology had, in the case of the psychoneurotic man, against the claims of most doctors." "I could say to myself: 'The kind of criticism that has been applied to your friend will be applied to you—indeed, to some extent it already has been.' And now I may replace the 'he' in the dream-thoughts with 'we': 'Yes, you are right, it's *we* who are the fools.' "

"There was a very clear reminder in the dream that '*mea res agitur!*' of this by Goethe's small, incomparably beautiful essay." And this is how Freud concludes his commentary: "for when at the end of my high-school days I was hesitating in my choice of a career, it was hearing that essay read aloud in a public lecture [*in einem populären Vortrag:* in a popular lecture] that decided me on taking up the study of natural science."

Freud's interpretation of his dream already contains a prescription recommending the application of "different interpretations" to the eighteen-year-old's diagnosis. However, this diagnosis has perhaps not gone far enough in Freud's commentary, for it still remains unclear precisely which predicament or which eighteen-year-old is thematized in the dream. In order to approach this and other enigmas that linger persistingly within Freud's text, I shall limit my interpretation of the dream and commentary, taken together, to two major possibilities, the first of which would be reducible to a sort of "anxiety of influence." The first interpretative stage is admittedly of less concern than the second, but will do much to clarify what follows.

Freud's asserted goal in the commentary is to justify his having made his friend's subject (*Sache*) his own in the dream. Indeed, one might quickly ask whose dream this will have been. Was Freud dreaming Fliess's Unconscious? For it is known that Freud could not entirely approve Fliess's book, and could have easily caused his friend, the professed "reader of his mind," a good bit of anxiety on this subject. In the commentary Freud places his desire and failure to write, calculate, or clarify (*aufzuklären*) close to Fliess's name. Considering that this follows upon the evocation of genitals to approach the issue of genius, we are reminded of something that the nexus gathering together enlightenment, writing paralysis, and genius recalls. Does it not recall Freud's other dream, reportedly provoked by Fliess's wish, in Italy? Was not the issue already linked to the question of genius? The word in German for Italy is *Italien*. The problem of *gen*ius, influence, and impotence with which Freud associates both Fliess and Goethe is linked in some specific way to a genre of *Gen-Italien* (genitalia).[5]

In the commentary, Freud, however, joins genius with a concept of irony when he quotes the dream as dealing with the relation of fools and madmen to genius. The irony would be, as Freud interprets it, that he and Fliess are the fools to Goethe's critical genius. But following a complicated maneuver, he suggests the relationship to be "the other way around," thus making Goethe the madman, and allowing Freud and Fliess to accept the attributes of genius. In any case, we seem to have a relationship of unsheathed brilliance traveling between Goethe, Freud, and Fliess.

Freud reveals time and again that he naturally identifies with his friend Fliess, thus effectively aiming the criticism that has been dealt to Fliess in the dream at himself. If, however, we bear in mind, as alas we must, that *two* friends figure in the dream interpretation, then a helpful confusion might ensue—namely, another pattern of identification emerges, taking place between Freud and the other friend, the exterminating editor, *against* Fliess. In this respect, it is important to note that the phrasing of Freud's relation to criticism (*so wird es auch dir mit der Kritik ergehen*) could well be taken to mean: your critique (of Fliess) will also follow along these lines and, to a certain extent, has already done so; i.e., you, Freud, are attacking Fliess with unjustifiable violence in Goethe's *Fragment*. In sum, Freud can now crush the mindful Fliess in the nature of Goethe. Put another way, and with less violence, Freud would here be borrowing the authority of Goethe's name in order to criticize Fliess, however fragmentarily.

Such an interpretation does not seem destined to go too far afield, especially when we take into account that the two doctors put an end to their friendship in August of the same year as the publication of this writing. This possibility is further betrayed by Freud's interpretative language: the editor, he says, cannot promise redress. Not only does the Latin word *Remedur* communicate in every sense with the single other Latin event in this text, *"mea res agitur,"* but it also belongs less to the sphere of critical judgment than to that of curative procedure, to Freud's "natural science." In other words, the editor-friend has recourse to Freud's language in order to attack Fliess, and the actual relationship about to be severed presently reigns between Freud and Fliess. Freud's identification with the other friend appears to fulfill the requirements for discovering the egotistical motor to his dream. If it were Freud's unarticulated and unarticulable desire to destroy Fliess and his book containing chronological data on Goethe's *Lebensdauer* (life-span, durability), he would be taking the part of Goethe and attacking Fliess in the name of the immortal name. Indeed, this would be the symbolic accomplishment of Fliess's wish that Freud be Goethe; but it was clear from the start that in this triangular arrangement one of the members would be necessarily sacrificed to the supremacy of the couple, be it pronounced as Fliess and Goethe, or Freud and Fliess, and so on. The attack would originate with the couple Goethe/Freud, but the victim's (Fliess's) "veneration for Goethe (/Freud) would not suffer"—that is, Freud would not suffer.

Now, there are at least three overt references to Goethe in the dream and commentary. In addition to Goethe's envisaged jawing of Freud—his censorial attack—there is Freud's conclusive "incidental" remark with which we have to contend: Goethe's *Fragment über die Natur* decided the hesitant (*schwankenden,* swooning) young Freud to take up what he here calls *natural* science. Everyone knows that the age of a high-school graduate is about eighteen, and a quick glance at Ernest Jones's chronology of Freud's life bears out the hypothesis that Freud was indeed approaching the age of eighteen when he was "thrust" upon (*drängen*) by the eighteenth-century genius.[6] In some way, then, the eighteen-year-old who cried "Nature!" upon reading the same *Fragment* prior to mutilating himself bears some relation to Freud himself. The work of tying together the interpenetrating issues of self-mutilation and Goethe must be left to the second interpretation. Suffice it to say, so that what we call the reader will not be left too unsatisfied, that well before the *Traumdeutung,* Freud writes to Martha Bernays that he has burned his papers and most of his letters on the occasion of Goethe's birthday anniversary. Here, Freud prefers to think that Goethe is in no way implicated in the young patient's outcry, despite the latter's intensive work on the decisive *Fragment.* Freud's preference lies instead with the *popular* meaning of the word, and with substituting his sexual etiology for the reference to Goethe. This substitution, as Freud reminds us in his commentary, amounts to something of a scandal. Now, the scandal, which Freud does not properly name, may lie in the fact that "Nature" can mean both semen and menses, male and female discharge, or, if we were to transpose this to the contextual filter of Freudian ideology, it suggests the specific sexual modes with which Freud has identified Goethe—namely, masturbation and mutilation. Engenderment will of course be another issue.

Perhaps Freud shows himself to be less concerned with protecting Goethe's name in this context than his own. For who demonstrates such fervor in refusing, repressing, or forgetting the connection between Goethe's *Natur* and its popular meaning? Indeed, who was so aroused so near the age of eighteen at a *popular* reading—Freud chose a most peculiar formula for designating "public" lecture—of the *Fragment?* Jones genially agrees with Freud that Goethe's dithyrambic piece exerted an immeasurable influence on the dream interpreter; but Freud ought to be shaken awake, as he seems to desire (*meine kritische Überzeugung im Wachen reicht hierfür nicht aus*); and let us, too, be alert to the nuance of *Überzeugung:* overengenderment or, as in the case of the *Über-Ich,* superengenderment, the one suggesting excess, the other a system of constraints. Both the dream and psychoanalysis return to Goethe's *Natur* as the source of their engenderment.

Throughout his commentary, Freud refrains from giving a reading of the fantasmatic cooperation that his relationship to Goethe assumes. And yet the dream proper points to the first manifestations of a union in which the anxieties of dependency and identification, as well as the neighboring ones of debt and guilt, are not spared. In order to throw some light on this particular formation of anxiety, let us consider briefly another dream that Freud recounts and comments upon.

This dream is about another type of calculation, whose protagonist is a taxi meter (*S.E.* 5: 637). In the commentary Freud remembers having left a party the night of the dream in the company of a friend. The friend had offered to hail a cab and see Freud home. " 'I prefer taking a cab with a taximeter [sic],' " the friend said, " 'it occupies one's mind so agreeably; one always has something to look at.' " When they had settled into the cab and the driver set the meter (which immediately displayed a first charge of sixty heller), Freud "carried the joke further." " 'We've only just got in, and already we owe him sixty hellers. A cab with a taximeter always reminds me of a table d'hôte [this table figures in the dream]. It makes me avaricious and selfish, because it keeps on reminding me of what I owe. My debt seems to be growing too fast, and I'm afraid of getting the worst of the bargain; and in just the same way at a table d'hôte I can't avoid feeling in a comic way that I'm getting too little, and must keep an eye on my own interests.' I went on to quote, somewhat discursively:

> Ihr führt ins Leben uns hinein,
> Ihr lasst den Armen schuldig werden.' "[7]

End of quote (how many sets of quotation marks should one care to place around Freud citing Freud reciting Goethe?). In the context of accumulating debt and guilt (*Schuld*), Freud goes on to cite Goethe "somewhat discursively." The debts start multiplying here, beginning with the friend who offers the cab and whose *délicatesse* dictates that he promptly direct Freud's attention to the meter, thus ushering us from the table d'hôte to a notion of parasitical desire, which in turn invites Goethe's participation. The taxi meter, while occupying the friend's mind so agreeably, reminds Freud of what he owes, or perhaps of a debt he might have forgotten. Freud acknowledges the debt somewhat discursively— that is, by changing courses to accommodate another discourse that, too, reminds him of a debt: to that discourse that, in a haunting way, knows and names nothing less than Freud's debt.

His commentary appears to have satisfied its interpretive hunger when Freud asserts: "Thus I was reminded of the duties of parents to their children. Goethe's words gained a fresh meaning in this connection" (p. 639). Thus Freud names the debt that he feels he had originally forgotten—namely, the debt that parents have toward their children. His own debts or duties are recalled to him after he is reminded by Goethe of the primal debt that children incur. While Goethe's words gained (a fresh meaning), Freud only has increasing charges to contend with; his debt seems to be growing faster, and Freud is naturally afraid of getting the worst of the bargain. In the dream as well as in the sources attributed to its content, the issue of debt emerges at the table; the matter of eating should be retained here, as well as the context of Freud's somewhat discursive citation, the harp player's song in *Wilhelm Meister*, which begins:

> Wer nie sein Brot mit Tränen ass . . .
> (He, who has never eaten his bread with tears . . .)

Mastery, poverty, bread, and tears: this is a large thematic within the Freudian text that is only beginning to open up. Some would like to see Wilhelm Meister come to life as Master Wilhelm Fleiss.[8] But Freud returns here to the family table, recalling in his commentary that on the evening of the dream his child had refused to eat spinach, just as he had as a child. Eventually Freud Sr.'s "taste changed and promoted that vegetable into one of my favourite foods" (p. 639). Can it be ascertained that Freud's slippage from father to child in this context has something to do with Goethe? In any case, we can now be mindful that taste is given to change, and what was once judged unappetizing can later be promoted to a favorite. In matters of aesthetic taste as well—for example, in the case of an eighteen-year-old who listened to a popular Goethe with some degree of apprehension and the forty-four-year-old who incorporates Goethe into the body of his oeuvre. Whichever meter has been ticking in Freud's unconscious and continues to tick in his discourse, Freud is not drawing interest in this bargain. Either as parent or child.

We have seen Freud link Goethe to a notion of originary debt or guilt (*Ihr bringt ins Leben uns hinein . . .*), and we know that Goethe is headed for the dirty business of *Totem and Taboo*, where great Fathers are murdered and great Sons consume the Father only to be cursed with the anxiety of radical guilt. Can Goethe (and Freud) be saved from this fate? Well, in *Totem and Taboo* Goethe intervenes at the moment of execution to save himself—and Freud. Here is how superego (which, let us not forget, is engendered by the son through identification with the father) saves his skin:

> Was du ererbt von deinen Vätern hast,
> Erwirb es, um es zu besitzen.
> (What you have inherited from your
> fathers, acquire it to make it yours.)
> [citation of *Faust*, I. i, in *S.E.* 13: 158]

Since Goethe intervenes here in his exemplary manner in order to give a sound interpretation of the birth of the superego, he escapes being repudiated by Freud or murdered as the Father. On the contrary, Freud cites him as someone who had intuited the systematized theory underlying *Totem and Taboo,* as someone whose truth had to await metapsychology in order to be discovered and interpreted: thus psychoanalysis becomes Father to Goethe. And we have already seen Goethe name his debt to psychoanalysis: *Ihr führt uns . . .* , you bring us [back] to life, we, these impoverished lines, in order to name our debt. Goethe names a debt, and it is not unthinkable that Freud would see himself as a cause for Goethe's admission. This would amount to just one of Goethe's belated births.

But if Freud agrees to be Goethe's creditor, to place himself in the position of Goethe's Father, he is now forever running the risk of being attacked, crushed, destroyed, and consumed by his guilty (*schuldig*) son. For if psychoanalysis is the Father of Goethe's intuitions, then that which surpasses or astonishes Freud in Goethe's text is equivalent to a neglect of debt with respect to psychoanalysis, or to Goethe's murder of the Father. And thus, Freud will have made himself exceedingly vulnerable to successive attacks (*Angriffe*).

Now that we have, or rather, Freud has, saved Goethe from the jaws of *Totem and Taboo,* let us return to the epicures of the family table and to the taxi meter that continues to tick. The issue was spinach and Goethe, and whether Goethe had begotten Freud's discursive style. Or perhaps the immortal Goethe, demoted to the great Goethe, has already been shown in Freud's commentary to be indebted discursively to Freud. For Freud is reminded of his parental duties, which he had somehow forgotten. This is perhaps the context in which Freud's earlier "confusion of temporal relations" should be considered.

Let us take Freud at his word. He is reminded by Goethe of his parental duties, of his duties as father. It is a commonplace of Freudian criticism, and of Freud's own Freudian criticism, to recognize Freud as the father of psychoanalysis. "For psycho-analysis is my creation," and "I have come to the conclusion that I must be the true originator of all that is particularly characteristic in it," are some of the terms Freud adopts in *On the History of the Psycho-Analytic Movement* and elsewhere. It may well be this child, psychoanalysis, toward whom Freud pleads guilty in connection with Goethe: guilty of abandonment, of abandoning his "own" stock, style, and discourse in favor of the adoptive child; guilty of leaving psychoanalysis at critical moments in its development in order to visit with those "incomparably beautiful pages" of poetry. Freud pays calls on poetry when he should be minding psychoanalysis; these calls are paid highly, as he reminds us: "Goethe's words gained." Indeed, the charges made against psychoanalysis would often be unsparing in singling out Freud's lack of scientificity at crucial junctures of his theoretical elaborations.⁹ Wouldn't Freud need to be constantly reminded of his parental duties to psychoanalysis and, therefore, somehow *need* to start calculating Goethe from his *Sterbejahr* within his first great text? In order to protect the child of whom Goethe reminds him, Freud will inscribe the date of death, presently.

The second interpretation, which forms a plausible couple with the first, begins where we left off, or so it seems. As everyone knows, Freud tampered with his first name. In 1870, he had his name changed back from Sigismund to Sigmund, thus leaving the *mund* intact. In any consideration of Freud's biography, this should, and no doubt has, become a matter of unsettling irony. For it is also well known that the part of his body destined to suffer gradual and painful decomposition would be concentrated around the area of his mouth (*Mund*). In her book on Freud (1949), Helen Puner goes as far as binding his subsequent illness with Freud's violent fall at the age of two, which left him with a lifelong scar along the jawbone. Her etiology has since been refuted, for as Jones pointed out four years later, the cancer began on the right side whereas the wound was inflicted on the left side of the jaw (Jones, 1953, p. 8). Puner, however, is certainly right in drawing our attention to the concrete mark of that early traumatism and in isolating, as her flair for continuity forces her to, the jaw area as a particularly fragile and enduring point of reference. Freud would have been beardless without that mark, Puner is careful to remind us. But it would not be until eighteen years after the *Traumdeutung* that the first cancerous manifestations emerged in the form of a palatal swelling. Indeed, the entire area around his mouth, and its many names, proffers a generous opening for speculative intervention while it also presents a screen—a certain pilosity, as it were, that would require our shaving the text.

This protuberance as well as this aperture continue to produce their effects in our interpretation as they may have, in some uncanny way, in Freud's dream of Goethe's attack. In order to remain within the precinct of that pain, one must poke at his mouth in a way the immortal Freud preferred to leave to the business of displacement: in German, then, *munden* means to please, as in matters of appetitive taste; *münden*, to flow or empty into; and *mündig* means coming of age, in the sense of no longer being a minor. The delicate tissues of genius, maturity, influence, or confluence of spirits can thus be grafted onto the physiognomy of our subject. Remembering that Freud feels attacked by Goethe's genius, let us now call forth the etymologically intimate horde cohabiting genius, generation, genitals, and genre. "*Mea res agitur*," Freud recalls, "this concerns me," literally, this is about my "thing" (and Goethe). Now in order to locate the *Remedur* for clearing up the obscurity, let us, at this point, admit the word *Angriff* in its medical sense. Let us now utter the unspeakable, but solely for experimental purposes: Goethe attacked or affected an organ, but this "did not change my veneration for Goethe": and "I hoped that our personal relations would not be affected by the event." Indeed, these frightfully personal relations appear to be consti- tuted by the event (*Vorfall*) and, it must be assumed, in the mode of suffering. Goethe's unjustifiably violent *Angriff* through the *Fragment* naturally destroyed, naturally too soon. Let us launch into the attack proper.

By almost universal agreement, Goethe's unfinished dithyramb on Nature can be classified as one of his early ventures into the natural sciences. Lionel Trilling goes as far as naming this piece an important and "elegant disquisition on Nature," though I wonder whether scholars have not been prejudiced by the force of Goethe's signature when they read the piece, which is neither properly scientific nor quite poetic for that matter. There are, however, other discursive ventures more plausibly attributable to Goethe's pen, but we shall return to this issue in a moment. In his commentary, Freud refuses to interpret the "Nature!" of the self-mutilating eighteen-year-old close to Goethe. However, the dream will be interpreted by the dreamer in terms of genius and geni- tals, both of which are troubled. Two patients are clinically linked to Goethe: the eighteen-year-old with whom we have joined Freud, and the one who masturbates to *Dichtung und Wahrheit*. If these two types of affinity to Goethe were presented in the form of an option, one would certainly prefer to evacuate Freud's name from the site of the first case, particularly since few have claimed to recover more pleasure in Goethe's "incomparably beautiful pages" than the analyst.

But however inclined we may be to invest Freud's reading of Goethe with a principle of pleasure rather than with one of irrepresent- able sufferance, we must nonetheless ask ourselves why he eliminated Goethe—the Goethe *Fragment*—from the context of mutilation, favor- ing instead the sexual "meaning" of "Nature" and its sexual interpreta- tion. And even if the patient's self-mutilation manifestly invites a diag- nosis dealing with sexuality—the attribution of sexual meaning to a symptom—the symptom itself seems to be more urgently bound up in Goethe's text than with a sexual question. If something is being repressed when Freud effaces Goethe here, would it not be a certain link between Goethe and the phantom of (self-)mutilation?

The binding terms of Freud's early engagement with Goethe, and his secretive espousal of his text, have barely come to the fore though it should have become clear by now that the bitter taste of Goethe's crush- ing genius will stay in Freud's mouth, if only to travel to the genitals and back. It is known that at the time of writing the *Traumdeutung*, Freud was suffering from a boil on the scrotum and, as the dream in which he dissects his own pelvis amply displays, Freud was very much focused on the greater genital area of his body, including the pelvic girdle. He was also at this time producing the insights that led him to believe in the veracity of Aristotle's assumption that dreams tend to harbor a sort of alert system for nascent illnesses. His own formula for at least three likely dream sources is listed in part I, C, of the *Traumdeutung* as (1) External Sensory Stimuli (*Äussere* [objektive] *Sinneserregung*), (2) Internal (Subjective) Sensory Excitations, and (3) Internal Somatic Stimuli (*Innerer* [*organischer*] *Leibreiz*). Bearing in mind the place of these dream incubators, and particularly the third of these, let us travel with Freud, if only momentarily, from the site of mutilated genitals back to the intact part of his name, to his mouth and text.

It cannot, of course, be ascertained whether the final mutilation of the maxillopalatal region was consciously felt by Freud some time before the first cancerous symptoms actually emerged from a state of latency; nor can it be ascertained which came first—the symptom or the identification of the symptom, the text that fabricated the disease or the disease that infested the text. This is where Goethe offers his prosthetic hand. For another of his scientific ventures in which he had made a mark for himself—now we arrive at a more plausible type of *"mea res agitur"*—involves his discovery of a specific articulation of the jawbone, the *os intermaxillare* (*Ein Zwischenknochen der obern Kinnlade*), written, incidentally, at about the same time as the *Fragment über die Natur*. To state this very summarily, Goethe had discovered that beltway of Freud's body which would be vulnerable to incessant mutilation. It was perhaps Goethe's most passionate discovery, surpassing in personal investment and importance any of his previous pieces of writing, including *The Sorrows of Young Werther*. It seems, indeed, that all of Goethe's systems were stimulated by this *os*, which, let it be remembered, also means an opening, as a mouth, or an entrance, as the orifice of the vagina. Goethe's agitation was so marked that he produced this unique and extraordinary confessional delicacy: owing to this discovery, he writes to Charlotte von Stein on March 27, 1784, "I am so joyous that all my bowels are stirred" (*Ich habe eine solche Freude, dass sich mir alle Eingeweide bewegen*). In a sense, then, Goethe has already arranged for a shuttle mechanism to travel between the upper maxilla and the lower stations of the body.

If Freud has been struggling to protect the name of Goethe from contamination by the episode of self-mutilation, he may have been doing so to insure his own name, which bridges not only the gaping memory of his body's somatic history but also that body of discursivity that he named psychoanalysis. For it should not be overlooked that Freud names his discursive body here and in numerous other contexts a *natural* science (as opposed to "philosophy," which is associated with the figure of the stricken eighteen-year-old). Indeed, the dark moment in which he is now writing requires him to elaborate a mode of fragmentation that contains within it, like a potential explosive, the possibility of mutilation. The fragment, Freud explains, is the mode of the dream, and the dream interpretation must proceed delicately by fragment. Yet some of the words ushered in to put a handle on the fragment could easily tip over into mutilation. What about the sentence, "the dream is a conglomerate which for the purposes of investigation should be once again *zerbröckelt*" (morcellated, *Traumdeutung*, p. 451)? How easily and how persistently will the fragment efface mutilation? At any rate, we can begin to perceive an unconscious strategy linking, however cautiously, the fragment, Goethe's *Fragment*, psychoanalysis, mutilated genitals, and the jaw. Will it not be one of the great ironies of psychoanalysis when, in the moments it succumbs to extreme fragmentation, it will call upon the prophet of the *Fragment* to hold together an edifice eternally prone to collapse? It will engender the fragment—as its paternity, its source, its child, as citation and absolute debt—constantly, obsessively to dissimulate its fear of mutilation. Freud and Psychoanalysis, as Freud and Psychoanalysis constantly remind us, name one and the same thing (see *"Selbstdarstellung"*—the quotes around this title have too often been forgotten).

But what had Freud and Psychoanalysis actually read when they said they were reading Goethe? We have long enough borne up with the supposed inspirational source of psychoanalysis, its founding text—or Goethe's supposed *Fragment*. The time has come to let Goethe attack the *Fragment*. Here is what he has to say, four years before his death, about Freud's presumed source of inspiration:

> That essay has been recently imparted
> to me from the epistolary legacy of the
> eternally venerated Duchess Anna Amalia. . . .
> I cannot remember having in fact written
> these reflections. . . .
> [*Commentary* to *Fragment*, p. 48]

Divided on the issue of the *Fragment*'s authorship, many scholars have worked under the assumption that Goethe had written the piece; however, the 1975 edition of the *Hamburger Ausgabe* and other authoritative sources attribute the *Fragment* to Georg Christoph Tobler, the Swiss writer who had borrowed Goethe's copyist. What Goethe remembers is that in the years "to which said essay might be attributed, I was principally occupied with comparative anatomy." In those years, Goethe adds, he was actually working on the *Zwischenkieferpublikation*: on the jawbone, his first and, for a long while, most secretly guarded discovery. The

secretive nature of this particular *Entsehungsgeschichte*, which later
became a well-known fact, and Freud (and Fliess's) elaborate readings of
Goethe's scientific works would lead one to suppose that Freud was
himself aware of Goethe's substitution of texts here. To pursue the logic
that Freud has bestowed upon us, it would be quite conceivable to
consider the *Fragment on Nature* as somewhat of a screen memory, a
Deckerinnerung for Goethe's text on the jawbone. Like the son in Kafka's *Judgment*, Freud will try to cover (*decken*) the father's corpus only
to witness its monstrous revival in the form of an enlarging organ.

To bring to light some of the components of the rapport between
Goethe's scientific discovery and the genesis of Freud, we would do well
to note first the context of Goethe's scientific pursuits. Until as late as
1791, Goethe was intent on making his mark principally in the sciences
and considered his artistic bent a "wrong tendency." His attitudes
toward his texts are revealing: Goethe was not the least concerned about
losing possession of the *Götz* and *Werther* manuscripts, but he did
everything to hang onto the text of the *"Knöchlein"* and assert its
priority.[10] Whatever the priorities, this double identity that Goethe
claims for himself cannot have been foreign to Freud, who at once
incorporates and problematizes the painful inevitability of the double
nature, the double genre, indwelling in his own discourse. Thus Freud
writes in the preliminary note to the *Traumdeutung*:

> With the communication of my own dreams it inevitably followed that I
> should have to reveal to the gaze of strangers [*fremden Einblicken*] more
> of the private aspects [*Intimitäten*] of my psychic life than I liked, or than
> is normally necessary for any writer who is a scientist [*Naturforscher*] and
> not a poet. Such was the painful but unavoidable task.

The *Naturforscher* is, however, forced into the role not merely of
Poet, but of arch-poet precisely "so that I would not have to renounce
the marshalling of evidence for my psychological conclusions." Yet,
when Freud does make a discovery, the evidence of its truth will frequently be said to hark from the poets. Thus, for example, when writing
on sexual repression in *"Selbstdarstellung,"* Freud, in order to found the
nasty theory of infantile sexuality, writes: "The results established con-
firmed what poets and keen observers of human nature had always
maintained." The language of Freud's exposition further recalls
Goethe's language in *Dichtung und Wahrheit* when he explains, for
example: "Childhood was supposed to be 'innocent' [*'unschuldig'*],
free from sexual lust, and the struggle with the demon 'sensuality' was
supposed to arise only at the *Sturm und Drang* period of puberty."
Besides its appeal to the *demon* of sensuality and to the literature of the
Sturm und Drang period from which Goethe's name is indissociable,

this passage reads much like a recollection from Goethe's *"Selbstdarstellung,"* *Dichtung und Wahrheit,* in which he explores his own case of infantile desire for his sister (see the section beginning with "that interest of youth, that awe before the awakening of sensual drives," part 2, book 6).

From another point of view, in the third Foreword to the *Traumdeutung,* Freud predicts that future editions of his text will require, of all things, a deeper investigation of the poetic resources on the one hand and scientific depth on the other. In the subsequent Forewords, Freud will begin to enmesh the two discourses (if they are indeed two) and refer to scientific material as *Literatur.* Indeed, the book proper begins with the bigeneric heading, "Die wissenschaftliche Literatur der Traumprobleme" ("The scientific literature of dream problems"), and the first paragraph of *Traumdeutung* ends, coincidentally, with a certain constellation that has occupied us here: "Having gone thus far, my description will break off, for it will have reached the point where the problem of dreams merges into [*einmündet*] more comprehensive problems, the solution of which must be considered [*in Angriff genommen,* lit.: taken in hand] in terms of other material."

The time has indeed come for us to prepare a solution for this material and to adjust the issue of Goethe's attack. The attack, the solution, the mouth, the jaw: do these features properly belong to Freud or Goethe? These features of a common text, of a doubly redoubled identity on both parts—on the part of the scientist and the poet— belonging to neither the one nor the other exclusively, this text begins or ends with the morphology of inaugural discoveries. I shall isolate a few sentences of Goethe's discovery without commentary for the moment:

1. This frontal section of the upper jawbone has been given the name of *os intermaxillare.* The Ancients already knew this bone and recently it has become especially noteworthy. . . .

2. The bone of which I am speaking derives its name from the fact that it is placed between the two primary bones of the upper jaw. It is itself composed of two parts which are joined in the center of the face.

3. Its foremost, widest and strongest part, which I call the body [of the bone], is determined according to the type of food intake. . . .

4. The second suture, which is located in the base of the nose, arises from the *Canali naso-palatini* and which can be traced as far as the area of the *Concha inferior,* was not noticed by [Vesalius]. On the other hand, both are found in Albin's great Osteology on Plate 1, designated by the letter *M.*

5. And so I conclude this small venture with the wish that it might not prove displeasing to connoisseurs and friends of natural philosophy [*Naturlehre*] and that it might accord me the opportunity to be more

closely bound to them and, as far as circumstances permit, to make
further progress in this enticing [*reizenden*] science.[11]

Thus Goethe makes his contribution to science, a science that cuts
as deeply into the Freudian body as one dare imagine. But could Freud
himself have imagined this uncanny link—one that privileges the initial
M, as in Herr M., that explores the buccal cavity to fix on the jaw, that is
preoccupied with modes of food intake (as Freud will have to be for a
good part of his life), that insists on naming and renaming the traumatized area—as early, say, as the time of his *Matura*?

I am certainly not the first to connect the name of Fliess with that of
his young friend Fluss, to whom Freud was writing at the time of his
exams. Freud was first, as usual, to draw attention to the jarring compati-
bility of the names of his most vital friends: Fluss, Fleischl, Fliess. Before
there was Fliess there was Fluss, and before Fluss (also "river") dissolved
into Fliess (also "flowing," "secretion"), there was Fleischl (also
"flesh," "meat"). And though we shall have to cut Fleischl out of the
picture, his name should resonate in the suture of Fluss and Fliess. The
remains of Freud's correspondence with Fluss date from 1872–74. At this
time Freud is preparing his *Matura*, reading for the first time Sophocles'
Oedipus Rex (of which he will be required to translate thirty-three lines),
very much enamored of Fluss's sister, signing his letters alternately Sigismund and Sigmund Freud, commenting on his exams, deciding upon a
career, and quoting Goethe. At the threshold of maturity, Freud substi-
tutes the natural for the legal process, abandoning his earlier goal of
becoming a lawyer—herein outdoing Goethe, who was obliged by his
father to study law at Leipzig. By 1874, he is writing a letter of apology
to Fluss with the intent of acquitting himself for having missed
a rendezvous:

> It was the final, feeble eruption of a formerly powerful crater, the last
> spasm from an area of my body [*Leib*] which, for a long while, has been in
> open revolt against the peace and order in my organism—I am speaking
> of my denture [*Gebiss*]. In this respect I'm in an embarrassingly sad
> dilemma; if man lives in order to eat, then I live in order to ruin my teeth,
> that is, in order to suffer from toothaches. . . . My life is, then, necessarily
> bound up with the toothache, of which, it follows, I shall nevermore in my
> life rid myself—such a sad destiny and as such worthy of your sympathy.
> [March 6, 1874]

Regardless of how witty Freud could prove with respect to the seedy
neighborhood of his mouth (Freud was also witty when the Gestapo
stampeded through his apartment),[12] he was certainly aware of the area

in which his body had chosen "openly" and "necessarily" to revolt against him. Perhaps it is unnecessary to trace the itinerary of Freud's pain, or to emphasize the duration of the symptoms that had been forming around the maxillobuccal region. Nor would it seem necessary at this point to make the connection, as Goethe does in the *Zwischenkiefer* study, between the mouth and nose and, in this connection, to remind anyone of Freud's experiments with cocaine, his addiction to cigar smoking, or to mention that Freud had considered Fliess, at least initially, merely as "a throat, nose and ear-specialist."[13] Officially, Freud's problems begin in 1923, under the diagnostic heading of epithelial cancer, requiring surgical intervention in the form of the resection on the level of the *maxillaris superioris* (which figures in Goethe's essay under *"Corpus,"* p. 186). The details of Freud's operation are dreadful enough, and leave one wondering why he had submitted himself to the butchery of a declared enemy without mentioning the illness or operation to his family. Details of this and subsequent operations—they were thirty in number—can be found in Max Schur's *Freud: Living and Dying,* which characteristically begins with a quote from Goethe. Schur is the physician whose injection brought Freud his final rest. Suffice it to say that his wife and daughter found Freud slumped in a chair, bleeding profusely at a run-down clinic on the wrong side of town. By tragic coincidence, Freud and his grandson, Heinele, were operated on the buccal cavity at the same time. The child died on June 19, 1923, leaving Freud as the guilt-ridden survivor of the double operation.

Schur promotes the hypothesis that Freud likewise would have a relationship of "guilty survivor" to the author of *Die Beziehungen zwischen Nase und weiblichen Geschlechtsorganen.* Should this be the case, then Freud's survival, as any survival inevitably does, already contains within it the seed of death. In order to place the deposited seed with some exactitude, however, we might first examine the opening and closure of the *Traumdeutung* itself. While giving birth to psychoanalysis as a discipline, this work will also leave a residue of traces indicating Freud's future disease, whose localization—the *maxilla* or *Kinnlade*—Goethe studied in the double and phantom of the *Fragment über die Natur.* The originary moment of the *Traumdeutung*'s genesis could thus be interpreted by means of a dream containing a foreboding or premonition of the disease. But what position does psychoanalysis take toward such dream contents? The closure of the *Traumdeutung,* its *Lösung* or solution, appears to have foreseen and foretold all the modalities of this question:

> And the value of dreams for supplying an awareness of the future? Naturally, one cannot think of such a thing.

Naturally, Freud estimates, this value is not thinkable. Then why does Freud think the unthinkable at the end of his thought? And why does he continue to think the unthinkable to the end? The slight hedging with which Freud proceeds initially to un-think the unthinkable should not escape us:

> One might say instead: they supply an awareness of the past. For dreams are derived from the past in every sense.

The dream descends from the past *in every sense.* Yet, Freud does not show himself averse to adding this declaration, at once timid and assertive:

> Nevertheless the ancient belief that dreams foretell the future is not wholly devoid of truth. By picturing our wishes as fulfilled, dreams are after all leading us into the future. But this future, which the dreamer represents as the present, has been moulded by his indestructible wish into a perfect likeness of the past.

Freud thus makes provisions for the futural dimension of dreams to flash before us, but only within the horizon circumscribed by the past. Nonetheless, this prospect does admit, however cautiously, a certain filtration of the future or fortune-telling elements of dream. Such ambivalence, it has been shown, hovers on the frontier between science and its others, be these poetry, superstition, or telepathy.

At this frontier and time, it would make sense to close our interpretation of Herr M.'s dream; to that end, it seems indeed necessary to take into account the possibility that the last page of the *Traumdeutung* leaves open. To proceed in the manner of Freud himself, we might first reassemble some of the fragments that make up the dream content. In this dream, Goethe violently submits Freud to an operation both critical and surgical in nature. Freud identifies one of the instigators of the dream as the eighteen-year-old who had read Goethe's *Fragment.* Another source is given as Freud's own reception of this *Fragment,* which he remembers as having taken place at a critical point in his development. Let us reconstruct the events.

At the age of eighteen, Freud is in the process of choosing a career. During this period he recognizes the first manifestations of pain, whose development he anticipated in a letter to Fluss, on the inside of his mouth. At this point he is incited by a public reading of Goethe's *Fragment* to opt for a career in the natural sciences; Goethe's text is thus perceived by Freud as the seed from which his future discoveries will be

engendered. This is also the age in which Freud decides upon the varia-
tions around the *mund* of his first name. About twenty years later, while
writing his magnum opus, Freud faces another decisive step in his career
in which Goethe once again makes an altogether striking appearance.
Freud begins openly to attach a good deal of anxiety to Goethe's name.
In the first place, Freud, troubled by his double nature of scientist and
poet, also dreams of a discovery at the Lido that might respond to
Goethe's injunction or in some way satisfy his demand. He develops a
theory of dream that retains the imprint of necessary fragmentation and
germinates precisely in his analysis of Goethe's attack. The disappoint-
ment he experiences in his scientific career reflects to a large extent the
sorrows of Goethe in the same field. Freud is at loose ends over the
fortune-telling aspects of the dream.

As for Goethe, his intervention in the history of psychoanalysis
proves to be as painful as it is paradoxical. The violence of his attack
appears to be linked to an act of mutilation and even to the self-mutilation of the patient with whom Freud is associated. To the multiple
determinations that make Goethe's attack intelligible we can add the
possibility of reading Freud's recollection of the *Fragment on Nature* as a
screen memory behind which another essay on nature, written at the
same time as the *Fragment* and to which Goethe attached the highest
value, can be discerned. This would be the essay in which Goethe names
and treats the *Zwischenkiefer* of the upper maxillary. If Goethe should
then appear to Freud as an unappeasable phantom, this is not only due
to the double trajectory that his genius had forecast—the same could
have been said of da Vinci—but also, most cruelly, because Goethe had
put his finger on Freud's indelible wound, placing the affected area
under the sign of his victim in Freud's dream ("M"). When Goethe
delivers his sentence, he pronounces with equal gravity his support and
condemnation of Freud. But he will also try to abandon Freud to his lot
by refusing to underwrite the text that, according to Freud, he had sired:
indeed, Goethe has withdrawn his signature from the founding text
upon which Freud and Psychoanalysis counted so heavily.

In this somber light, one could read the *Traumdeutung* according to
the terms retrospectively suggested by Freud himself, as an epitaph for a
father whose irremediable loss gives rise to desperate calculations but
who nevertheless continues to infest Freud's text and body, where he has
deposited the seed of death. This is where Fliess comes in, for he will
have made explicit the synonymity of Goethe with catastrophe and death
as early as the dream of neurotic impotence, for example, when he sent
Freud to seek Goethe's "light" on the Lido. However, it should suffice
to remain within the context created by the dream of Herr M., where
Fliess is shown in the light of his speculations, which turn out to be as
"mortifying" as the dream of the Lido: Freud identifies the book under
heavy attack by Goethe as the one dealing with Goethe's *Sterbejahr*.

Thanks to Fliess's studied calculations of the same genre, Freud was scheduled to die in 1907, an eventuality that Freud took very seriously. Despite Fliess's sadistic statistics Freud and Goethe will of course have had the same *Lebensdauer*. Nonetheless, the chronological data with which Fliess computes Goethe's life-span provides the grounds for legitimizing his sentencing Freud to death. Under the circumstances, Freud will have to stave off Fliess's as well as Goethe's frontal attacks, and he will have to screen himself and his text from their acts of mutilation.

For Freud, then, Goethe intervenes as the name of the *Sterbejahr*, as the instance from which the deadline must be calculated. This is as true of the dream in which Goethe attacks him as it is of the one in which a taxi meter imperturbably reminds Freud that the time for settling accounts is nearing. For us, too, the stakes are high and the calculations difficult, all too difficult. In order to appreciate them, one has to renounce safeguarding or even saving the text from the pressure exerted by a question of timing and, perhaps necessarily, of bad timing. The question involves knowing at which point calculations must begin in order to account for the apparition of a syndrome, a complex, or even of what we call a cancer.

If the operation to which Freud has been submitted is too dreadful because too real, and if Goethe has been brought in to give his light to Freud's unspeakable afflictions, it is only because the proliferation of Freud's disease cannot be stopped—certainly not with Goethe, where it all began. Nor can the fragile opening from which Freud's growth issues be blocked or silenced. This opening of many names speaks to us in different voices. One is the *Traumdeutung* itself, on whose inner limits scattered references to Freud's future disease mercilessly proliferate. Consider for instance Freud's demonstration of the Dream as Wishfulfillment in chapter 3, where he devotes merely three sentences to interpreting a dream about the opera. The patient who had dreamt of going to the opera had also just undergone an unsuccessful jaw operation (*einer ungünstig verlaufenen Kieferoperation*). Freud resolutely overlooks the possibility of linking the opera with the operation or of exploring the implications of a botched operation for his own interpretative work or *opera*.

While the *Traumdeutung* closes with the hypothesis that illuminated our way through the cavernous premises of a "wish-fulfillment" dream, it opens with a mutilated entry about another dream—another mouth or cavity which communicates in a vital sense with the female cavity. At the end of the opening dream and commentary, Freud writes: "I have now ended the [I]nterpretation of [D]reams [*ich habe nun die Traumdeutung vollendet*]." This opening will therefore also have been a closure, and will continue to open and close like one of the mouths it investigates.[14] Freud himself calls this opening a *Mustertraum* (model or exemplary dream; *S.E.*: specimen dream). It is a monstrous dream, impregnated with the future and marked with the agonies of guilt and birth. It is the dream whose inscription Fliess is known to have mutilated. But the mutilation is multifaceted. Fliess certainly compelled Freud to excise substantial portions of the dream for publication purposes; he had also received Freud's patient, whose name appears in the entry as "Irma" but whose actual name was "Emma." Freud's substitution of *Ir* for *Em* (as in Frau "M" perhaps) would be a story in itself—one that he only intimates at several junctures of his commentary, for example, when writing of diagnostic error (*Ir*rtum der Diagnose, pp. 114, 119). The story of the maltreatment to which Fliess subjected Irma is no longer a secret: Freud had referred Irma to Fliess, who then operated on her nose. In the course of the operation, Fliess had inserted a tampon in Irma's nose, which he later forgot to remove. As a consequence, Irma was afflicted with a serious infection that almost cost her (and Freud) her life. This, then, is the story of Irma's infection, which Freud, however, calls Irma's injection. To Freud's dismay and astonishment, Fliess was cavalier about his error and failed to see the need for Freud's fuss over the matter.

Fliess's double mutilation of the Irma episode takes place behind the preface, as the *Hintergedanken*—behind the hall, the passage, the colonnade of a Belle Vue or a canal. By now we are removed from the canals of Venice drifting toward another topography of the canal on whose bridge the nose, with its extension into the buccal cavity, very literally continues to scent the trail of Goethe.

Now the dream narrated as Irma's injection takes place in a large cavity, *"eine grosse Halle,"* a type of vestibule where Freud or rather "we" receive Irma as well as other guests. His word for this reception is *empfangen,* whose other strong meaning in German is "to conceive," "become pregnant." Irma, as we later discover, is a young widow; in the commentary Freud will substitute his wife for Irma, without however linking up the obvious: Freud is treating a young widow, maybe his own wife, on the event of his wife's birthday (*Analyse,* p. 113). The reception takes place, according to the commentary, in some great hall resembling Freud's summer residence, Belle Vue. But what is the *belle vue* that Freud cites in a dream connecting his wife's birthday with Irma's injection? Well, he tells us in so many ways, without ever saying so. The first motive assigned to the dream is that he wanted to respond orally to Irma's letter. His response takes the form of reproaches (*Vorwürfe*), for Irma has not yet accepted his "solution" (*"Lösung"* is placed in quotation marks)—or, since Freud himself lifts the word out of its comfortable context, the young widow has not yet accepted his "unraveling," "dénouement" (*"Lösung"*).

Freud's principal gesture consists in taking the young woman aside
to tell her, "If you are still in pain, then it's really only your own fault
[*Schuld,* guilt, debt]." She replies in the dream, "If only you knew the
suffocating pain I am suffering in my throat, stomach, womb [*Leib,* also
'body']." Freud, frightened by this profession of pain, wonders whether
"in the end I have overlooked something of an organic nature" and
begins to look: Escorting the young widow to the window, he finally
looks into her throat. "At this, she shows some resistance, as do women
who wear prosthetic devices [*wie Frauen, die ein künstliches Gebiss
tragen*]. I think, she does not need it, however." Freud, who will himself
wear and endure a prosthesis as a consequence of his cancer, thinks to
himself that this young widow—also his wife—does not need it. In the
commentary that follows, he does explain the dream as having something to do with his own health; but when localizing the traumatized
area, he places or displaces the pain onto his own shoulder, which is
frequently cramped after long writing sessions. In the dream, however:
"the mouth then opens easily [*der Mund geht dann gut auf*]," permit-
ting him to discover, on the right side, a large spot, and elsewhere he also
spots scab formations "upon some remarkably curly structures which
were evidently modeled on the turbinal bones of the nose." He immediately calls over another guest, Dr. M., who, pale and limping, joins the
couple to concur with Freud's opinion: they are undoubtedly faced with
an infection. Dr. M., by the way, is "beardless along the chin [*am
Kinn*]," as Freud might have been without his ineffaceable wound. They
both are aware that Irma had recently received an injection of "*Pro-
pylpräparat . . . Propyl. . . .*" The needle with which the injection had
been administered was also probably unclean, impure.

When analyzing the dream, Freud merely attaches a footnote to the
passage dealing with Irma's mouth: "I suspect [*ahnen,* to have a presentiment or premonition] that the interpretation of this piece [*Stück*] of
the dream has not been carried far enough in order to pursue the whole
of its hidden meaning [*Sinn*]. . . . Each dream has at least one spot at
which it is unfathomable [*unergründlich*]—a navel, as it were, that is its
point of contact with the unknown." This note of presentiment could
not have found a more ominous opening. Nonetheless, Freud does make
his allowances, and concedes that the dream may have some bearing on
the future in terms of wish-fulfillment. With respect to this dream he,
however, announces its result thus: "that I am not guilty [*Das Ergebnis
des Traumes ist nämlich, dass ich nicht schuldig bin*]." So it would seem
that on one level the result and resolve of the dream eliminates the
premonition of the future. On one level, that is.

The *Muster* or monster dream requires Freud to peer at formations
taking shape on the right side of the mouth, proximate to the maxillary,

and to localize his sense of guilt and the name that he attaches to that guilt in the mouth, the *Mund*—which in turn designates the area of future devastation.

In the analysis of the dream, Freud claims that he has been exercising vengeance against Irma, the disobedient patient with whom he identifies his wife as well as his daughter, Mathilde. The word he uses to designate "disobedient" is *"unfolgsamen,"* which can be broken down into *unfolg-samen*: the semen that does not follow. We know that Freud's reference to his wife does not limit itself to the event of her birthday but includes the fact of her present, unwanted pregnancy—that is, unwanted by Freud. Thus, we approach the abyssal moment of the dream whose cavity is conceived not only as mouth and nose, but as the womb and its unwanted secretions: we are before two horrors of future engenderment, consigned to the cavities of the nasal-palatal region and womb. And right now Fliess's nasal secretions also preoccupy Freud— Fliess who, as Freud reminds us (p. 122), had opened up (*eröffnet*) the terrain upon which these secret relationships between the nose and the female organs take form. As Freud does not remind us, Fliess's book holds birth and abortion to amount to the same phenomenon (Fliess, p. 12). Fliess could have caused Freud discomfort on yet another count, for it is he, Freud's "first public" and "highest judge," whose censorial injection into Freud's dream left Freud with the consequences of impurity on the threshold of Freud's first substantial work of maturity. The preparation of this work, as of the propyl injection, had been submitted to Fliess's judgment. With this injection, we are introduced into the bottomless moment, the omphalos in Freud's analysis, which begins: "with a preparation of propyl . . . propylen. . . . How did I ever get to that? [*Wie Komm ich nur dazu?*]"

On the same evening as the dream, Mrs. Freud had opened a bottle of liqueur the label of which read *Ananas* (pineapple). In his sleep, Freud then substituted *Propyl* for *Amyl*, the scent of the *Ananas*: "I certainly undertook a substitution; I dreamt *Propyl* after I had smelled *Amyl*, but such substitutions are perhaps only admitted in organic chemistry." Organic chemistry indeed.

In pathology, amyloid degeneration is a change of structure by which amyloid is formed and deposited in the tissue or organ affected. This is the albuminoid developed in diseased degeneration of various animal organs. Now, in botany, albumen is the substance that surrounds the embryo in many seeds; it is also, for instance, the white of an egg. Albumen is thus the endosperm or perisperm. Freud himself mentions albumen, or egg white, but in the context of a sinister joke prompted by Dr. M. and a colleague. These two doctors visit a gravely ill patient, at which occasion Dr. M. feels called upon to play a diagnostic joke. Dr. M. tells his colleague that he has found egg white in the patient's urine. But the colleague would not be led astray (*liess sich aber nicht irremachen,*

p. 120) and responded calmly: "That doesn't matter, Herr Colleague, the egg white will be expelled! [*ausscheiden*, eliminate]." Freud cites this example to expose his scorn for colleagues ignorant of hysteria, and explains that it had worked itself into his dream in the form of the guest whom he consults when looking inside Irma's mouth. But whether we are speaking of urine or sperm, it all comes down to the discharge of the male organ contaminated with properties of the female organ—something Freud does not say. This discharge will contain something like albumen, covering the egg, which, as Freud remembers, can be eliminated or, we might add, removed, from the vagina, the limit (*Scheide*). In his dream and commentary, Freud thus eliminates (or represses) the amyloid or the diseased organ and the prospect of birth to replace them with another type of birth, bringing to light another type of child. This is the dream of the double birth of the *Traumdeutung*, the dream of Irma's injection that will engender the exemplary and initiating dream text after which the *Traumdeutung* will have reached fruition, "completion." And it is Irma, but really Emma, who, on the event of his wife's birthday and Freud's *Sterbejahr*—for Irma is a young widow—will act as midwife and wet nurse to the dream of dreams, the story of the semen that did not follow. Others have already mentioned the inversion of Emma that produced *Amme*, midwife and wet nurse, while elucidating Freud's marked attachment to his own wet nurse (*Amme*).[15] We have not yet left the scene of Goethe's double birth and of Freud's repression of Textor, who had intervened in the education of the *Heb-amme*, literally, the wet nurse who lifts the child into existence. Let this scene be projected on a backdrop while we continue to pursue Freud's *Amme*, who brings the *Traumdeutung* into this world.

Freud receives and conceives Irma or *Irrmama* at the threshold of the third part of his book. But according to his description, Irma is received and conceived in a *grosse Halle*. As vestibule or cavity, as architectural or anatomical structure, *Halle* is never quite inside or outside the body, quite like a mouth or vagina. Nor is the narration of Irma's injection *qua* dream either quite inside the body of the *Traumdeutung* or part of the somewhat external, preparatory pages that lead into the analysis of dreams. In fact, the Irma dream, while making up the last part of *"Die Methode der Traumdeutung"* with its principal emphasis on methodology, and while holding the rank of Freud's *Mustertraum*, somehow introduces or introjects, without entirely belonging to, the subsequent chapters demonstrating the varieties of dream and dream analyses. At once the threshold and the completion of the *Traumdeutung*, it arrives before the interpretation of dreams actually begins; it neither belongs to the history that precedes the *Interpretation* nor takes part in the section devoted to *Dream*. It begins as a *Vorbericht* (preliminary report or preface), where we learn that Freud had begun to dream his great vestibule as a *correspondance manquée*: his dream will have been, within the dream, the response to Irma's unanswered and perhaps unanswerable letter.

To find the way to the underbelly of the *Propyl*-solution in the text of Irma, I propose that we enter with Freud another great *Halle* on the occasion of another birthday and letter which, on the face of it, is an *open* letter, a kind of Carte Postale, reinscribing the earlier thematics of an Italian Voyage along the lines of finality and powerlessness: "My powers of production are at an end," Freud begins, ending: "I myself have grown old and stand in need of forbearance and can travel no more." Nonetheless, Freud is still Goethe-bound.

The letter, written in January 1936, is occasioned by Romain Rolland's birthday. Freud's title: "A Disturbance of Memory on the Acropolis." To his French correspondent Freud explains that in 1904, Alexander and Sigmund Freud visited Trieste, where they were presented with the long-desired prospect of spending some time in Athens—three days, to be exact. As the certitude of seeing the Acropolis increases, they inexplicably find themselves in "remarkably depressed spirits." The entire letter is taken up with investigating the causes of this depression. Freud's text proves rich in allusion to French terms such as *"déjà vu," "fausse reconnaissance," "déjà raconté"*; yet he has difficulty determining why he would be *triste* at Trieste. The sense of *déjà raconté* which he mentions may not appear to join up with the name of Goethe per se, but Freud does illustrate the sensation of encroaching joy and present sorrow as "an example of the incredulity that arises so often when we are surprised by a good piece of news, when we hear we have won a prize, for instance" (*S.E.* 22: 242). This would comprise the only apparent allusion to "Goethe." For although Freud was repeatedly nominated for the Nobel Prize in literature, of all things, the only award of considerable prestige that would ever be granted to him was the Goethe Prize in Frankfurt, just three years before his books were burned in Berlin. Freud writes of the "too good to be true" effect of this visit and of the disbelief associated with hope that one would live long enough actually to view the Acropolis. The sense of a double consciousness or split personality, of guilt and inferiority, assails him as he reconnoiters the Greek military ensemble. He describes the experience of derealization which emerges as a sort of propylaeum of defense for the ego.

In order to urge the point, Freud cites the lament of the Spanish Moors *"Ay de mi Alhama,"* which tells how King Boabdil received letters (*cartas*) announcing the fall of his city, Alhama: "he determines to treat the news as *'non arrivé.'* [The King] threw the letters in the fire and killed the messenger." In so doing, "he was still trying to show his absolute power." This passage suggests itself as an allegorical reading for the genesis of the Irma dream, insofar as the dream is said to arise from Freud's concern about the relativization of his power (*Autorität*) and from his anger toward the messenger, Otto, who informs Freud of Irma's fallen state (cf. *Vorbericht*). But the messenger is somehow adopted by the unconscious; thus only the dream itself secures a certain fictional "arrival of the message"—in fact, it begins, we may recall, as a compensatory form of epistolary exchange.

When he himself arrives at his troubling destination in Athens, Freud is in awe "that I should 'go such a long way.'" For when he was a mere schoolboy "the limitations and poverty of our conditions" appeared to preclude the possibility of his ever traveling this far. Freud remembers that he "might that day on the Acropolis have said to my brother: '... And now, here we are in Athens, and standing on the Acropolis! We really *have* gone a long way!'" He also remembers that just as he was about to be coronated emperor, Napoleon remarked to his brother at the threshold of Notre Dame: "What would *Monsieur notre Père* have said to this, if he could have been here today?"

Past this apt comparison, Freud arrives at a solution for

> the little problem of why it was that already at Trieste we interfered with our enjoyment of the voyage to Athens. It must be that a sense of guilt was attached to the satisfaction of having gone such a long way: there was something about it that was wrong, that from earliest times had been forbidden. . . . It seems as though the essence of success was to have got further than one's father, and as though to excel one's father was still something forbidden. . . . The very theme of Athens and the Acropolis in itself contained evidence of the son's superiority. [p. 247]

It should be remembered, however, that his father "had been in business, he had had no secondary education, and Athens could not have meant much to him." Thus filled with filial pity, Freud names the symptom "filial piety."

One can hardly wish to engage Freud in a debate on a subject so properly his own. But it does seem odd that he would not have had occasion to feel such pangs of "filial piety" prior to Athens, say, in Venice or Rome or even in America, where he was honored by no less an institution than the university. As for the father in question, it seems reasonable to suppose that Freud had excelled him considerably simply by crossing the Vienna streets over to the Rathausstrasse and opening his practice with the title of Herr Doctor Freud. It would seem that Freud had already crossed the paternal threshold long ago, when receiving his Matura, for instance, which he had already termed, at that time, his "Martyr."

Perhaps the single other figure who had reason to stir in Freud a feeling of deep filial piety was Goethe. Of course, the closest he ever came to Athens was through Lord Byron's catastrophic voyage to Greece.

Goethe knew about Greek art, of which he wrote so imposingly, mostly through literature—Wincklemann would be a prime example—and through his friends Mayer and Moritz. Thus beyond or along with his own father, Freud was no doubt excelling another, very powerful *Monsieur notre Père,* the one who had been his judge and aggressor since at least the time of his *Matura.* Indeed, Goethe may have recalled to Freud, as he was standing before the Acropolis, the name of Napoleon, which, at least on that side of the Rhine, was culturally entwined with that of Goethe, whom the emperor met privately in 1808.[16] Perhaps, too, the source of the phantom reference that Freud makes in the open letter to the Frenchman, and that can be linked to his sense of *"déjà raconté,"* is to be found in the corpus of a father who foretold this moment in a celebrated essay whose history has been marked by a long series of interceptions before reaching its self-addressed destination at the Acropolis. It is entitled *"Einleitung in die Propyläen"* ("Initiation [or Entrance, Introduction] into the Propylaea"). We are standing before the father complex and the solution of the *Geheimrat,* whose preparation had begun in Italy, long ago, but this time consolidating in *Tries*te: before the third gate—the Propylaeum—of the Acropolis.

In his essay Goethe names his debt to a past whose grounds he would never tread: "What modern nation does not owe its artistic formation to the Greeks; and, in some disciplines, who more so than the Germans?" The richness of this essay can scarcely be gathered up in a few remarks, but for our purposes we can mark some key moments in a work that, in the first place, gives focus to the exchange of ideas and letters (*Ideen- und Briefwechsel*), to the meeting grounds for the arts and sciences, to the framing of judgments, indeed, to the need for bringing questions before a higher authority or court.[17] The essay makes claims for a psychological-chronological procedure (*psychologischer-chronologischer Gang*), speaks for the transference of the self into works of nature and art (*in die höchsten Werke der Natur und Kunst überzutragen*), struggles with great models (*grossen Mustern*), situates comparative anatomy, and imputes to the genuine artist a capacity to penetrate the depths of his own mind (*in die Tiefe seines eigenen Gemüts zu dringen*). This text consecrates a ground of speculation whose highest priest and cultivator would be Freud; it initiates themes that would reach maturation under Freud's tutelage, and one finds Freud treating and retreating from many of these themes in his oeuvre, the way a master accepts and abandons certain disciples. But the particular enticement that this essay offers for our study unfolds in the beginning of the initiation to the Propylaea:

> The young man who begins to feel the attraction of Nature and Art
> believes that active [*lebhaft*] striving alone will enable him quickly to

penetrate to their innermost sanctuary; but the man discovers that even
after lengthy wanderings, he is still in the forecourts [*Vorhofen,* also
"vestibules"].

Such a consideration has occasioned our title. Rung, portal [*Tor*], entrance,
vestibule, the space between the inside and this outside, between the
sacred and the prosaic: only this can be the place where we shall commonly
dwell with our friends.

If there is someone for whom the word Propylaeum more specifically
recalls that structure through which one arrived at the Athenian citadel,
then this, too, is not contrary to our intention.

. . . . Under the name of the site [*Ort*], let one understand what might
have transpired only there: let one await interlocution and discussion that,
perhaps, would not be unworthy of that place.

This moment of Goethe's solicitation speaks for itself, and speaks for
Freud, I believe. It is the unlived memory of the Acropolis, the remembered dialogue that Goethe would never travel far enough to hold; it is
perhaps the paternal spirit with whom Freud uneasily communed that
day in Athens, remembering indeed his school days, but blotting out the
image of "the youth attracted by Nature and Art," the young man
strangely drawn by Goethe's Nature to erect an "edifice" which, according to the *Traumdeutung,* "is still incompleted."

We have at once discovered and returned to the space between the
inside and the outside, the portal, the mouth, the text, the anatomy of
the *Propyläen,* the forgotten injection into the initiating *Mustertraum.*
The Irma dream had already brought us somewhere near the third gate
of Freud's inaugural work. We were at the end of the second chapter,
searching for the *"Propyl-präparat . . . Propyl,"* how did Freud ever get
to that? This would be one passageway, or to speak in the manner of
Freud and Goethe, one portal, entrance, vestibule.[18] The Irma text is
constituted in and by that vestibule, and besides being the second chapter, it is also the third gateway to the text. For the *Traumdeutung* begins
with an unacknowledged chapter, if one agrees to count the section
containing the prefaces. And though I have emphasized the opening in
terms of initiation and birth, this moment resembles the two processes
only insofar as birth, like initiation rites, cannot be conceptually limited
to the bringing about of something. But something is usually removed,
and usually from the body, be it the child who formerly filled the womb
or, as in the rite of circumcision—to take just one example—a part of the
male organ. This emptying or loss usually makes up the entrance fee; it is
the fee that life pays to death at the macabre festival which Freud will
call *"fort-da."*

One can never lose sight of the fact that the *Traumdeutung* as such
is profoundly concerned with and even built upon the notion of a *Ster-*

bejahr—one that is by no means restricted to Goethe, though he may be its unique point of articulation. Freud is himself reminded of the centrality of the *Sterbejahr* when he writes the second preface to the *Traumdeutung* in the summer of 1908, and traces the work's genesis to the trauma or *Trauerarbeit* over his father's death. Though the period in which Freud began writing his great work coincided with his abandonment of the trauma theory, the transference from *Trauma* to *Traum*-work remains engraved in his project. The *Traumdeutung* not only contains the first seeds of the Oedipus complex, but also shows Freud's entire perspective on literature to be shaped by the haunting event of the Father's Death. This comes to light in Freud's interpretation of Sophocles, to be sure, but also in his interpretation of *Hamlet* whose origin Freud assigns to the death of Shakespeare's father in 1601 as well as to the untimely end of his son, Hamnet. It is of little importance whether Freud was correct in his assumptions; what is important is that these deaths make up an integral moment—a kind of invisible matrix— for his overall strategy. Freud introduces his interpretation of *Hamlet* by way of Goethe, whose binary scheme opposing the pensive with the active Hamlet Freud lays to rest. The word employed by Goethe and Freud for "action" in this case is *Tat*, which resounds death—*Tod*—in hushed tones, particularly when one considers Freud's spelling of death as *Tot*—the adjectival dative of which would be *totem*, as in *Totem and Taboo*. Indeed, *Totem* is the work that ends with Faust's beginning, allowing us to hear the beginning as the end, the deed as the dead: "In the beginning was the Deed" (*Tat,* I.iii). Swaying from *Tat* to *Tot*, the beginning of Freud's deed and legacy is already entangled in the active movement from "a-a-a" to "o-o-o," from *da* to *fort*, to which Freud, as occasional father to Goethe and grandfather to himself—for sons become the father of the father, he tells us in *Totem and Taboo*— earnestly commits us.

When citing a certain line from Shakespeare's *Henry IV,* Freud would make a curious lapsus of which a good deal has been said. Quoting, "Why, thou owest God a death (V.i)," Freud would repeatedly replace "God" with "Nature." Was Freud thinking of Goethe's "Nature" each time he put this citation to paper? Did psychoanalysis owe a death to its begetter and child, to its dreadful initiator whose mark would sear Freud's corpus for good, as it were? The memory of a response has been peeled away from our writing blocks. But a response is there, though the Prince has left the stage to join his father: Falstaff's response to Prince Hal's admonishment will be, at this time, in honor of deferral,

'Tis not due yet;
I would be loath to pay him before his day.

NOTES

This work has undergone one of Goethe's "terrifying operations," which, he explains to Eckermann in conversation, consists in cutting a text down to size. In this case, the text has been extracted from a chapter in a forthcoming book on Goethe. The operation also involved leaving traces of the German language wherever the English rendition seemed to require some strengthening.

1. Of his visit to Freud in 1927, the prominent biographer Emil Ludwig tells the following:

[Freud] did not seem satisfied and asked why I had not dealt with the psychological aspects of Goethe's childhood in my book on Goethe.
"Because there are no documents," I said.
"But there is one," he said, "and moreover in a very prominent place, just at the beginning of Goethe's memoirs." And he cited the anecdote in which the three-year-old Goethe, to his great delight, throws some dishes out of the window. When I asked him the meaning of this incident, he proceeded to explain it in great detail—I did not comprehend his explanation. At that time I was not aware of the fuss [*Zirkus*] which had been made about Goethe in Freudian circles.

First published in E. Ludwig, *Der entzauberte Freud* (1946). Translated in *Freud as We Knew Him*, ed. H. M. Ruitenbeck (1973), p. 214.

2. All Goethe quotes, unless otherwise noted, are taken from Goethe's *Werke*, Hamburger Ausgabe, vol. 9 (1974).

3. I am assuming, of course, that Derrida's message regarding this scene has been received in one form or the other. *La carte postale* (1980).

4. Freud, *Aus den Anfängen der Psychoanalyse* (1962), p. 277 (my translation).

5. Freud himself makes the connection between *Italien* and *Genitalien* fleetingly and with reference to a woman patient, though never with reference to his own difficult rapport with Italy (*Traumdeutung*, p. 237). I am grateful to Maria Torok for this reference.

6. See also Anna Freud Bernays, "My Brother, Sigmund Freud" (1940), in *Freud as We Knew Him* (Ruitenbeck, 1973); "At eighteen, Sigi passed all his examinations at the Gymnasium *summa cum laude*" (p.1 44). The prevalence of the number or age eighteen should be considered in readings of Freud's texts: his father's date of birth, though according to Freud on April 1, 1815, was actually on December 18. Dora is eighteen in 1900. Koller, Freud's early rival on the anesthetic properties of cocaine, who was responsible for the deeply felt delay of Freud's fame, was eighteen months younger than Freud. Schur indicates that Freud translated "18," via Hebrew, into "Life." These are just a few examples.

7. We can profit here from an editor's note (*S.E.* 5: 637–38), which explains, "In the original the words are addressed to the Heavenly Powers and may be translated literally: 'You lead us into life, you make the poor creature guilty.' But the words '*Armen*' and '*schuldig*' are both capable of bearing another meaning. '*Armen*' might mean 'poor' in the financial sense and '*schuldig*' might mean 'in debt.' So in the present context the last line could be rendered: 'You make the poor man fall into debt.'—The lines were quoted again by Freud at the end of Chapter VII of *Civilization and its Discontents* (1930)."

8. Patrick Lacoste, *Il écrit: Une mise en scène de Freud* (1981).

9. For just one such example, consider Jean-Michel Rey's discussion of "an *uneven development* of Freudian theory" in "Freud's Writing on Writing" (1977), pp. 303 ff.

10. The circumstances surrounding Goethe's discovery multiply certain fantasmatic connections made in my discussion thus far. Three days before the discovery was made, on March 24, 1784, the five-year-old princess, firstborn daughter of the ducal pair, died suddenly of a suffocating catarrh (*Stickfluss*). Goethe himself had to arrange for most of the ceremonies and even to select, with Herder, the place in the church where she was buried. Although Goethe was particularly attached to the child, he makes no mention of the event of her death in his many letters written at that time—that is, not until his letter of March 31 to Jacobi, who had lost his wife, and then again on April 24, in a letter to Knebel in which he devotes only one sentence to "the death of the little Princess." Goethe had observed the same kind of epistolary silence when his father died and when his sister, Cornelia, died. In the section of his book dealing with the intermaxillary bone and "the psychology of scientific discoveries," Eissler observes that "there is an uncanny connection between the child's death and the discovery. The organ whose pathology killed the child was, according to the official diagnosis, the throat, and the discovery pertains to a structure in closest proximity to the fatal area, namely, the upper bone of the jaw" (p. 857). Even for Goethe, then, the birth of the *Knöchlein* followed on the steps of death. The cause of Goethe's own death would be officially published by Ottilie von Goethe as *Stickfluss*.

11. The quotation is taken from Goethe's *Werke,* Hamburger Ausgabe, vol. 13 (1975).

12. Upon learning from Anna that the Gestapo had stolen a considerable wad of money, Freud remarked that "they get more for a house-call than even I do."

13. *Sigmund Freud in Selbstzeugnissen und Bilddokumenten,* ed. K. Kusenberg (Hamburg: Rowohlt Taschenbuch Verlag, GmbH. 1971), p. 43.

14. In fact, the *Traumdeutung* is riddled with teeth marks. In the section devoted to "Internal Organic Somatic Stimuli," Freud describes "typical" (his quotation marks) anxiety dreams of appreciable frequency as "the familiar dreams of falling from a height, of teeth falling out, of flying and of embarrassment at being naked or insufficiently clad" (*S.E.* 4: 37). In "A Chemist's Dream" (chap. 6), the dental impressions left by Freud become more prominent. First he recounts the dream of a man who "was attending a performance of 'Fidelio' and was sitting in the stalls at the Opera beside L., a man who was congenial to him and with whom he would have liked to make friends. Suddenly he flew through the air right across the stalls, put his hand in his mouth and pulled out two of his teeth" (*S.E.* 5: 385–86). Needless to say, Freud's analysis of the dream skirts the mouth but lands on masturbation. The dream that Freud quotes immediately after this one suggests, at least in terms of succession, the link that he prefers to leave missing: a young man being treated by two university professors, one of whom "was doing something to his penis [*Glied,* member]. He was afraid of an operation. The other was pushing against his mouth with an iron rod, so that he lost one or two of his teeth." By 1914, Freud affixes this footnote to his interpretation: A tooth being pulled out by someone else in a dream is as a rule to be interpreted as castration (like having one's hair cut by a barber, according to Stekel)." His interpretation gives signs of edginess: "I cannot

pretend that the interpretation of dreams with a dental stimulus as dreams of masturbation—an interpretation whose correctness seems to me beyond a doubt—has been entirely cleared up. I have given what explanation I can and must leave what remains unsolved" (*S.E.* 5: 387–88). A footnote that he adds in 1909 to his resignation before the enigma of this type of dream will have a place in our analysis: "A communication by C. G. Jung informs us that dreams with a dental stimulus occurring in women have the meaning of birth dreams." If Freud must desist from interpreting these kinds of dreams in his name, by 1911 he has inserted the accounts of other signatories—who even cite him in the third person (i.e., "Freud has written")—like a prosthetic device. Freud takes sudden leave of his text, in this case handing it over to Otto Rank, who works on a dream regarding the jawbone, with elements of teeth being crushed and pulverized but in which "the decisive factor was the birth of a child." We find Freud repeatedly expiring ("Freud has written . . . ") at such critical junctures in "his" text.

    15. See Lacoste (1981) and Granoff (1976).

    16. The connection is far from being severed. The most recent book-length study of his radical attachment to Napoleon, and Goethe's corresponding demonology, is Hans Blumenberg's *Arbeit am Mythos* (1979).

    17. When Freud returns to the dream of Goethe's attack after his initial commentary, his insights are guided by a notion of "acts of judgment" (*Urteilsakten; Urteilsäusserungen*) which he finds to be active in the dream (*Traumdeutung;* pp. 450–51).

    18. Freud himself finally has second thoughts concerning the proper place of "propyls" in chap. 6, when explaining "the work of condensation." He appends "the following addition to the analysis of the dream. When I allow my attention to dwell for a moment longer on the word 'propyls,' it occurs to me that it sounds like 'Propylaea.' " This rendition of 'propyls' now guides his interpretation; however, he quickly passes over Athens and goes to Munich, where he had visited a friend who was seriously ill: "but there are Propylaea not only in Athens but in Munich." It might be added that the Propylaea in Munich stand as a perpetual reference to the citadel in Athens, on which they are modeled.

REFERENCES

Blumenberg, H. *Arbeit am Mythos.* Frankfurt a.M.: Suhrkamp, 1979.
Derrida, J. *La carte postale.* Paris: Flammarion, 1980.
Eissler, K. R. *Goethe: A Psychoanalytic Study.* Detroit: Wayne State University Press, 1963.
Freud, S. *Gesammelte Werke.* Frankfurt a.M.: Fischer Verlag, 1946.
    Die Traumdeutung, vols 2, 3 (1900).
    Über den Traum, vol. 3 (1901).
———. *Standard Edition of the Complete Psychological Works.* London: Hogarth, 1953–74.
    The Interpretation of Dreams (1900), vols. 4, 5.
    On Dreams (1901), vol. 5.
    Notes upon a Case of Obsessional Neurosis (1909), vol. 10.

Totem and Taboo (1912), vol. 13.

On the History of the Psycho-Analytic Movement (1914), vol. 14.

"A Childhood Recollection from *Dichtung und Wahrheit*" (1917), vol. 17.

Civilization and its Discontents (1930), vol. 21.

The Goethe Prize (1930), vol. 21.

"A Disturbance of Memory on the Acropolis (1936), vol. 22.

————. *Aus den Anfängen der Psychoanalyse: Briefe an Wilhelm Fliess, Abhandlungen und Notizen aus den Jahren 1887–1902.* Edited by M. Bonaparte, A. Freud, and E. Kris. Frankfurt a.M.: S. Fischer Verlag, 1962.

Goethe, J. W. von. *Werke.* Hamburger Ausgabe. Munich: Verlag C. H. Beck. Vol. 9, 1974; vol. 13, 1975.

Granoff, V. *La pensée et le féminin.* Paris: Les Editions de Minuit, 1976.

Jones, E. *The Life and Work of Sigmund Freud,* vol. 1. New York: Basic Books, 1953.

Lacoste, P. *Il écrit: Une mise en scène de Freud.* Paris: Editions Galilée, 1981.

Ludwig, E. *Der entzauberte Freud.* Zurich: Carl Posen Verlag, 1946. Translated in Ruitenbeck (1973).

Puner, H. *Freud, His Life and His Mind.* London: Gray Walls Press, 1949.

Rey, J.-M. "Freud's Writing on Writing." *Yale French Studies,* nos. 55/56, 1977.

Ruitenbeck, H. M., ed. *Freud as We Knew Him.* Detroit: Wayne State University Press, 1973.

Schur, M. *Freud: Living and Dying.* New York: International Universities Press, 1972.

Index

Chaos *(continued)*
 mythology of, 87
 in Renaissance literature, 96
Childhood
 and debt, 44, 156
 infantile sexuality in, 163–64
 truth in, 102
Christianity, 113
Clinamen
 of atoms, 7
 and Epicurean doctrine, 10
 and freedom, 7
 and mark, 15–16
Coding, 2
 decoding, 126
 postal code, 52–56
Coincidence, xiv, 6–7
 in Poe, 14
Communism, 113
 authority in, 114
Compulsion, 22
 repetition-compulsion, 43
Conscience, 3, 45
 in *Being and Time,* 60
 and *Dasein,* 62
 guilty, 45–47
Consciousness, genealogical, 48
Context, 4
Contradiction, and unconscious, 74
Cosmogony, 102
 and atomism, 95–96
Criticism, 72
 deconstruction and, 125, 128
 Newer, 132n

Dasein, 59–61
 analytic of, 9
 double meaning of, 60–63
Davenant, William, 97
Death
 and anality, 91
 being-to-death, 62
 death-drive, 43, 68
 epitaphs, 92–95
 of Freud, 159, 165
 of Goethe, 146

 in the Renaissance, 90
Debt, 156. *See also* Guilt: and debt
 borrowing and, 40
 in childhood, 44
 of deconstruction, 33–65
 to Democritus, 19
 Goethe's, to his past, 176
 and guilt, 52, 179n
 inauthenticity in, 63
 of psychoanalysts, 28
 and secrecy, 44
 and suffering, 50
 theory of, 45
Decisions, 72
 suspension of, 81
 unconscious, 141
Decoding, 126
Deconstruction, xiv
 and affirmation of text, 80
 and atomism, 87
 brand name of, 44
 in *La carte postale,* 44
 as criticism, 129, 132n
 debts of, 33–65
 and exteriority, 64n
 of Freud's text, 42
 of Lacan's position, 118
 of logocentrism, 74
 of mark, 25
 and metaphysical values, 75
 and philosophical speculation, 54
 and psychoanalysis, 75, 80, 129
 purpose of, 127
 and self-reflexivity, 132n
 strategy of, 42
 of thought, 69
de Man, Paul, 133n
Democritus, 7, 9–10, 14, 89, 94
 and Plato, 18
 as psychoanalyst, 19
 repression of, 25
Demultiplication, 37
Derealization, 174
Derrida, Jacques, 33–65
 La carte postale, 38, 63, 136
 concept of text, 119

Freedom
  and *clinamen*, 7
  in literature, 28
Freud, Sigmund, 29
  on the Acropolis, 101
  analysis of dreams by, 121–22
  assumptions vs. principles in, 56–58
  Autobiographical Study, 36
  avoidance of philosophy by, 54
  Beyond the Pleasure Principle,
    37–42, 52–55, 55–57
  on Charcot, 84
  Civilization and its Discontents,
    112, 114–16, 130
  death of, 159
  debt of, to Nietzsche, 35–65
  and Democritus, 19
  denial of superstition by, 23–26
  Derrida's indebtedness to, ix
  determinist conviction of, 24
  disease of, 165–66
  and Fliess, 150–54
  and Goethe, 146–50
  and Heidegger, 35
  *On the History of the Psycho-analytic
    Movement*, 158
  *Interpretation of Dreams, The
    (Traumdeutung)*, 41, 69, 121–22,
    151–52, 160–68
  on *Kultur*, 111
  and Lacan, 120
  *Leonardo da Vinci and a Memory of
    his Childhood*, 28–30
  mode of analysis by, 121
  on oceanic feeling, 114–15
  as poet, 131n
  on projection, 26
  *Psychopathology of Everyday Life,
    The*, 17, 25
  Theme of the Three Caskets, 29
  Totem and Taboo, 27, 157–58, 178
Future, 6
  in dreams, 167

Galileo, Galilei, 9
Game
  double. *See* Doubleness
  of *fort-da*. See *Fort-da* game
Game theory, 17–28
Gassendi, Pierre, 17–18, 94
  atoms of, 97
Genealogy
  of consciousness, 48
  of Derrida's themes, 87
  of resentment, 49
Genetics, 11, 30, 41
Genitals
  double meaning of hymen, 72–73
  etymological associations, 159–60
  female, 172–73
  Freud's focus on, 161
  mutilation of, 152–53, 170
Gods, role and origin of, 48–52
Goethe, 116, 146–82
  authorship of *Fragment*, contested,
    160–63
  Dichtung und Wahrheit, 148, 163
  Faust, 116, 148
  scientific pursuits of, 162–63
  Wilhelm Meister, 116, 148, 157
Goethe Prize, 174
Guilt, 45, 47–48
  and debt, 50, 52, 59, 157
  of Freud, 171, 174
  in Nietzsche's works, 40
  of survival, 166

Hardy, Thomas, 135–45
  Far from the Madding Crowd, 140
  Torn Letter, The, 138–44
Hartman, Geoffrey, 126–29
  *Psychoanalysis and the Question of
    the Text*, 129
Hegel, G.F.W., 16
  and Derrida, 79
  on double meanings, 73
  master-slave dialectic, 51
Heidegger, Martin, 29, 58–59, 81
  on authenticity, 9
  Being and Time (Sein und Zeit),
    45, 59
  on conscience, 62
  and Derrida, 79
  Die Frage nach dem Ding, 9